'Crossing the Acts'
The Support and Protection of Adults with
Mental Disorder across the Legislative
Frameworks in Scotland

Tom Keenan

Contents

Preface

It is often said that the measure of a society is how it treats its most vulnerable members. Although language has changed and we now speak of people at risk the sentiment holds true. So much so that we have legislation to provide protection, care, support and treatment as necessary. Mental health laws are by far the oldest and were originally introduced in the UK to protect the property of the 'mad'. The 1714 Vagrancy Act, whose main purpose was punishment, excluded the 'furiously mad' from such punishment, allowing for them to be locked up until such 'lunacy' had passed. Although specific mental health legislation was introduced in the 19th century it took until the 21st century for laws to be introduced to protect and support people who lack capacity and those at risk of harm or exploitation.

In Scotland the three main pieces of legislation are the Adults with Incapacity (Scotland) Act 2000, the Mental Health (Care and Treatment) (Scotland) Act 2003 and the Adult Support and Protection (Scotland) Act 2007. These three Acts together form a network of powers to support and protect people with mental disorder. They have at their heart a set of principles, which was not common at the time of the passing of the 2000 Act. Central to these principles is the primacy of the individual, the person to whom the Act will apply; to engage the person, so far as is possible, with the measures being taken on his or her behalf.

Not everyone will want to engage with services and it is at such times that sensitive and balanced use of legal provisions is necessary. Whilst it is important to protect people unable to make decisions for themselves, or who are at risk, protecting their rights means that over protection is as problematic and dangerous as poor protection or neglect. Within a society which values the liberty and autonomy of the individual people with a mental disorder should have as much right to make mistakes, be imprudent or have things go wrong and be disappointed as everyone else – within the same parameters.

Applying one law can be difficult, working between three laws, which are both distinct and have areas of overlap can tax even the most able. If it is difficult for professionals to understand and apply it is even more so for people with a mental disorder and their family and friends who support them. Yet protecting their rights means empowering people to understand what rights they have and ensure that they are used in their own best interests- as defined by them.

In this book Tom Keenan tackles the unenviable task of leading us through the Acts, showing how they work together and when and why the powers of one Act may be more appropriate than another. If the Scottish Parliament is to be congratulated on its vision in introducing these three important Acts in the first decade of its existence then it is up to us to make sure that the powers in the Acts are used appropriately and sensitively to support and protect those with mental disorder and Tom is to be congratulated on helping us do this.

Jacqueline M Atkinson, Professor of Mental Health Policy,
University of Glasgow,
April 2011

INTRODUCTION

This work explores the risks of adults with a mental disorder and how the relative Scottish legislation, policy and practice frameworks interrelate to provide them with support and protection. The main Acts in Scotland which support and protect adults at risk with mental disorder are:

Primary:

   a)   the Mental Health (Care and Treatment) (Scotland) Act 2003 Act (the 2003 Act);

   b)   the Adult Support and Protection (Scotland) Act 2007 (the 2007 Act);

   c)   the Adults with Incapacity (Scot) Act 2000 (the 2000 Act);

Seeking, primarily, to explore the practical application of duties and powers across the interface of these Acts, this work explores their links and relationships, their thresholds, and their effect on the lives of adults with mental disorder.

The tenet of this work is that adults at risk with mental disorder require a dedicated and, sometimes, a specialist approach to support and protection; primarily because their needs and risks are particular and can be complex in nature. A response to risk in many cases may need access to a comprehensive range of legislative provisions and a broad framework of care and support. This is not to minimise generic adult protection; much of which can be supported by the 2007, 1968, 1990 and 2002 Acts, in the context of health and community care frameworks and adult care services.

The work concerns adults, i.e. over 16, affected by mental disorder, taken from the definition within the 2003 Act (section 328), which includes mental illness, learning disability and personality disorder, who are at risk to their health, welfare, safety, finance and property, and the primary legislations response to this range of risk.

Many adults with a mental disorder need access to care and treatment and adequate support and protection. Often, however, no one legislative framework neither meets all the needs of an adult with mental disorder nor responds to all risks associated with the effect of the mental disorder on an adult's life. Consequently, given the range of Scottish legislation which now applies, key practitioners, such as social workers and mental health officers, consultant psychiatrists and general practitioners, are pivotal in ensuring an accurate response to the risk associated with adults with mental disorder at risk.

A predominant problem experienced by the Mental Welfare Commission when conducting deficiency in care inquiries was not about the availability of legislative powers and provisions in Scotland for adults with mental disorder, but a lack of knowledge (and application) of these provisions. This work seeks to respond to the challenges associated with this lack of knowledge and application.

Whereas other work concentrates on the law of Scotland as it relates to adults at risk, this work progresses this by concentrating on how the law is or should be applied *in* practice and by the key practitioners and agencies concerned, i.e. practical application of Scottish law rather that only what the law is and what it provides, thereby exploring a practical response to the risks and needs of adults affected by mental disorder in the community.

Navigating a course, however, through and across legislation provisions can be challenging for practitioners, and confusing and disempowering for the adults concerned. Applying collective powers and provisions is like negotiating a legislative maze, which requires safe and informed decisions, in particularly on a collaborative way between health and social care practitioners.

This work will be informed by risk. In the same way community care is provided relative to need, adult protection is delivered relative to risk. Risk, therefore, governs protection *and* support, and this work will endorse this view. The work will explore the dilemmas, difficulties and deliberations, for those who protect and support adults at risk across the Acts.

For key practitioners, this work has a four part objective:

- to confirm what the powers and the provisions are available across the Acts;

- to assist practitioners decide which provisions and powers are best suited to respond to the risk posed to adults with mental disorder;

- to assist practitioners to apply legal provisions in a safe and productive way, in suited risk management and care management systems; and

- to set all legal responses in suitable risk management and care management.

Note

This work is provided in good faith to assist practitioners in their role of supporting and protecting adults at risk who are affected by mental disorder and to applying legal provisions. It does not seek to advise practitioners to act in a particular way or to make particular decisions, nor does it seek to be the final authority on the subject. It seeks to illustrate the options and opportunities available by working across the Acts and by applying certain frameworks and processes. Practitioners will make decisions, formulate opinions, make judgements and take actions based on their understanding of the area. As such, this work cannot be responsible for the actions of practitioners or agencies, nor held accountable for actions that go wrong. The work seeks to explore developing practice, to provoke a debate and to ask agencies and practitioners to consider how to apply these acts in a collective way.

Please also note that this is 'work in progress' where developing practice, policy and ideas will inform further editions, and indeed other and alternative works may develop this theme further.

Tom Keenan

Summary and Order

The order of the book follows a process from setting the context, explaining what is available in respect of legislative provisions, how they interact, then to how the powers and provisions in the Acts can be applied practically and simultaneously 'Across the Acts'.

Part One of the book provides an exploration of risk and harm as it relates to adults affected by mental disorder, emphasising that for such adults there are particular risks with which they are exposed, in a sense inhabiting a risk landscape. The Part also explores the problems and gaps in supporting and protecting such adults, and provides typical case examples to inform this work.

Part Two covers the primary Acts (the 2003, 2000 and 2007 Acts) in their generality and their relationship with relevant and supportive legislation, e.g. the Social Work (Scotland) Act 1968 (the 1968 Act); the NHS and Community Care Act 1990 (the 1990 Act); and the Community Care and Health (Scotland) Act 2002 (the 2002 Act). It considers the relative duties of the Acts, in particular those that support and protect, e.g. duty (or mandate) to inquire and criminal offences available to protect adults with mental disorder.

Part Three moves progressively to consider the application of the powers of the Acts against the risks associated with mental disorder and the duties of the agencies to support and protect such adults. It explores the orders individually, their liner application from immediate to long term orders, and how to apply the orders in a multiple and simultaneous way.

Part Four explores the interrelationships and their relative powers. Having revealed and explored the powers and duties in the context of risk and harm in previous parts, this part explores the 'crossing of the Acts', in the context of adult protection frameworks, and offers practical guidance on how this might be achieved by agencies and key practitioners.

The Writer's Experience of the Subject Area

The writer is an independent consultant, trainer and social worker practitioner in the area of adult protection, specialising in the support and protection of adults at risk with mental disorder. He was a member of the Scottish Government's code of practice working group on the 2007 Act, having a particular remit for the protection orders aspect of the code of practice. He was a part time Commissioner with the Mental Welfare Commission from 1998 to 2006, and worked temporarily for SHAS and NHS QIS. He was chair of the British Association of Social Workers Strathclyde branch for five years. He has trained health and social care staff in local authority, health, voluntary and private agencies across Scotland, in particular key practitioners, such as mental health officers, social workers and health care practitioners, and has delivered independent training events. Additionally, he acts as an independent social worker preparing community care assessments and reports on adults at risk and adults with mental disorder for solicitor agencies, and acts as a safe guarder in Glasgow Sheriff Court in relation to adults with incapacity. He is a former independent convener of an Adult Protection Committee (2010 to 2012). In 1999, the writer completed a master of community care degree at the University of Glasgow, writing a thesis on the predominant use of emergency detention under the 1984 Act. He has contributed to consultations for the 2000, 2003 and 2007 Acts, and has practised as a social worker, consultant and trainer, in respect of all the primary Acts. He has practised as a social worker since 1984 and a mental health officer (MHO) from 1985 until 2001, when he became an independent social worker. He has acted as a MHO under the 2003 Act and mentors MHOs in local authority areas. He leads Mental Health Law in Practice, a consultancy and training organisation specialising in the practice based application of mental health, adults with incapacity and adult at risk law.

List of Abbreviations

AMP: Approved Medical Practitioner

APC: Adult Protection Committee

ARBD: alcohol-related brain damage

ASD: autistic spectrum disorder

BASW: British Association of Social Workers

CCP: crisis contingency planning

CCTO: community-based compulsory treatment order

COP: code of practice

CPA: care programme approach

CTO: compulsory treatment order

EDC: emergency detention certificate

GP: general practitioner

JIT: Joint Improvement Team

MHO: Mental Health Officer

MHTS: Mental Health Tribunal for Scotland

MWC: Mental Welfare Commission

OPG: Office of the Public Guardian

PEP: Psychiatric Emergency Plan

RMO: Responsible medical officer

SLC: Scottish Law Commission

STDC: short-term detention certificate

SWSI: Social Work Services Inspectorate

The 1948 Act: the National Assistance Act 1948

The 1968 Act: the Social Work (Scotland) Act 1968

The 1984 Act: the Mental Health (Scotland) Act 1984

The 1990 Act: the NHS and Community Care Act 1990

The 2000 Act: the Adults with Incapacity (Scotland) Act 2000

The 2002 Act: the Community Care and Health (Scotland) Act 2002

The 2003 Act: the Mental Health (Care and Treatment) (Scotland) Act 2003

The 2004 Act: the Vulnerable Witnesses (Scotland) Act 2004

The 2007 Act: the Adult Support and Protection (Scotland) Act 2007

The 2009 Act: The Sexual Offences (Scotland) Act 2009

WOS: West of Scotland

PART ONE

THE RISK ENVIRONMENT

Chapter 1

THE EVOLVING LEGAL FRAMEWORK

In highlighting the development of legislative frameworks throughout the first decade in this millennium, the gaps and deficiencies in service response and practice over the past twenty years, and exploring the risks associated with mental disorder, the writer seeks to illustrate a context within which to consider the collective application of the primary Acts.

The developing legislative context

Throughout the end of the last millennium and the beginning of this, there was a growing awareness in the protection of vulnerable adults, in particular regarding adults with mental disorder. Major deficiencies of care were in the public domain and television documentaries highlighted neglect and abuse in care settings and from care providers. The Mental Welfare Commission (MWC) conducted major inquires such as the Ms P case (1998), where a homeless woman with mental disorder was physically and financially abused. This case highlighted failings of the statutory agencies to take action, such as not pursuing welfare guardianship, which was eventually taken, and her subsequently being transferred into a care environment.

The National Assistance Act 1948 (the 1948 Act) had a provision (s47), which was repealed by the 2007 Act, to remove to suitable premises 'persons in need of care and attention' and had a duty of Councils to provide temporary protection for property of persons admitted to hospitals (s48).

Most provisions, however, out-with the 1948 Act were to be found in the Mental Health (Scot) Act 1984 (the 1984 Act), e.g. emergency detention and entry on premises and warrant to search for and remove patients, who may be ill-treated, neglected or unable to care for himself. However, the Act's most used formal provision was on providing treatment on a compulsory basis following an emergency detention (Keenan, 1999 i[i]).

The 1984 Act (a consolidation Act for the 1960 Act) lacked essential measures to protect mentally disordered people from harm and suffered from a lack of duties to investigate (inquire) and lack of provision to enter to assess. Powers in the Act concentrated unduly on removing the person from harm (SLC 2001 ii[ii]), and protection provision were limited to offences related to inappropriate sexual intercourse with 'mentally handicapped females' and ill treatment of inpatients. Guardianship, however, was available within the 1984 Act, but this had static powers of (a) residence, (b) attendance, and (c) access to the patient. The Act, however, offered little to protect for those who may be incapable because of mental disorder, other than a duty to protect property and affairs.

The advent of community care following the 1990 Act offered new care and treatment provisions for people with mental disordered other vulnerable groups. Local authorities were given a duty to assess the needs of 'a person in need' who may require community care services. It did little, however, to protect adults at risk with mental disorder, other than providing additional services to meet need at home.

This was a time and context where many mentally disordered people were being resettled in the community from large long stay hospitals. Whilst this was unarguably correct, offering many people the opportunity to live normal lives, it increased the number of vulnerable adults with complex needs in the community, including those open to harm and exploitation. Adding to this, there was (and remains so) a developing and ageing population, with more frail older people living alone, and an increase in people affected by dementia and mental disorder associated with drug and alcohol abuse.

For adults affected by mental disorder, particularly risk factors are relative, e.g.:

a)   adults with a learning disability appear particularly open to a variety of harm, such as highlighted by the Scottish Border's case (MWC 2004 iii[iii]); such as those open to physical harm and financial exploitation, sexual exploitation and harm (predominantly for females), and generally an inability to self-protect;

b)   adults with mental illness, with conditions such as dementia, neglect and financial exploitation appears prevalent; and for adults with conditions such as bipolar disorder, a lack of insight and disinhibition adds to their risk; and

c)   adults with personality disorder are open to self-harming behaviour and chaotic lifestyle, adding to their risk.

For all of these groups, the use and abuse of alcohol or drugs appears to increase the potential for physical, sexual and financial harm.

Throughout the period of developing legislative context, in protecting adults with mental disorder, finding an appropriate response between the least restrictive option, i.e. not going too far and infringing a person's human rights and liberties, to not going far, or assertive, enough where vulnerable adults could be placed in serious risk, is (and will always be) a difficult balance to achieve for the key practitioners. However, certain cases highlight an inhibition to pursue powers, e.g. the Ms P case (MWC 1999) where there was 'ill-informed assumptions about guardianship', where practitioners believed guardianship might not have worked (or benefited her); and, therefore, it was not pursued.

The primary Acts introduced in this decade, however, offer a new set of options, and importantly are governed by applied principles, such as obtaining benefit and minimal intervention, which may help practitioners with adult protection dilemmas.

The 2000 Act arrived in the new millennium, seeking to offer a more specific provision for those adults incapable because of mental disorder (and physical disability) across the range of health, welfare, property and finances, including a new duty to inquire and a range of provision, which included a more flexible set of guardianship powers. Its primary parts, which concerned adults with financial or welfare needs (Parts 2, 3 and 6), were implemented between 2001 and 2002.

In 2004, summary findings iv[iv] were produced by the Scottish Executive examining the operation of these Parts. 'Learning from Experience' said, in broad terms, the 2000 Act was meeting its central aims to provide enhanced protection for adults. However, it said 'when to invoke the Act', primarily referring to welfare guardianship, was a major issue for local authorities, whereby 'perceived barriers' in its use may just be as important as realised ones in hampering access to the Act. Additionally, this was mentioned in the Border's Reports (2004) where guardianship was not pursued, there being failings in the understanding of provisions for guardianship, where many practitioners and local authority agencies were sceptical about its use.

In 1997, the Scottish Law Commission (SLC), in its report on vulnerable adults[v], recommended a new legal framework to protect vulnerable adults, to include defining the term "vulnerable", which had long been linked with mental disorder, to be included in reviews of mental health policy, such as were prompted by the Millan Report (2001 v[vi]).

Through 1999 and 2000, the Milan Committee explored the provisions available to protect vulnerable adults with mental disorder, and through the Millan Report recommended the SLC's proposals relating to vulnerable adults should be accepted in respect of adults with mental disorder, which were adopted in the 2003 Act, including the power to enter and to be assessed by a mental health officer. The SLC consultation of 2001 recommended a new power to exclude a suspected abuser from a home occupied by a vulnerable adult, including an adult with mental disorder. This, however, had to wait until the 2007 Act was implemented.

The 2003 Act, implemented in 2005, introduced enhanced provisions to protect vulnerable adults with mental disorder, including:

a)   a new local authority duty to inquire (s33);

b)   powers of entry and to conduct a medical examination (s35);

c)   removal to a place of safety (ss293 and 294); and

d)   a new set of offences against mentally disordered adults (ss311 to 318).

There was no power, however, to protect mentally disordered persons from harmers, in particular to exclude a harmer from the premises of a vulnerable adult, with options limited to that of removing the adult from his/her home to protect from harm from others, considered by many to be an overly restrictive use of the Act.

Primary protective provisions, therefore, prior to the 2007 Act, available to statutory authorities, were to be found in (and across) the 2003 and 2000 Acts, e.g.:

a)   a duty to inquire (2003 Act, s33);

b)   separate powers i) of forcible entry to premises where a mentally disordered person is (2003 Act, s35[1]), ii) to carry out a medical examination (s35[4]; and to have access to the person's medical records (s35[7];

c)   removal of a mentally disordered person to a place of safety (2003 Act, s293 and s294);

d)   a police power to take a mentally disordered person found in a public place and in need of care to a place of safety (2003 Act,s297);

e)   short term detention (2003 Act, s44) and emergency detention (2003 Act,s36) in hospital;

f)   long term powers to detain a mentally disordered person in a hospital for treatment or to impose measures in the community on a mentally disordered person such as to attend for treatment and community care services (2003 Act, s63); and

g)   powers to require an incapable adult to accede to a welfare or financial guardian's directions(2000 Act, s57).

On 1 March 2002, a woman with learning disabilities was admitted to Borders General Hospital, having suffered extreme levels of physical and sexual abuse within her home over an extended period. Three men were subsequently imprisoned for the abuse; one of whom was the carer of the woman. The Social

Work Services Inspectorate (SWSI) and the MWC undertook inquiries, summarising their findings and recommendations, which was released in the Borders Reports of 2004 (MWC 2004).

This case, and a serious of consultations, set the context for the 2007 Act, which was implemented in October 2008. This was, in Part 1, the first legislative framework in Scotland designed solely to protect adults at risk.

The 2007 Act offers new options and new responsibilities to protect adults at risk, significantly with a mental disorder and introduced a power to ban a perpetrator of harm from being in an adult at risk's premises. It also seeks to protect adults at risk out-with the range of mental disorder, including those adults with mental infirmity, which poses an interesting consideration of the Act's application for those not affected by mental disorder, but affected by varying degrees of mental frailty and/or vulnerability.

There was a sense, however, that a primary legislative framework evolved rather than was developed or planned; a sense of one Act 'leapfrogging' the other or 'hop-scotching' in respective directions, leading to the present set of Acts; where each Act has distinct care groups and provisions, but where no one Act met the needs of all adults with mental disorder for support and protection.

At the time of the Millan Report it had been hoped that a consolidation Act may have been conceived, which would have spanned the provisions as they relate to people with learning disability. So far, of course, this has not occurred.

Currently, moreover, there may be problems protecting adults with incapacity within the 2007 Act, where there is no particular statutory provision inbuilt there, out-with an amendment to the 2007 Act Code of Practice (COP vii[vii]), to allow cases of adults with incapacity to go before a Sheriff, and where there is no compulsory provision if adults (capable or incapable) refuse the protection power.

Additionally, there may be a gap because of the repeal of the 1948 Act, which offered some protection (but minimal legal rights) for those 'in need of care and attention ... living in unsanitary conditions ... unable to devote to themselves ... not receiving from other persons, proper care and attention', e.g. a capable adult, affected by mental disorder (thereby ruling out the 2000 Act), not needing treatment in hospital nor meeting grounds for removal under the 2003 Act, i.e. not 'likely to suffer significant harm' (thereby ruling out the 2003 Act), who may not meet the criteria for the 2007 Act.

Moreover, adult at risk procedures are in early implementation and need to be fully and practically tested over time. Many adult at risk procedures and investigation processes follow a child care perspective, e.g. case conferences governing decisions, where adult protection is predicated on obtaining individual consent and empowering the adult to take their own steps and decisions to manage risk.

It is likely, therefore, that developing practice and case law, and continuing deficiencies of care and protection, will prompt further changes to the legislative and procedural framework for adults with mental disorder.

Legislative implementation

Each of the primary Acts has some provisions to protect adults at risk with mental disorder. However, how are they used and how are they performing in this respect?

Within the 2000 Act, it has long been the case that use of welfare guardianship to provide a framework to manage risk to incapable adults at home is of minimal use in comparison to its predominant use in transferring incapable adults out of the risk environment to a care environment. Over 90% of applications seek a residence power (MWC Annual Report 2003-2004) to transfer adults to a residential home, where it is clear for many practitioners(and the MWC) such a framework can be a useful and certainly a less restrictive option to support and protect an adult at risk at home.

However, the MWC, in its annual report of 2008-9, indicated that overall a previous downward trend in the use of welfare guardianship (fallen by 20% in the year following the 2007 Act's implementation), may have resulted from the introduction of the 2007 Act, where duties placed on local authorities for tighter procedures for investigations is ultimately informing decisions to seek welfare guardianship.

Moreover, there has been a 24% growth in welfare guardianship for adults with learning disability, and although cases of Alcohol Related Brain Damage (ARBD) have doubled from 32 in 2007 to 61 in 2008, it remains only 5% of overall welfare guardianship cases. A surprising low rate, the Commission said, given the risks associated with this group.

Adults with dementia, however, account for 53% (663) of the guardianship cases and adults with learning disability account for 31% (377) of the cases. Significantly, adults with mental illness only account for 4% (46) cases of welfare guardianship.

Within the 2003 Act, the Commission's annual report of 2008-9 indicates that, overall, compulsory treatment under the 2003 Act (4143 episodes) has reduced by 13% to that of the 1984 Act. Short term detentions have now become the primary vehicle to formally admit and detain people in hospital, with short term detentions rising by 12% since the Act was introduced. In that year, the Police took 192 places of safety under section 297, with 7 of these adults going to a police station, which can only be used by exception. From the overall statistics it can be seen, therefore, the 2003 Act is being used predominantly for people with mental illness (98% of all detentions).

Moreover compulsory treatment orders (CTOs), at the time of writing, are predominantly used to treat persons in hospital, i.e. where of 1105 new CTOs granted, only 138 were community based(MWC 2009). However, more people are receiving compulsory powers in the community, which may be viewed as a less restrictive option (minimum restriction) than having to be detained in hospital.

The MWC says that the proportion of women detained under emergency provisions has risen steadily over the past three years, where the figures suggest mental health services should look at how well they respond to women at times of crises. Furthermore, 42% of people admitted under emergency detention were aged from 25 to 44 and 26% aged from 45 to 64, with 70% of total emergency admissions occurring out of hours.

Therefore, for emergency detention certificates (EDC), the adult is more like to be a woman, aged from 25 to 44, and admitted after hours, which has significance for adult protection work out of hours. For short term detentions certificates (STDC), however, the majority (36%) were used for adults aged from 25 to 44, and of total admissions 98% are people with mental illness, where only 4% are affected by learning disability, and even less so (3%) for those with personality disorder. Significantly, 80% of STDCs are granted during office hours, where the certificate is viewed to be the primary route to hospital for people with mental disorder, where many adult at risk scenarios occur after hours.

The 2007 Act was implemented in October 2008, and at the time of writing it is in early days of implementation. From the introduction of the Act to the end of November 2009 (around 13 months) the number of protection orders recorded as considered, applied for and /or granted were: 9 assessment orders; 5 removal orders and 133 banning orders (including temporary banning orders). However, at the time of writing (September 2010), only around 38 banning orders, which include 11 temporary banning orders, are known to be in existence.

Although there is some activity considering adult at risk cases in the context of the Act, this is not reflected in actual orders, i.e. there is much more support in the context of the Act rather than 'protection', i.e. using the orders of the Act. There is no information of how the orders are being used to protect adults with mental disorder, in particular. Anecdotal information suggests there is a lot of activity around assessing and investigating under the Act, leading to case conferences in many cases; however, protection orders are rarely sought. The writer has knowledge of two recently approved banning orders, where there was an issue related to risk associated with mental disorder, i.e. 1) to protect a woman with a disability who was being harmed by her daughter who had mental health problems; and 2) to protect an older woman at risk because of her physical and mental health, where there had been a long history of violent behaviour from her son.

Recent Strathclyde Police figures say that there have been 375 adult at risk referrals to local Councils, with 32% of the total referrals relating to adults with 'mental health conditions' and 18% of the total who are self-harming and17% attempting suicide, both groups which would include those at risk with mental disorder. From its figures, Strathclyde Police ascertain that a 'typical adult at risk' would be: a female, aged between 36 to 45, living alone, self-harming, and affected by mental health problems.

This work pre-dates the biennial reports which will be provided by the 32 Adult Protection Committees (APCs) throughout Scotland, however recent information received from one APC indicated that from 124 adult at risk referrals, 74 related to adults with mental disorder (learning disability [10], mental health [52], older persons with dementia [11] and acquired brain injury [1]). Therefore, it would appear (at least for one area) at least 60% of adults at risk referrals relate to adults with mental disorder. From the same area, relative to the type of harm reported in 84 cases, self-harm was evident (others: physical harm: 22; psychological harm: 12; and financial/material harm: 13). Therefore, close to 70% referrals related to self-harm. From investigations (18 cases), 7 had learning disability, 3 were older people with dementia, and 1 had acquired brain injury; cases indicative of adults who may have issues related to incapacity. So clearly, a) adults with mental disorder, potentially with b) incapacity issues, and b) self-harm are significant aspects of (and challenges for) adult at risk practice.

The minimal use of the protection orders, however, appears to be related to the majority of cases being resolved by informal means, i.e. 'support' rather than 'protection (protection orders)'. Only 25% of the authority indicted, referrals resulted in formal actions. Most 'formal' action in the 2007 Act, therefore, appears to be contained within the 'inquiry/investigation/support services' component of the Act, in the context of local adult at risk procedures.

Anecdotal information suggests that using the 2007 Act to protect adults with mental disorder presents certain problems, in particular where they may lack capacity to consent to support and protection. It would appear that some authorities take the view that the 2007 Act doesn't cover adults with incapacity. The Scottish Government's Legal Division, however, says adults with incapacity should be protected under the Act, that it was intended in the Bill of the Act that such adults would be covered by the Act.

The Act is predicated on obtaining the consent of the adult (unless undue pressure prevents this). However, some adults with mental disorder lack capacity, in respect of understanding or making a decision to consent or not. The code of practice of the Act was amended to allow such cases to be taken to the Sheriff, but the Act has no compulsory powers to require adults to accede to the protective powers. This appears to be an anomaly in the drafting of the Act, i.e. protecting adults with incapacity, who are incapable of giving consent and/or refuse to comply with any direction under the Act. The 2000 Act may appear to be the correct framework here, but there are no emergency provisions there, nor powers to ban harmers from the homes of adults incapable because of mental disorder.

Equally, other groups may not be well protected under the 2007 Act, e.g. adults with mental illness with a lack of insight into their circumstances, such as produced by serious mental illness, e.g. schizophrenia or bipolar disorder, who may be affected by hallucinations or delusions and open to harm, but might not see the need for support or protection under the 2007 Act. Such adults, therefore, may not comply with any powers or provisions pursued there. The 2003 Act may be suitable here, but again this Act has neither banning provision norsubstantive provisions to protect welfare, finances or property.

In respect of finances and property, the 2000 Act could be used, but a lack of insight (i.e. not recognising the need for support and protection) or an inability to understand the needs for treatment, and lack of capacity (i.e. to make protective decisions, etc.) may be different things. Interestingly the 2003 Act COP (Vol2) vii[viii] considers the difference between incapacity (a criterion of the 2000 Act) and significantly impaired decision making ability (a criterion when pursuing the powers of the 2003 Act), arguing that the latter is primarily a 'disorder of the mind', on the basis of 'reasoning coloured by a mental disorder', where the former (incapacity) 'broadly involves a disorder of the brain and cognition' which 'prevent or disrupt the decision making process'. This distinction may refer to some adults affected by a mental disorder, who may not understand the need for protection, and therefore refuse it, but be capable of making a decision vis the protection provision, e.g. a woman with bipolar disorder being exploited sexually, lacking insight into the fact she is being exploited, but viewed as capable of making a decision over banning him from her house.

Problems also relate to some adults who are viewed as incapable in respect of giving consent for protection, but non-compliant or unwilling to do what the Sheriff requires of them, e.g. going to a place for assessment or agreeing to removal, or indeed dealing with a harmer on a banning order. There are problems also for adults who lack insight, at risk in terms of the 2003 Act, but where the provisions of the Act do not offer anything to manage this risk, e.g. emotional harm.

Progressing policy and practice

The implementation of 2007 Act, and the findings and recommendations contained in the Scottish Border's case required all local authorities to review procedural arrangements for adults at risk in their areas. At the time of writing, most (if not all) local authority areas have prepared interagency adult at risk procedures. A collective approach to local arrangements is evidenced by the West of Scotland Adult at Risk procedures, which involves 13 local authorities and 5 health boards, which at the time of writing was on its 7th draft and was being finalised.

For adults with mental disorder at risk, practice procedures and guidance on how to seek and use formal provisions across the Acts need to exist together. Procedures which don't relate well to the powers and provisions in the Acts will lead to problems, e.g. being unclear of who should do what formally and why, and how this should be done, can lead to inaccurate assessments and failed actions. Additionally, allocating practitioners to adults with mental disorder at risk, who are not trained in the primary Acts, or indeed in crossing the Acts, could equally be problematic, if not catastrophic, for adults at risk.

Procedures for adults at risk need to consider and respond well to the complex matters relating to adults with mental disorder, and should assist practitioners to cross the Acts. Where child care procedures rely on parental consent or Tribunal (children's) or Sheriff authority (involving the child as much as possible), adult protection procedures are based on consent. Local practice and procedures, however, need to consider issues arising for mentally disordered people who lack insight or are incapable of giving consent. Recent adults at risk practice, governed by procedures, appears to be designed based on those used within child protection, e.g. investigations based on securing evidence which will stand up in Court, case conferences, protection plans, etc.

Additionally, practice experience and training appears variable in adult protection work. Designated Council staff (council officers) may not have the same experience as MHOs (or social workers in child protection) in seeking or exercising powers, such as MHOs and consultant psychiatrists often do. Additionally, council officers, although appointed under the 2007 Act, may be trained to seek protection orders under this Act, but lack knowledge of other Acts, such as the 2000 or 2003 Acts, and lack experience in crossing the Acts, as indeed MHOs often need to do.

Chapter 2

DEFICIENCIES, NEEDS AND LEARNING

Cases of concern

Practice in adult protection needs to be informed by learning arising from previous cases that have gone wrong. No more so than in the area of mental disorder, as highlighted by a number of deficiency of care enquiries by the MWC, in particular risks relevant to a lack of legislative response, i.e.:

i)   The MWC Deficiency in Care Inquiry of Ms P (MWC 1998) confirmed Ms P had a learning disability, lived in a homeless persons' hostel and was open to physical, sexual and financial exploitation. In the case, there was a failure to protect her from financial exploitation and physical harm. Findings include:

   a)   a lack of local standardised, multi-agency procedures for the protection of vulnerable adults;

   b)   poor communication between agencies; and

   c)   ill-informed assumptions and attitudes about guardianship.

Recommendations included a need to consider adult care and protections procedures.

ii)   In 2001, the MWC Inquiry on Mr B was released, which concerned a young man with learning disability who lacked capacity to manage his financial affairs. He had spent an inheritance of over £50,000 over a 15 month period, where there were concerns over his capacity to manage this inheritance. The Commission said there was a failure to protect his finances. Findings include:

   a)   a lack of clarity about his learning disability;

   b)   a lack of assessment of capacity; and

   c)   no comprehensive multidisciplinary assessment.

iii)   In 2003, a man with ARBD was subject to a MWC Inquiry. Here the key issue was a deficiency in care to assess capacity in people with serious and long-term alcohol problems. Recommendations include:

   a)   better assessment, care management and information sharing for people with ARBD;

b) agencies to give their staff better training in ARBD; and

c) departments of medicine for the elderly need better procedures for assessing capacity and investigating impaired brain function in people with alcohol problems.

iv)   In 2004, the Scottish Border's reports (Ms H and Mr E) confirmed serious failings, which include:

a) a lack of risk assessment, failure to consider allegations of sexual abuse;

b) a lack of understanding of the legislative framework for intervention and its capacity to provide protection; and

c) a failure to consider statutory intervention at appropriate stages.

v)   In 2007, the MWC Ms A(Justice Denied) Inquiry highlighted serious concerns about services and systems and the use of legislation, where a 67 year old woman affected by a learning disability was sexually assaulted by a number of men in her local community. Services responsible for Ms A had been unable to protect her from a series of serious sexual assaults. The case highlighted problems in the criminal justice system regarding vulnerable victims of abuse and crime. The MWC indicated, however, that offences under the 2003 Act (s.311) might have been an alternative means to pursue convictions.

vi)   Additionally, the MWC investigated the care and treatment of Mrs T (2007). It was worried that despite indications Mrs T was a very vulnerable woman (with Alzheimer's disease), probably lacking capacity and living with a potentially abusive son, no multi-agency adult protection case conferences were held. This meant that there was no clear strategy to monitor her risks or to protect Mrs T where there was concern over the adequacy of the assessment of capacity.

In 2009, the MWC asked Glasgow University to review its past 10 investigations (at that time). The Commission believed that similar issues had been at the root of problems with care and treatment in all the cases they had looked at. They wanted to identify those common issues so that they could share that information and help services to address their key risk areas. The report said that many of the people whose care the MWC investigated had complex needs, and they faced situations where their health and safety were at risk. It said that assessment of needs *and* risks is the key to good care planning. However, the report identified five key risk areas for services:

1. problems around diagnosis and assessment of capacity had often prevented people from getting the right care and treatment;

2. poor practice in assessment and care planning that had led to people being neglected and suffering harm;

3. failures in recording vital information about individual care and treatment in all of their investigations and there are often problems with sharing information between health and social care providers;

4. limited knowledge of the laws which can be used to safeguard the welfare of individuals with a mental disorder, and often, laws that are designed to protect are not used at an appropriate time, leaving an individual at risk; and sometimes the failure to act at an early stage also means that more restrictive orders are put in place when legislation is, eventually, used; and

5.   different professional cultures could get in the way of effective communication and can distract attention from the needs of the individual. Where staff from different organisations disagreed, the investigations often found there was no way to resolve conflict. This led to serious gaps in the care of people whose cases they investigated.

vii)   Just before submission, this work became aware of an additional MWC inquiry 'Loss of Focus (Ms Z) ix[ix]' which concerned a woman who had died due to self-injury. The findings of the inquiry indicated 'the need to identify and try to manage risk for Ms Z was essential', and recognised the 'importance of risk assessment and development of a risk management plan'. Additionally, it emphasised the Care Programme Approach (CPA) might have resolved some of the problems identified in the case.

Importantly, however, the Scottish Border's case illustrates that it was not so much the lack of available statutory powers that led to the failure to act rather there was a lack of understanding of those powers and how to implement them. Indeed, many of the recommendations related to the practice of professionals and the systems in place in the local authority and health board.

These failings present a clear challenge to contemporary and future adult protection services, where many of the recommendations relate to the practice of professionals, and their knowledge of the laws available and how to apply these.

The major difference between a thing that might go wrong and a thing that cannot possibly go wrong is that when a thing that cannot possibly go wrong goes wrong it usually turns out to be impossible to get at or repair.' Douglas Adams

Needs

From the above, it is axiomatic to indicate that a) many adults affected by mental disorder need care and treatment *and* support and protection, and b) a lack of care and treatment can lead to the need for protection, as an adult's condition or circumstances deteriorate, and c) preventative measures may stave off the need for more restrictive provisions.

However, what do adults at risk need by way of support and protection, and where are the gaps in this provision? Well, from the above cases of concern, they certainly need responsive legislation; however, in applying legislative options, they need practitioners knowledgeable both in the Acts and their practical application, and these practitioners need to work well together across the spectrum of health and social care. They also need good risk assessment and risk management, access to specialist assessment, confident staff prepared to pull out all the stops and be tenacious in protecting vulnerable adults. These practitioners need a good understanding of mental disorder and its effect on safety, health, welfare and finances. Adults need access to good care and protection planning; and a trusting relationship, between protector and protected, needs to be formed, which promotes autonomy and empowerment.

'Your problem is to bridge the gap which exists between where you are now and the goal you intend to reach.' Earl Nightingale

Learning

Practitioners need to learn from previous failings in the adult care and support system, and according to the MWC inquiries there is a poor knowledge of relevant laws and safeguards, and failure to consider statutory intervention at appropriate stages. There have been ill informed assumptions and attitudes about powers, e.g. the use of guardianship and failure to consider offences under the Acts. Additionally, there has been a lack of procedures, a failure to consider and investigate appropriately serious allegations of abuse, a lack of information-sharing and co-ordination within and between key agencies, and failures in recording vital information. There has been poor practice in assessment and care planning, poor assessing of capacity, and a breakdown in care planning and care management, and problems in the criminal justice system regarding vulnerable victims of abuse.

In practice, there is often poor communication between agencies, a lack of clarity around mental disorder, a failure to consult specialist workers, a failure to act at an early stage, and different professional cultures getting in the way of effective communication. Practice, therefore, needs to develop to meet needs *and* risk associated with mental disorder, through the appropriate use of the primary Acts.

The use of the 2000 Act needs to develop for adults able to communicate and act, but with impaired decision making in aspects of their life, which might expose them to risk. The Act may be used to protect vulnerable (incapable) adults, to control problem behaviour, and to authorise actions, and it should focus on risk and its management. However, there needs to be a better assessment of capacity as recommended by the guidance produced by the Scottish Government [sx]. There needs to be continuing practice development in applying the Act, in particular a more creative use of guardianship to manage risk to incapable adults at home; especially where applying welfare guardianship alongside imaginative care plans, which might include Tele-care equipment, to assist vulnerable adults to remain at home safely.

Practice development under the 2000 Act also needs to consider adults within the range of functional mental illness, which impairs capacity. This only accounts for minimal use of welfare guardianship, where the Act is primarily used for adults with dementia, learning disability and ARBD.

In the 2003 Act, a short term detention is the primary vehicle to formal admission and treatment. However, it is only available (predominantly) during office hours. What happens after hours for such adults at risk? The use of community based orders (CCTOs) is gradually increasing; however, how are these orders used creatively to protect adults at risk in the community? Police powers to remove an adult from a public place primarily transfer adults to a hospital. However, how does this relate across health and social care services, where the adult needs access to support and protection services, and not only to medical examination in a hospital? The Act is predominantly used for people with mental illness; but does practice need to develop in the use of the Act for adults with other forms of mental disorder, such as adults with learning disability and personality disorder?

In the 2007 Act, there appears to be strenuous activity around assessing and investigating under the Act, leading to case conferences, but less so in seeking protection orders, which are rarely sought. Practice in the Act needs to consider and respond accordingly to how the Act is used for adults at risk with mental disorder, with the risk associated with the effects of mental disorder, e.g. incapacity, self-harm, and lack of insight.

Generally, use of legislation sets quickly in the early days of implementation, e.g. the predominant use of emergency detentions under the 1984 Act, the poor use of STDCs after hours under the 2003 Act, the lack of use of welfare guardianship in the 2000 Act for adults at home, and the lack of use of protection orders in the 2007 Act for people with mental disorder. It appears clear, if it is not used (legal provision), practice in its use doesn't develop (application of the law). In summary, there appears to be a lack of creativity in the use of the legislation and of the powers and provisions of the primary Acts.

Agencies need to be mindful of the findings of inquiries and research into the use of the Acts to avoid the pitfalls that exist in protecting adults at risk, e.g. the failure to allocate appropriately trained and knowledgeable staff, lack of collective working, poor communication, and lack of care planning, risk assessment, risk management, etc., and, in particular, a lack of practice development in both the application of the Acts *and* across the Acts.

Practitioners need to be aware of and avoid the pit falls of adult protection as they concern the area of mental disorder. One pitfall community care has is the delivery of care, which is predicated by available resources, thereby fitting the person's needs to the resource, whether the resource fully meets the persons' needs or not. In the same way, a pitfall of adult protection may be to apply the provision or power, primarily because it is expedient or convenient to the services to do so, which is not reflective of the risk experienced by the adult.

Another pitfall is to liken adult protection to child protection, i.e. (a) confirm the need for protective action; (b) source evidence to obtain this; and (c) pursue and expedite the power. While this may be necessary and appropriate where there is parental consent or where the Children's Panel of Sheriff's authority is required, adults have a right, unless incapable of making decisions in this regard or have lost insight because of mental illness, to lead their lives as they see fit, including dealing with *their* risk and making decisions about *their* lives.

The writer has knowledge of these pitfalls in practice; for example, where an investigation interview with a vulnerable woman was governed by a determination to obtain evidence that would stand up in Court. Whilst this led to a banning order being granted, it did little to confirm the range and degree of risk with which she was exposed, including the risk of losing the relationship of her son, the harmer; nor did it empower her; nor did it consider the range of options in which to deal, and to help her deal, with the risk to her. By going straight for the banning order, which protected the woman, it left this as the only available option for her future safety, and did nothing to resolve the risk scenario on a long term basis. This is presupposing, however, there is no on-going work with the adult and the harmers to resolve the harm over time.

Another pitfall is where agencies or practitioners go 'down the wrong road', where the wrong Act or provision is used over a more suitable or reflective (of need and risk) power or provision. Pursuing the wrong provision can lead to problems, which may leave practitioners in a position where the power or provision does not achieve the objective of the care or risk management plan and them having to seek other powers.

For example, an older woman with dementia is taken into hospital for respite, where there are concerns related to her husband's care of her and potential harm from him. She is thought to lack capacity but she agrees to the admission then wants to go home; a short term detention is taken which leads to a hospital based CTO, with the view she should move to nursing home, to continue to receive 'treatment'.

Her needs are for care and protection, however, and the CTO proves not to have suitable powers to make decisions about her welfare. Therefore, welfare guardianship is considered necessary, and an application is made to the Sheriff Court, which proves distressful for the woman and her family. Additionally, there is a challenge on the need for nursing home care by the husband's solicitor, who obtains independent reports which suggest her needs can be met at home provided the risks associated with her husband's lack of care and any potential risk from him is managed. Ultimately, she returns home with guardianship powers and a full care package. This case illustrates that had an adult at risk approach been taken earlier, perhaps initially (for respite, protection, assessment) by moving her to a place of safety or a suitable place either (with consent) under a removal order (2007 Act) or a removal order (2003 Act) without consent, and urgent application is made for welfare guardianship powers to effect her return home and to protect her there. The former approach meant that she was away from home for many months, with the resultant effect on her ability to return, and weeks in the latter way, with more appropriate powers sought to manage risk at home, assisted by a full care plan.

'Good things do not come easy. The road is lined with pitfalls.'

Desi Arnaz

Chapter 3

RISK AND HARM

ASSOCIATED WITH MENTAL DISORDER

Generally, vulnerable adults or adults at risk may be exposed to a variety of risk, such as an adult with physical disability who may be exposed to neglect or physical abuse. Adults affected by mental disorder, however, have particular risks associated with the effect of mental disorder of their health, welfare and safety. They may lack insight into their predicament, as many people with mental illness, such as with bipolar disorder, may have. They may have disordered thought processes, as many people with schizophrenia may have. They may lack memory and capacity to take decisions, as many people with alcohol related brain damage or dementia may have. They may have problematic behaviour as many adults with learning disability or personality disorder may have. They may be particularly open to harm and abuse from others, sometimes to financial exploitation, as many adults with dementia are, or open to sexual exploitation, as many women with learning disability may be. They may be open to self-harm, as many adults with mental illness, such as adults with severe depression, personality disorder, or eating disorder, often are.

Generally, types of risk and harm associated with vulnerable adults often include abuse, neglect and failures to act. Adults with a mental disorder, such as those affected by learning disability, however, are often at risk of psychological and emotional, physical, financial, material and sexual harm; primarily all forms of exploitation. Adults with a mental disorder are often open to domestic violence, abuse of civil and legal rights, inequality and discriminatory abuse, and social exclusion and marginalisation. This requires a greater degree and depth of response from across the Acts, and from the operative practitioners which seek to support and protect such adults.

Supporting and protecting adults at risk affected by a mental disorder can take on a number of forms and aspects. Some adults may need support to take the steps necessary to respond to and manage risk, and others may need protection against risk arising from the effects of mental disorder on health, safety, welfare, property and finances, self, and to others. Adults with mental disorder may need care and treatment on a voluntary; or, by exception, on a compulsory basis, i.e. risk to safety and protection, health, welfare, and risk of losing house, home, finances, employment and relationships.

However, what is the spectrum of risk within which an adult mental disorder may be particularly exposed? One can draw from the risk highlighted in the primary Acts, e.g. from others, from self, to welfare, to health, to property and finances, and to others; as well as on relative aspects of a person's life, e.g. employment, relationships and social circumstances.

The Acts comprehensively span these aspects of risk relative to respective duty to inquire and powers in each Act, i.e.:

a)   In the 2000 Act, under section 10, the local authority shall 'investigate any circumstances made known [to it] in which the personal welfare of an adult (with impaired capacity[predominantly because of mental disorder]) seems to be at risk', and where [the local authority] needs to take action 'necessary for the protection of the property, financial affairs or personal welfare of the adult (e.g. guardianship, s57)', and where there is an offence relating to the 'ill-treatment of wilful neglect' of an adult by a person exercising powers (s83)'.

b)   In the 2003 Act, within the local authority duty to inquiry (s33), there are terms employed such as 'ill treatment, neglect, deficiency in care or treatment, property at risk or has suffered loss or damage, living alone or without care and unable to look after property or financial affairs, and safety of some other person may be at risk'; and where the grounds for compulsory powers include (in the short term detention, s44) 'significant risk to health, safety or welfare, or the safety of any other person', and (under emergency detention, s36) where there is 'a matter of urgency'. Of course, these are terms significant across the range of mental disorder and not just to adults with mental illness, which accounts for the predominant use of orders under the Act.

c)   In the 2007 Act, there are significant terms to be found, such as in the Council duty to inquire (s4), if the Council 'knows or believes the adult is at risk (of harm)' and it 'might need to intervene to protect the person's wellbeing, property or financial affairs'. 'Adults at risk' (s3) are defined as adults who 'unable to safeguard their own well-being, property, rights, other interests', and are 'at risk of harm', and because they are affected by 'disability, mental disorder, illness or physical or mental infirmity', are 'more vulnerable to being harmed than adults who are not so affected'. Where 'another person's conduct (or is likely to cause) is causing the adult's harm' or 'the adult is engaging (or likely to engage) in conduct which causes (or likely to engage) self-harm. Here 'harm' includes (under s53) 'all harmful conduct, conduct which causes physical harm, conduct which causes psychological harm(e.g. fear, alarm or distress), unlawful conduct which appropriates or adversely affects property, rights of interests, (e.g. theft, fraud, embezzlement or extortion)' and 'conduct which causes self-harm'.

Drawing from these terms, we find key words and consistent phrases appearing, e.g.: ill treatment, neglect, conduct which causes physical harm, psychological harm, fear, alarm or distress, unlawful conduct which appropriates or adversely affects property, risk to health, safety or welfare, and personal welfare of an adult at risk. From these, we can develop a list of risks associated with mental disorder, from which to draw when considering a legislative response, i.e.:

a)   Risk from others: e.g. risk of abuse, assault, neglect, to personal welfare;

b)   Risk from self: a risk of self-harm, self-injury, or self-neglect;

c)   Risk or harm caused from a lack of (or deficiency in) care or treatment: e.g. from neglect, or from living alone, or unable to care, or ability to protect oneself, or to care, or to one's health or personal welfare;

d)   Risk to welfare, health and wellbeing: i.e. a risk to housing or physical health problems or quality of life;

e)   Risk to safety: e.g. a risk of causing, or placing oneself in, a risk situation;

f)   Risk to or harm to property and/or finances: e.g. a risk from financial exploitation and abuse, and to property and finances; and

g)   Risk to or harm of others: e.g. causing a risk to carers, children, family members, the public, because of mental disorder and arising from incapacity.

Other forms of harm or risk, associated with mental disorder, may be included within the above categories, e.g. a lack of opportunity or ability to develop, to human rights, of poverty and debt, and living in squalor, from chronic disease or physical illness, from poor or insecure housing and homelessness, or of falling into the criminal justice system.

*

In placing risk areas relative to the primary Acts, we see predominant and secondary Acts, powers and provisions, appearing (see appendix 4), i.e.:

a)   Risk from others; in particular harm (abuse) perpetrated by another adult, e.g. assault, etc.; which may be best responded to by the 2007 Act, because a) the range of harm in this Act is extensive, i.e. physical, sexual, financial, psychological and b) the Act offers relative powers, e.g. access and entry, assessment and removal orders, and/or a banning order. As the 2003 Act also offers protective measures, however, e.g. sexual offences (and penalties), this may Act may also be used to respond to this form of harm. Here, however, the 2003 Act may be viewed as a secondary option to that of the 2007 Act;

b)   Risk from self (or self-harm); which may be dramatic such as para-suicide and suicide attempts (e.g. taking pills or cutting wrists), may be best responded to by the provisions of the 2003 Act, again because the powers are relative to the risk and need, e.g. short term detention for treatment for mental illness. The 2000 Act may be appropriate if the adult is incapable and the self-harm is related to consequential behaviours, e.g. disinhibition or hitting the head with fists or against hard objects or walls, or where access or removal is required, for example where there is self-neglect or an ability to self-care, where other provisions of 2003 Act, i.e. entry, assessment and removal to a place of safety, may be needed. So, here, the 2003 Act may outweigh the others;

c)   Risk to personal welfare; such as, because of incapacity, the adult is unable to self-care; e.g. not looking after self, may be best dealt with under the 2000 Act, where there is relative welfare provision such as guardianship (welfare), or where the adult is capable although mental disordered, e.g. affected by bipolar disorder, where a relative provision under the 2003 Act may be more appropriate, e.g. a short term detention;

d)   Risk to health; where there is a need for treatment, either as a result of incapacity and where the powers of the 2003 Act aren't necessary to deliver this treatment, this may prompt treatment under the 2000 Act, i.e. where section 47 treatment for an incapable adult may be authorised, or where compulsory treatment is required to treat mental illness the provisions of the 2003 act may be needed. Where there is an abuse of medication, either by over medication overly sedating or overdosing the adult, thereby posing risk to the adult's health or life, the use of the 2007 Act may be considered;

e)   Risk to property and/or finances; where there is a need for a protective measure e.g. where the adult is incapable, unable to manage or protect property or finances, a relative provision may be found in the 2000 Act, e.g. Part 3, Access to Funds or Part 6, Guardianship (financial), or where there is financial abuse, requiring access to the provision of 2007 Act, where orders such as a banning order may be considered; and

f)   Risk to others; where there is a need to protect others from the adult affected by mental disorder; e.g. the use of the 2003 Act, where there are relative powers, e.g. short term detention; or where the adult's behaviour arises from incapacity caused by mental disorder, e.g. learning disability, where the 2000 act may have a relative power, e.g. welfare guardianship, to respond appropriately to these risks, or where other powers or provisions (out-with the primary Acts) are necessary, e.g. a) criminal justice or child care legislation, or b) to carers, or c) of because of fire due to misuse of cigarettes or cooker, etc.

*

However, often no one legislative framework neither meets the needs of an adult with mental disorder, nor responds to all risks associated with the effect of the mental disorder on an adult or on other person's life. Practitioners, therefore, working across the range of mental disorder, may need to navigate a course through the legislations, looking for resolutions to meet particular needs.

Seeking appropriate powers in this way can be like negotiating a legislative maze (or minefield!), requiring informed decisions, in particularly on a collaborative way between social workers, mental health officers, consultant psychiatrists and general practitioners, and sometimes legal advice to assist these practitioners is necessary.

'There are risks and costs to a program of action. But they are far less than the long-range risks and costs of comfortable inaction.' John F. Kennedy

Typical cases and exemplars

There are some particular groups of adults with mental disorder who appear open to risk and in need of support and protection (as well as care and treatment), across the Acts, e.g.:

a.   Adults with functional mental illness (35 – 59) (e.g. bipolar disorder, schizophrenia, depression), e.g. often living alone, affected by poor insight; potentially at risk to welfare (self-care; losing job, house, relationships), or to health or safety (frequent admissions to hospital; of self-harming/suicidal), or to sexual exploitation (in particular woman [disinhibited] with bipolar disorder), or of sometimes to physical abuse (sometimes in a domestic violence situation); of financial problems, debts, and open to financial exploitation; and sometimes using/abusing alcohol;

b.   Adults with organic mental illness (45 – 59), most commonly alcohol related brain disorder, or acquired brain injury (ARBD) or dementia; often living alone, where there are major risks to welfare (e.g. self-care; losing house / tenancy); where there is a risk to health or safety (e.g. from associated physical health problems), often affected by alcohol abuse; or open to financial exploitation and financial problems, such as debts, etc.;

c.   Older adults with organic mental illness (60 – 85), most commonly affected by Alzheimer's / dementia, often living alone, affected by major memory problems and affected by a lack of insight and incapacity (actions and decisions); often exposed to a risk to welfare (e.g. to self-care and personal hygiene) and health (e.g. poor physical health or poor nutrition), or to safety (e.g. from frailty, falls or wandering); who are often open to financial exploitation; and sometimes physical and emotional harm/abuse;

d.   Adults (16 – 55) with learning disability or autistic spectrum disorder (ASD), often living with carers or in family group, potentially lacking capacity, open to sexual harm and /or exploitation, and open to emotional, physical or financial abuse (e.g. from maladministration of benefits and funds to major theft/criminal activity); often where there is an infringement of human rights, e.g. liberty, privacy, and restrictions of independence; often affected by mental illness and/or mental health problems; and a potential lack of ability to self-care and/or to manage independently; and sometimes posing a risk to others (predominately male to female);

e.   Vulnerable adults (25 – 65) living together with mental disorder, sometimes affected by mental illness and/or learning disability. Often using alcohol and having needs for support and care. Often they have spent a good part of their lives in long term hospital care and sometimes non-complaint with services. There may be a risk posed or aggressive domination from one to the other. There may be fire risks, e.g. from cookers or dropped cigarettes, and their house may be in a poor condition with minimal furniture or equipment, and there may be little evidence of food or provisions; and

f.   Male adults (21 – 55) with mental disorder, posing risk to others, often posing risk to women and open to attack by others. Most probably adults affected by mental illness or learning disability, who have health and welfare needs which are not met, and who need treatment and care; however, may be unwilling to accept these. Sometimes the Police is involved.

*

As this work concerns 'crossing the Acts' these cases best demonstrate the issues arising in this respect and case examples will be drawn from them to assist the understanding of this work. Some case scenarios and case exemplars used here are fictitious and some generalised to preserve confidentially and anonymity. They seek to highlight the range of risk issues typical of adults affected by a mental disorder in in need of support and protection, and the groups are most likely to involve the crossing the Acts to seek appropriate provisions. These cases will cover and inform the main aspects of this work, i.e. the crossing of the Acts while exploring:

a)   inquiries and investigations;

b)   immediate powers;

c)   short term powers; and

d)   long term powers.

Particular emphasis will be given to the application of these powers across this range of scenario identified above, across the Acts, in an adult protection / risk management framework, and in the context of local adult at risk procedures. The case examples (1 to 5) summarised here, will encapsulate the circumstances, scenarios and risks highlighted, and will inform this work from this point on; and, in particular, to highlight the issues and practice application of the Acts. In addition, to ensure this work is informed by cases which have gone wrong, two MWC cases will also be added (6 and 7).

Case examples *(full descriptions on see appendices)*

1. **Walter**, a vulnerable man of 57, who has alcohol related brain damage and is affected by agitation and depression. His alcohol abuse manifests in self-harming and behavioural difficulties, disinhibition and poor self-care. He has heart disease.

2. **Wilma**, a vulnerable older person of 72, who has dementia, heart disease and abuses alcohol which manifests in poor self-care. She is generally non-compliant and resistant of supports. Her house is continually untidy and is very basic. She is thin and unkempt. She doesn't do much each day and remains at home most of the time, because she can't walk very far because of her asthma. A younger man visits her for sex.

3. **Mary**, a vulnerable adult of 23, who is affected by learning disability, which affects her ability to make important decisions regarding her safety and welfare. She lives with her aunt and uncle. They are emotional harming her, threatening to throw her out of the house and financial abusing her. Her cousin is sexually abusing her.

4. **Lesley**, a vulnerable adult of 34, living with Tom who seriously abuses alcohol. She is affected by learning disability. There has been a fire in their house caused by Tom's drinking and Lesley has sustained burns. He is known to be aggressively dominant of her. The house is in a deplorable and unsafe condition.

5. **John**, a man of 24 with learning disability and asperger's syndrome, who poses risk to women and consequently is open to attack in his local community. He has welfare needs, and needs for treatment and care on a compulsory basis.

6. **Mr H**, a man in his mid-70s with a long history of alcohol abuse. His circumstances include suicidal wishes, overdoses, duodenal ulcer, non-insulin-dependent diabetes, arthritis and various injuries, including fractures resulting from fights and falls, most often associated with alcohol abuse. The MWC found that health and social care services did not pay enough attention to his mental function and capacity (Mr H MWC).

7. **Ms A**, a 67 year old woman with a learning disability, who had been in the care of the local authority since she was eight years old. She reported being raped. Similar assaults were alleged to have taken place previously. It appeared from initial investigations, that the services responsible for her had been unable to protect her from a series of serious sexual assaults. The responses of health, social care and criminal justice services combined to deny her access to justice (Ms A MWC).

The risk or harm environment

From the above we can see certain risk factors emerging, which taken together form a collection, i.e. a risk landscape or an environment of within which an adult with mental disorder may be exposed (see appendix 1). Confirming an environment of risk, populated by the typical risks an adult with a mental disorder may be exposed, helps us to see the relative range of risk factors associated with mental disorder on such adults, to assist in the preparation of relative and responsive risk assessments and protection planning.

From this landscape, one can see certain clusters of risk appearing (see appendix 2), which formed around primary risk aspects, may be viewed as primary risk domains (see appendix 3), i.e.:

Physical harm: e.g. from assault, e.g. punching, slapping, burning, pushing, grabbing, biting; or ill treatment, abuse of medication, use of weapons, use of physical force, restraint, force feeding or starving;

Risk to finances: e.g. from theft, exploitation, forcing to give money, misappropriation (of funds), extortion, embezzlement; abuse of powers (e.g. DWP appointee, intromission with funds, power of attorney or financial guardianship); to savings, accounts, benefits, rent, security; or from imprudence or debt;

Risk to property: such as to housing, residence, tenancy, mortgage, or inheritance; and movable property and personal things, such as equipment, goods, pets, and clothes;

Sexual harm: from sexual exploitation to multiple rape, from the use of sexual language, forcing to watch pornography, lack of consent or incapacity to consent; touching and trying to touch; and sometimes from disinhibition or a lack of insight into safety;

Psychological harm: e.g. using force/abuse, emotional harm, causing fear, alarm and distress; the use of blackmail, threatening to harm adult and to harm others the adults care for, excluding the adult or preventing contact with others, to dashing confidence, undermining, running down and belittling, treating with a lack of dignity, and the application of tyranny;

Risk from neglect of needs: e.g. wilful neglect, needs not being met, lack of care and support, a lack of personal care (washing, getting out of bed, dressing, eating, toileting, housework, travel); lack of treatment and mismanagement of medication; causing squalor, lack of hygiene, insanitary condition, or services being cut off;

Self-harm: e.g. from para-suicide, suicide attempts, cutting parts of body, overdosing, or a reluctance or inability to self-care, etc.;

Verbal harm: e.g. from shouting, swearing, brow-beating, or name calling;

Risk to health: e.g. from abuse of alcohol or drugs, lack of treatment, from cold or hypothermia; from poor diet and nutrition; or causing physical illness, mental illness or relapse;

Risk to safety: e.g. from frailty (falls), fire: from dropped cigarettes, cooker and fires; or from wandering and traffic;

Risk to welfare: e.g. losing relationships; causing divorce, unemployment, homelessness; or from abuse of powers (e.g. welfare power of attorney);

Risk to other persons: e.g. to carers, family, children, e.g. lack of childcare or education, to public and neighbours; causing emotional harm, stress, fatigue, from behaviour (anti-social), or sometimes causing sexual or physical harm;

Risk to rights: e.g. civil and legal; to being protected; to education, independence, privacy, social contact, social inclusion, leisure, choice, control, friends, employment, ownership, freedom; or from abuse, discrimination, inequality or stigma;

Institutional harm: e.g. from harmful care services, strict systems and regimes, neglect or abuse or from poor standards and patterns of care; and

General aspects or effects of harm: e.g. arising from a crises or short term episode of risk; from committing offences and falling into the criminal justice system; from a long term risk scenario; to harm being perpetrated in a particular way; or from bodies, persons or proxies, or from persons (third parties) promoting or facilitating the harm.

Signs and indicators

To explore risk, practitioners need to be aware of and sensitive to the signs of financial, physical, sexual, or emotional risk and harm, and how these types of harm manifest on the lives of adults with a mental disorder. Generally, signs of abuse of vulnerable adults or children may be quite explicit such as bruising and injury, etc., or they may express something is happening to them in a variety of ways. However, for adults affected by a mental disorder, there may be particular circumstances which may need to be observed, e.g.:

a)   for adults with a learning disability, who are being harmed, the signs may be less explicit, e.g. indicators may be expressed by emotions, such as distress, anger or withdrawal, or behaviour such as self-harming or hitting out, or sometimes by inappropriate behaviour, such as overly sexualised activity; or

b)   for adults with dementia, signs may be agitation or depression, or confusion over what is happening, or where self-care, health or personal hygiene deteriorates. Physical signs may also be observed, e.g. sleepiness, which may indicate over medication being applied, or health problems, losing weight, infections occurring (sexual) unusually; or

c)   for adults with mental illnesses, such as bipolar disorder or schizophrenia, already with disordered thoughts about others, feeling persecuted or harmed by others, care has to be applied, both not to disregard any real harm, where there are unreal thoughts, or by regarding unreal harm as real.

Practitioners should allow the benefit of the doubt until proved otherwise. Additionally, there may be anxiety or signs or demonstrations of fear towards others, or the adult may not be letting people into his/her house, or there may be indicators from others of undue pressure or over dominance or control of the adult. There may be signs of financial harm demonstrated through poverty or debts. Whatever, practitioners need to keep their eyes, ears *and* mind open to signs, which may not be so apparent for this vulnerable group.

'Everything is dangerous, my dear fellow. If it wasn't so, life wouldn't be worth living.'

Oscar Wilde

PART TWO

THE PRIMARY ACTS

Chapter 4

THE ACTS IN GENERAL

The primary Acts

The 2000, 2003 and 2007 Acts are the primary Acts that protect adults with mental disorder in Scotland. They also provide support, care and treatment, alongside the 1968, 1990 and 2002 Acts, which seek to ensure access to care and support services. Combining the primary Acts, with which this work is concerned, with this range of supportive legislation, offers a comprehensive range of legislative provision across support, protection, care and treatment.

See Appendix 4 for a full description of general provision 'across the Acts'

In their application, however, there is often a mesh of response to risk between formal and informal provisions; however, before formal or compulsory actions are pursued, practitioners need to rule out supporting and protecting an adult at risk on a voluntary, informal and consensual basis, in keeping with the principle of the least restrictive approach, a principle common to all the primary Acts. Furthermore, accessing legislation involves confirming respective access criteria or crossing thresholds to access the powers or provisions of the Acts.

The 2000 Act

The 2000 Act protects the welfare, finances and property of an adult incapable because of mental disorder (and physical disability). It provides authority to treat mental disorder (s47), but it does not offer compulsory powers in this regard, and certain (safeguarded) medical treatments are out-with the scope of this Act, in particular those specified in the 2003 Act. Across an adult's range of decisions and actions affected by incapacity, and its effect on health, welfare, finances and property, the 2000 Act has provisions that both support and protect. The provisions of the Act, however, should be implemented in the context of local interagency working and assessment and care management functions, and delivered within the context of the local authority COP for the Act (Scottish Government, 2008b). Local authority functions under the Act include, where necessary, applying for a guardianship order to safeguard and protect the adult's welfare or financial interests. In practice, guardianship is used predominantly to protect adults with dementia, adults with learning disabilities, adults with ARBD, adults with acquired brain injury, and some adults with severe and enduring mental illness (MWC, 2008b). One of the 2000 Act's deficiencies, however, is that it lacks emergency powers; for example, it has no warrants for entry or removal. This is where consideration should be given to moving across to the 2003 and/or 2007 Acts, which have such powers.

The 2003 Act

The 2003 Act has provisions across health, safety and welfare risk, which both support and protect, and which provides treatment and care, and which gives greater rights to services and provides a range of powers in response to risk to an adult or the safety of other persons. It also specifies a range of special criminal offences (Part 21) where mentally disordered adults are open to sexual exploitation, abuse, ill-treatment and neglect.

The 2003 Act, however, has no civil powers against harmers, e.g. to ban (now in the 2007 Act), nor has it powers to manage finances or to protect property (in the 2000 Act for adults with incapacity). Where it is clear after inquiry/assessment under the 2003 Act, action under the 2000 or 2007 Act is necessary, in particular where the powers therein to protect are more appropriate, e.g. welfare guardianship (s57, 2000 Act) or a banning order (s19, 2007 Act), or where the duty to protect falls more appropriately within either of these Acts, the relevant Act would be used.

There are three primary compulsory powers in the 2003 Act, i.e. (a) a short-term detention certificate (STDC) (s44); (b) an emergency detention certificate (EDC) (s36); and (c) a compulsory treatment order (CTO) (s63). Depending on the adult's needs and risks, these provisions may be applied in isolation of each other or applied consecutively, and also may follow inquiry and investigation, perhaps where an adult has been removed to a place of safety (ss293/294/297).

The 2007 Act

The 2007 Act protects a range of adults at risk, including those affected by mental disorder and those incapable because of this. It has a range of duties and powers, which include investigation and the banning of harmers from being in an adult at risk's premises. However, it has to be viewed in the overall legislative context, which includes the 2000 and 2003 Acts, when relating to those affected by mental disorder.

The 2007 Act, however, lacks powers to provide care or treatment, or to protect welfare and finances on a long-term basis. This is where consideration needs to be given to the powers of the 2003 Act and/or the 2000 Act, particularly where immediate action is required under the 2003 Act, where long-term action is needed under the 2000 Act, or where long-term action combining the 2000, 2003 and 2007 Acts is necessary.

*

Taken together, the primary Acts provide a comprehensive response to the range of risk with which an adult with mental disorder may be exposed. Certain Acts respond in a primary way to particular types of risk and 'risk domains' described earlier, e.g. the 2007 Act is designed primarily to respond to risk from others and its primary power, a banning order, seeks to protect the adult from a harmer. It is useful, however, to know what Act responds best to which range of risk because it helps the practitioner to move quickly to that particular Act.

Appendix 5 highlights the range of risk that is covered across the Acts, i.e. from others, from self, to personal welfare, to health, to property and finances, and to others. It also encapsulates some of the types of harm contained therein (e.g. from self: self-neglect or lack of self-care), and also gives examples to assist understanding. The 'primary (or predominant) Acts' that respond in a primary way to the types and examples of risk are also indicated, e.g. risk from others: 2007 Act (predominant Act) and 2003 Act (secondary Act), because the 2003 Act also offers a response to risk from others, e.g. duty to inquire and sexual offences. Appendix 5 takes this a step forward, where powers and provisions relative to particular risks are indicated.

In its composite form, key practitioners need to be comfortable with responding to the range of typical risks with which an adult with mental disorder is exposed, and of using the primary or predominant Acts and relative provisions that respond best to this risk.

Thresholds and entry criteria

In crossing the Acts, the primary common criterion to access any of the primary Acts is 'mental disorder'; this is because it features in the criteria of each of the primary Acts as it affects adults. However, each Act has specific entrance criteria, i.e. a set of conditions that need to be met to allow the adult access to the provisions (and powers) within.

Where affected by mental disorder, an adult may have access to the 2003 Act, which would offer care and treatment, and a range of rights, duties and provisions to assist them to cope with the effect of the mental disorder on themselves, their carers and their families. In accessing the 2003 Act, this does not need to determine severity as a means to access its services nor does it require a confirmation of risk; being affected by a mental disorder is enough. Mental disorder is defined under s328 as:

- mental illness;
- personality disorder; or
- learning disability; or
- a multiple combination.

According to the 2003 Act, 'mental disorder' is 'however caused or manifested, but not just by reason of sexual orientation, sexual deviancy, transsexualism, transvestitism, dependence on, or use of, alcohol or drugs, behaviours that cause, or likely to cause, harassment, alarm or distress to any other person, or acting as no prudent person would act'.

Access to the 2000 Act, for a person or an organisation acting on behalf of an 'adult with incapacity', and to the provisions of the Act, relies on confirming an adult with incapacity, so defined in the Act (under s1) as a person who has attained the age of 16, who is incapable of:

- acting; or

- making decisions; or
- communicating decisions; or
- understanding decisions; or
- retaining the memory of decisions,

in relation to any particular matter, by reason of 'mental disorder'(or of inability to communicate because of physical disability), and 'incapacity shall be construed accordingly'. To access the 2007 Act, an 'adult at risk' has to be confirmed as an adult, so defined (s3), who:

- is unable to safeguard her/his own well-being, property, rights or other interests;
- is at risk of harm; and
- because s/he is affected by disability, 'mental disorder', illness or physical or mental infirmity, is more vulnerable to being harmed than adults who are not so affected.

An 'adult at risk' of harm, for the Act's purposes, is if:

- another person's conduct is causing (or likely to cause) the adult to be harmed, or
- the adult is engaging (or likely to engage) in conduct which causes (or is likely to cause) self-harm.

The term 'abuse' is not favoured within the 2007 Act. 'Harm' is, however (defined in s53), which includes all harmful conduct, including neglect and other failures to act and, in particular (a) conduct that causes physical harm; (b) conduct that causes psychological harm; (c) unlawful conduct that appropriates or adversely affects property, rights or interests; and (d) conduct that causes self-harm.

Medical assessment is required to confirm (formally) access to the 2000 and the 2003 Act, but not so the 2007 Act, which requires the local authority to confirm an 'adult at risk'; however, confirming the adult is so affected by mental disorder may require medical assessment.

A practitioner or agency may, of course, access (a) one Act, e.g. the 2003 Act, where a person may be affected by mental disorder, but not incapable nor at risk of harm, or (b) a combination of the Acts, e.g. where a person who is affected by mental disorder, incapable because of this, and is at risk of harm.

Having access to any or all of the Acts not only allows access to the services and provisions within the Acts, but also the formal measures and legal rights therein. Access to the formal measures of the Acts, however, requires further access conditions to be applied (criteria or grounds), e.g. under the 2003 Act, where the person has to have mental disorder, where there is a risk to health, safety or welfare, and where informal treatment is not possible, etc.

Equally, an adult at risk with mental disorder may need support and protection under the 2000 or 2003 Acts, but may not be confirmed as an 'adult at risk' under the 2007 Act. For example, a mentally disordered adult may be at risk from others, but able to safeguard their own well-being, thereby falling out-with the terms of the 2007 Act, but potentially falling within the terms of the 2003 Act. Furthermore, an adult with impaired capacity because of mental disorder may not be at risk of harm as defined by the 2007 Act, but may need support and protection under the 2000 Act. So a selective use of the Acts, based on access criteria, is necessary to ensure correct access to the legislative framework which bests supports and protects the adult.

See Appendix 7 for a 'side by side' description of the general access criteria.

Supportive and underpinning legislation

No protective legislation can exist without the assistance of supporting and underpinning legislation, i.e.:

- Community care legislation (i.e. the 1990 Act), which amends the 1968 Act (s12) makes provision for assessment and care management, and health and community care services;
- Social work legislation (i.e. the 1968 Act), which, in many cases, provides a 'duty of care' (i.e. s12) and other duties to provide services for vulnerable people; and
- Carers' legislation (e.g. the 2002 Act), which requires social work agencies to consider the needs of carers while assessing vulnerable people.

The Social Work (Scotland) Act 1968 (the 1968 Act) remains the fundamental tenet, within section 12, to provide 'a duty of care', where there is a duty of every local authority to promote social welfare by providing advice, guidance and assistance; and under section 12A (amended by the NHS and Community Care Act 1990) where it appears to a local authority for whom they are under a duty or have a power to provide, or to secure the provision of, community care services, the local authority shall make an assessment of the needs of that person for those services, and shall then decide, having regard to the results of that assessment, and taking account of the carer's needs (amended by the Community Care and Health (Scotland) Act 2002) (the 2002 Act), whether the needs of the person being assessed call for the provision of any such services. Section 13 ZA of the 1968 Act allows local authorities to provide services to adults affected by incapacity who cannot authorise these services. The 2002 Act also introduced free personal care, and creates expansion of direct payments.

Carers of adults with mental disorder at risk have a unique role caring role and, of course, have particular needs and require an assessment reflective of their needs and their role in protecting the adult at risk. Carers, relatives and friends of people with mental disorder have features in common with other carers, but with needs that are distinctively theirs, where having to cope with difficult behaviours, delusions, hallucinations and indeed risk presents particular personal and emotional stress. Their needs for information and support are very much tied to the needs of the adult at risk, indeed often acting as proxies in the care and treatment of people with mental disorder; all the more important to provide appropriate support after assessment.

Carers, however, can also be harmers, whether it is either intentional or unwittingly done. The harm, however, can also arise from fatigue or tiredness, or anger or frustration in or from the caring role. Key practitioners need to find a balance between the needs and risks of adults at risk in this caring scenario, and, again, find the appropriate legislative framework to protect the interests of the carer and cared for.

The supporting 1968, 1990 and 2002 Acts offer a range of services, e.g. assessment and access to services; care management; a duty of care (and protection); the care programme approach (CPA); services in the community, at home or in residential or nursing home care; carer assessment/support; direct payments; care management; single shared assessments; and access to treatment following community care assessment.

Other supportive provision includes the following:

- The Human Rights Act 1998: all modern legislation should be compatible with this and be tested against it. The Act enshrines the European Convention on Human Rights, which includes, e.g. the right to life (article 2); freedom from torture and inhuman or degrading treatment or punishments (article 3); the right to liberty and security of the person (article 5); the right for private and family life (article 8); freedom of thought, conscience and religion (article 9); all inalienable rights, which of course can be abused by others.

Interestingly, article 8 is an important determinant when considering protecting an adult who does not consent to action but appears to lack capacity to make that decision. Does taking action to remove this adult contravene his/her human rights (article 8)?

Constrained or denied human rights obviously falls within the context of harm and abuse of vulnerable adults, and 'public authorities' have to 'act in a way which is incompatible with Convention rights'. Human rights are enshrined within the primary Acts (the 2000, 2003 and 2007 Acts) discussed, which are exercised by 'lawful' bodies, i.e. the Sheriff Court and the Mental Health Tribunal for Scotland (MHTS), where adults may exercise their legal rights such as a right of representation and appeal, etc. A 'human rights' test may also assist practitioners when confirming the most suitable provision across the Acts, e.g. which Act or provision restricts the adult's rights less, e.g. to liberty? However, the Acts also enshrine these rights as articulated through principles such as minimum restriction.

- The Vulnerable Witnesses (Scotland) Act 2004 (the 2004 Act) (a) formalises the existing special measures that are available to vulnerable witnesses when giving evidence in the High Court, Sheriff Court and children's hearings; (b) extends the definition of 'vulnerable witnesses' where there is a significant risk that the quality of their evidence will be diminished through fear or distress and (c) introduces new special measures and provides other provisions designed to help child and vulnerable adult witnesses give their best evidence. Clearly, this Act has significance in vulnerable adult cases and, in particular, adults affected by a mental disorder who have been harmed, where criminal justice action is necessary. The Ms A case (MWC, 2008a) indicated concerns in the criminal justice system in supporting the evidence of Ms A. The term 'justice denied' highlights this. The MWC recommended that 'guidance should take account of the special measures which are now available for vulnerable adult witnesses in criminal cases under the Vulnerable Witnesses (Scotland) Act 2004, as well as the need to consult with relevant others involved in the protection of vulnerable adults on a case by case basis' (MWC, 2008a, p5), thereby guiding key practitioners in their support and protection of adults at risk.

- The Appropriate Adult Scheme (Scottish Government, 2006) also has relevance here, where the police, when interviewing an adult with mental disorder should refer to the local Appropriate Adult Scheme, to ensure the allocation of an 'appropriate adult' to be present during interviews of the adult by the police, to assist and support the adult and to ensure good communication between the adult and the police officer(s). This has obvious importance where interviewing an adult with mental disorder, e.g. an adult with a learning disability who may not understand the nature or consequence of the interview questions.

- The Protection of Vulnerable Groups Act 2007, and the Protection of Vulnerable Groups Scheme (Scottish Government, 2008c), helps 'to ensure that those who have regular contact with children and protected adults through paid and unpaid work do not have a known history of harmful behaviour'; again, having significance for the support and protection of adults at risk with mental disorder.

- The Regulation of Care (Scotland) Act 2001 established a system of care regulation in Scotland. The Act's purpose is to provide greater protection for people in need of care services. The Care Commission (Scottish Commission for the Regulation of Care) registers and inspects services against a set of national care standards. The standards outline the quality of service that care service users have the right to expect. They have been developed with the intention that the quality of care provided and received throughout Scotland will be consistent. The standards also ensure that all care services are measured against a set of general principles. Significantly, the Care Commission may conduct investigations into the professional conduct and competence of care staff, to establish the facts of an incident or complaint prior to any consideration being given to the need for disciplinary action being taken against an employee, which may also lead to de-registration from the council's register or other appropriate register. This mainly concerns professional staff and is related to professional conduct or competence in the carrying out of duties in situations where it is considered advisable to have the matter investigated and a report prepared by officers qualified to do so.

*

Additionally, there is a range of disability, housing, homelessness and equalities legislation, all of which support vulnerable adults at risk. Key practitioners need to be mindful of these when supporting and protecting adults at risk, to ensure that adults' rights are upheld and public authorities meet their respective duties towards adults.

The United Nations Convention on the Rights of Persons with Disabilities places a duty on public authorities to ensure access to justice (as mentioned in the Ms A case: MWC, 2008a) for adults with a learning disability, e.g. 'recognising that discrimination against any person based on disability is a violation of the inherent dignity and worth of the human person'; and recognising that women and girls with disabilities are often at greater risk, both within and outside the home, of violence, injury or abuse, neglect or negligent treatment, maltreatment or exploitation.

These legislations, working in synthesis, provide a framework for support and supplement the range of primary adult protection legislation.

Chapter 5

DUTIES TO SUPPORT AND PROTECT

Duties to provide

There is a range of care and support services across the primary Acts that underpins and supports any adult at risk response. The primary Acts also, however, have a range of provision and duties, which both support and provide:

- The 2003 Act, which 'supports and provides', e.g.:

  - access to key practitioners such as MHOs, responsible medical officers and general practitioners;
  - access to an independent advocacy service (s259); and
  - access to the range of duties applied on the local authority and health board, i.e. the local authority has a duty under the 2003 Act to provide care and support services (s25) and services designed to promote well-being and social development (s26);

This is the basis for provision of services and support for people in the community affected by mental disorder, thereby supporting and protecting the person on an informal basis in the context of a care arrangement; the duty to provide such services is to all people, including children and young people, who have or who have had a mental disorder, and not just those subject to (or who have been subject to) compulsory measures;

  - an assessment of needs for community care services where an MHO notifies the local authority that a patient in respect of whom the authority is under a duty or has a power to provide or secure the provision of community care services may be in need of such services. In those circumstances, the local authority must carry out an assessment of needs under section 12A of the Social Work (Scotland) Act 1968(s227); and
  - where a written request for an assessment of the needs of a person with a mental disorder has been received by a local authority or health board, provided the circumstances referred to in section 228(2) are met, the local authority or health

board is under a duty to respond to the request within 14 days, indicating whether or not they intend to carry out the assessment and, if not, why not (s228).

- The 2000 Act, which is set in the context of the relevant COPs, in particular (respective of adults at risk) the COP of the local authority, ensures assistance, information and advice from local authority officers, such as social workers and MHOs, and health care practitioners, such as GPs and consultant psychiatrists. Other local authority duties under the Act, include:

  – investigating complaints in relation to those exercising welfare powers, where powers are wrongfully, inappropriately or dangerously exercised in respect of the adult's welfare (s10);
  – supervising private welfare guardians in the exercise of their functions, and to supervising a welfare attorney where ordered to do so by the Sheriff (s20);
  – providing information and advice to carers and relatives, or proxies with welfare powers, e.g. where an adult is losing decision-making capacity, or appears to have lost the ability to make some or all decisions for themselves, or has never had full capacity to make decisions; and
  – consulting the Public Guardian and/or MWC where there is, or appears to be, a common interest.

- The 2007 Act imposes a duty on the council to have regard to the importance of the provision of appropriate services (including, in particular, independent advocacy services), where the council considers that it needs to intervene in order to protect an adult at risk of harm (s6).

Other services are not defined in the 2007 Act, but thought should be given to practical and emotional supports that may be provided by social work and health care services, and from voluntary sector and private sector providers, e.g. the provision of mainstream health and social care services, such as housing, independent living, financial services, occupational therapy, counselling, support for carers, and Community Health Partnership services. Other useful services may include Victim Support Scotland, which provides emotional support, practical help and essential information to victims, witnesses and others affected by crime, and the Vulnerable Witnesses (Scotland) Act 2004, which provides support measures to help vulnerable adults participate more fully in court proceedings.

The primary Acts also both support and confirm medical treatment for adults at risk with mental disorder. Medical treatment is confirmed and defined under the 2003 Act (s329), i.e. nursing, care, psychological intervention, habilitation and rehabilitation (including education, training in work, and social and independent living skills). Provision of treatment for mental disorder is also governed by (a) advance statements (s275) and (b) safeguarded treatments under the Act, e.g. ECT, treatment over two months, certain surgical treatments, etc.; and (c) compulsory powers (where necessary).

The 2000 Act may authorise treatment for the physical or mental health of the adult incapable because of mental disorder (s47); and, in the context of proxy powers, e.g. welfare power of attorney (Part 1) or welfare guardianship or intervention order (Part 6), medical practitioners may be required to consult these parties over the adult's treatment. Within the 2007 Act, medical examination in the context of inquiry is available, which can be provided through the overall inquiry or based within assessment orders. In this context, where an adult at risk needs medical treatment, this should be provided.

The informal and voluntary approach

Non-compulsory, or informal, measures, with the consent and full involvement and participation of the adult, should be the prevailing principle of adult protection whenever possible. Much of the basis of informality, of course, exists within the 2003 Act, which succeeds the 'informality' rule in previous legislations, i.e. the 1984 and 1960 acts, where formal powers were to be used by exception. This informal approach is augmented by the 2003 Act duty of the local authority to provide care and support for persons in the community who have or have had a mental disorder (s25).

The 2003 Act was implemented 'with inclusion in mind' (Scottish Government, 2007), a Scottish Government policy to promote involvement, participation and control for all who might fall within the Act's remits. It offers a way of improving the quality of life of those affected by mental disorder and espouses, in its principles and philosophy, a determination not only to offer new and innovative care and treatment options, but also to promote the mental health, well-being and social development of people affected by mental disorder, reaching every aspect of life that promotes well-being rather than just the elimination of symptoms. It seeks to move away from segregated services, strengthening inclusive opportunities, and promoting access to universal services rather than just specialist services.

The 2003 Act confirms a duty of local authorities to provide services that offer care and support, services designed to promote the well-being and social development of such persons, thereby supporting and protecting the person on an informal basis in the context of a care arrangement.

Care and support services include 'residential accommodation and personal care and personal support, but not nursing care'. Personal care means 'care, which relates to the day-to-day physical tasks and needs of the person (such as eating and washing) and to mental processes related to those tasks and needs (such as remembering to eat and wash)'. Personal support means 'counselling, or other help, provided as part of a planned programme, which is important where an adult may need a programme of counselling or therapy, which may assist an adult regain ability and confidence, or to desist from self-harming behaviour'. Care and support services provided shall be 'designed to minimise the effect of the mental disorder on such persons and give such persons the opportunity to lead lives, which are as normal as possible'. A local authority shall provide, or secure the provision of, services to promote the well-being and social development of persons who have or who have had a mental disorder who are not in hospital. These services include the provision of social, cultural and recreational activities; and training and assistance in obtaining and undertaking employment for such of those persons as are over school age. Adults in need of support and protection may be assisted here, where an adult's well-being may be advanced through access to day services, including day care, recreational opportunities, drop-in centres and support services, and cultural enhancement through services that reflect and support minority cultures.

The 2007 Act consolidates the need to pursue voluntary support and protection wherever possible; indeed, consent of the adult is required, with a couple of exceptions, i.e. undue pressure or incapacity to consent. It is envisaged (and established in practice) that the provision of 'appropriate services' (s6) in the majority of cases will be the primary means to support and protect adults at risk, including those with mental disorder, rather than pursuing formal protection powers under the Act. Informal assistance or intervention must be well assessed and planned so that the adult is provided with the right kind of support, particularly in cases of harm where the adult must feel supported and listened to, and able to be in control of any potential process towards protective action.

Supportive provisions (in the primary Acts)

Each Act has a range of supportive provisions, some of which may need additional authority, e.g.:

- The 2003 Act has a range of non-compulsory and supportive provisions, which may assist to support and protect adults at risk with mental disorder, e.g.:

  - advance statements, which are 'wish lists (wishes on how to be treated and wishes on how not to be so treated)' made by the adult, where the medical practitioner has to 'have regard to the wishes specified' (s276); being mindful that 'medical treatment' covers 'care', which might include the support and protection of the adult, e.g. the adult may indicate that they should not be admitted to a care setting for treatment, which may be an issue when pursuing protective powers, e.g. an assessment order (2007 Act), for a medical examination;
  - access to independent advocacy services, where the Act requires health boards and local authorities to collaborate with each other to secure the availability of independent advocacy services and to make sure that mentally disordered persons have the opportunity to make use of the services (s259). These services are essential in the support and protection of an adult at risk with mental disorder, by empowering them to take steps to protect themselves from harm or in supporting the adult through any formal process, e.g. appearing in court or a tribunal; and
  - access to a 'named person' (s250) who the (capable) adult nominates and who has a role in the formal provisions of the Act, e.g. seeking assessments or appeals.

- The 2000 Act has a range of non-compulsory provisions with which to protect adults whose capacity may be impaired because of mental disorder, i.e.:

- Part 2: Powers of Attorney:
    - a welfare power of attorney (s16), which may provide a useful provision where a capable adult grants authority to a person to manage or protect their welfare on incapacity, or sometimes where there is the potential of losing capacity, and
    - a continuing power of attorney(s15), which may be a useful provision where a capable (mentally disordered) adult needs a person to manage or protect their finances before or on enduring incapacity;
- Part 3: Access to Funds, where the accounts and funds of an incapable adult may be managed, following authority given by the Office of the Public Guardian: this may be a useful provision to protect the (limited) financial management of an adult incapable due to mental disorder;
- Part 4: Management of Residents' Finances, which is a useful provision where there is no one managing the resident or patient's money or where there is a risk caused by a person or organisation mismanaging the adult's finances;
- Part 5: Medical Treatment and Research, where an adult with impaired capacity has health needs or health care risks, e.g. an adult with mental illness who needs medication for the illness, where there is no need to pursue compulsory treatment under the 2003 Act; and
- in the context of the 2000 Act, the informal provisions of the 1968 Act, i.e. s13ZA; e.g., to provide a framework of care and support to an adult with incapacity, which offers a less restrictive and less formal provision than that of welfare guardianship. This approach is applied, of course, where the adult is compliant, and where all parties agree that the approach is suitable.

The 2007 Act imposes a duty on councils (s6) to 'have regard to the provision of appropriate services', including independent advocacy services, where the council considers it needs to intervene to protect an adult at risk of harm.

In this context, the provision of an independent advocacy worker is a valuable way of empowering an adult and helping them to get the information needed to make choices about services available, to make views known and to take independent steps to remove themselves from risk of harm.

Other services are not defined in the Act, but consideration should be given to practical and personal support provided by social work, health, the voluntary sector and private sector providers, including the provision of mainstream health and social care services such as housing, independent living services, financial and benefits advice, occupational therapy, counselling, support for carers and Community Health Partnership services.

The principles

The principles of the Acts are the guiding lights of good practice in the application of the primary Acts, emphasising the primary principle of non-compulsory care and treatment wherever possible when responding to risk. The principles are in the Acts and not outside in a code of practice, and therefore they have statutory significance, setting legal precedent, and are a formal requirement, where powers can be challenged on their application or not.

Practically, they support, protect and inform the use of the statutory provisions; having critical significance in (a) the application for statutory orders, (b) the protection of rights of persons subject to powers and (c) the supervision and monitoring of powers by private proxies, agencies or practitioners. Individually (and collectively) they ensure that:

- the intervention will produce benefit (maximum benefit in the 2003 Act) to the adult, where such benefit cannot be reasonably achieved without the intervention (2000 and 2007 Acts);
- practitioners consider a range of options (2003 Act), likely to fulfil the object of the intervention;
- the intervention is the least restrictive to the adult's freedom (2000 and 2007 Acts), thereby discharging in a manner that involves minimum restriction where subject to compulsion (2003 Act), consistent with the purpose of the intervention (2000 Act);
- the adult's ascertainable wishes and feelings (2007 Act), past and present (2000 Act) are regarded, by any means of communication/in a way most likely to be understood (2003 Act);
- where intervention is to be made (2000 Act), account shall be taken of the views of others (relevant persons: 2003 Act) including nearest relative, primary carer, guardian/attorney, and others with an interest (2007 Act);
- the patient participates in the discharge of the function, providing the adult with such information and support as is necessary to participate (2003 and 2007 Acts);
- equality and diversity are respected (2003 Act); ensuring that the adult should not to be treated less favourably than any other in a comparable situation (2007 Act);
- the adult's abilities, background and characteristics are respected (2007 Act), encouraging the adult to exercise whatever skills they have, and the development of new skills (2000 Act); and
- regard is given to the provision of appropriate services and continuing care and the needs and circumstances of the patient's carer (2003 Act).

See Appendix 8 for the respective principles across the Acts 'side by side'.

Chapter 6

INQUIRY

The range of inquiry duties across the Acts is contained in:

The 2000 Act	The 2003 Act	The 2007 Act
Duty to investigate (s10)	Duty to cause inquires to be made (s33)	Duty to make inquiries (s4)

Duty to inquire

In each of the primary Acts, there is a duty of the local authority to inquire as it relates to adults at risk and, particularly, those affected by mental disorder. Inquiry, of course, has formal significance, involving investigation. The confirmation of a duty to inquire, however, also provides a mandate to inquire and an authority within which to conduct an investigation.

Each duty to inquire has to be considered in its own right, assessing the adult against the criteria provided in each Act, thereby responding to the corresponding duties to inquire and other duties contained in COPs and other Scottish Government guidelines, e.g. an inquiry under section 10 of the 2000 Act requires the local authority to provide a report to the MWC (see Scottish Government, 2008b).

There may be occasions where an adult's circumstances fits more than one duty to inquire, so agencies may be operating within more than one duty to inquire and responding to the respective duties in each. Almost a 'blended approach' may be necessary in certain circumstances, e.g. where the personal welfare of an adult seems to be at risk or there is a complaint against a welfare proxy under section 10 of the 2000 Act, and where the adult is an adult at risk under the 2007 Act and meets the duty to inquire there under section 4 of that Act. As discussed earlier, there is a danger, moreover, of 'going down the wrong road', for example where section 4 of the 2007 Act is used exclusively over s33 of the 2003 Act or s10 of the 2000 Act, which might identify and confirm duty respective of 'adults at risk', however may miss those adults whose 'personal welfare' is at risk (s10) or where 'some other deficiency of care and treatment (s33)' is not sufficient to be confirmed as 'harmful conduct (under s4)' or an adult is posing risk to others (s33). 'Going down the wrong road' may also leave practitioners without proper mandate and authority; for example, where a council officer, in conducting an inquiry under section 4 finds him/herself in the context of a section 33 inquiry and needing access to corresponding powers, e.g. warrants under section 35 (which require a MHO to obtain), would have to either draw in a MHO or transfer the case thereto.

The respective duties to inquire are covered in section 33 of the 2003 Act, section 10(d) of the 2000 Act, and section 4 of the 2007 Act. In their common application, they apply to adults, i.e. aged sixteen and over, and primarily they are duties of the local authority, in this respect the social work department, which would relate to an adult within the local authority area.

They provide a respective duty to:

– 'investigate the circumstances of an adult' (s10 [d] 2000 Act), made known to it, and in some cases to 'investigate any complaints' against a welfare proxy (s10 [c]);
– 'cause inquires to be made' (s33, 2003 Act);and to
– 'make inquiries about a person's well-being, property or financial affairs' (s4, 2007 Act);

where any of the following circumstances apply:

– the adult is at risk of harm (s3(1), 2007 Act); and
– the council might need to intervene in order to protect the adult's well-being, property or financial affairs (s4, 2007 Act);
– the person may be or may have been subject, or exposed, to ill-treatment, neglect or some other deficiency in care or treatment (s33, 2003 Act);
– that because of mental disorder, the person's property may be, or may have suffered, loss or damage, or may be, or may have been, at risk of suffering loss or damage (s33, 2003 Act);
– the person may be living alone or without care, and unable to look after themselves or their property or financial affairs (s33, 2003 Act);
– that because of mental disorder the safety of some other person may be at risk (s33, 2003 Act); or
– where the personal welfare of an adult (incapable [mental disorder] s1, 2000 Act) appears to be 'at risk' or is 'in jeopardy' or 'where the adult, impaired by incapacity, needs support and protection' (s10, 2000 Act).

And where:

• 'it appears' the adult has mental disorder and risk circumstances (above [2003 Act]) apply (2003 Act);
• an adult (2007 Act):
  – 'is unable to safeguard her/his own well-being, property, rights or other interests;
  – is at risk of harm (defined s53); and

- because he/she is affected by disability, mental disorder, illness or physical or mental infirmity, is more vulnerable to being harmed than adults who are not so affected; and
- an adult (incapable, 2000 Act):
  - whose living circumstances has deteriorated or is at risk of harm from others, (e.g. financial or sexual exploitation);
  - is at risk from poor safety and security, e.g. wandering, mismanaging cookers, fires, etc.; or
  - is being neglected or ill-treated; or
  - has a proxy misusing powers against them under the Act.

'Harm' is defined under section 53 of the 2007 Act, which includes:

all harmful conduct [which includes neglect and other failures to act], and, in particular includes:

(a) conduct which causes physical harm;
(b) conduct which causes psychological harm (e.g. by causing fear, alarm or distress);
(c) unlawful conduct which appropriates or adversely affects property, rights of interests (e.g. theft, fraud, embezzlement or extortion); and
(d) conduct which causes self-harm.

(s53 2007 Act)

The adult is at risk of harm for these purposes if:

(a) another person's conduct is causing (or is likely to cause) the adult to be harmed, or
(b) the adult is engaging (or is likely to engage) in conduct which causes (or is likely to cause) self-harm.

(s3 (2), 2007 Act)

Confirmation of the duty to inquire needs to (a) confirm the respective legal duty of the local authority to inquire, which may lead to (b) confirming the need (or not) to take action under either the 2000, 2003 or 2007 Act to safeguard the health, safety, personal welfare or property of the adult; thereby making available the respective powers and provisions of the Act concerned.

See Appendix 9 for a full description of these duties to inquire across the Acts.

Confirming a mandate for inquiry

Where it is clear that the person's circumstances and risks are matched by the criteria of a particular Act, e.g. the 2003 Act, the local authority may conduct an inquiry within that Act's context. Where, after engaging in an inquiry under a particular Act, it is, or becomes, clear that the person's circumstances more accurately relate to the criteria of another Act, e.g. the 2007 Act, the local authority may progress the inquiry under that Act, or pursue action or provisions or meet other duties or functions in that Act's context and framework. In essence, each Act may act as a gateway to other Acts.

Each 'duty to inquire' has particular criteria that need to be met, which include primary aspects. For example, where it appears that an adult has a mental disorder, then other individual criteria that confirm the areas of risk that prompt the need to inquire, e.g. exposed to ill-treatment, etc. (s33) need to be confirmed.

See Appendix 10 for primary and individual criteria to be confirmed.

Duties to inquire have similarities, but they also have distinctions, which may move the practitioners from one Act to another, e.g. the 2000 Act does not deal with risk for other reasons other than related to incapacity. In such circumstances, intervention within the 2003 Act or the 2007 Act may be more appropriate. However, where an adult lacks capacity due to mental disorder, an intervention under the 2003 Act may be also considered. The common aspect here is 'mental disorder', which prompts assessment across all the primary Acts' of their grounds and criteria, and careful consideration of respective inquiry needs to be given by the local authority concerned, and here a flexible and pragmatic approach should be taken. Where there is an indication of mental disorder, a MHO may direct the inquiry towards the most appropriate legislative framework.

In assessing and confirming appropriateness thereof, it is useful to apply the key terms of the respective duties to inquire in each of the Acts and thereby match these with the adult's circumstances and risks. The closest match would point towards the most appropriate duty to inquire. This should be achieved, following assessment, on a collaborative and interagency basis. Thereafter, the combined application of the Acts may be necessary to meet the range of the needs arising for an adult at risk, e.g. an adult with incapacity, because of dementia, living alone, at risk of exploitation or harm from others, with major risks to her/his welfare, who has a need for care and treatment, and there is a need to protect her/his property or finances: potentially, in effect all the primary (2000, 2003, 2007) Acts.

The Lesley case (4) indicates the dilemmas for practitioners in deciding which duty to inquiry has precedence, to ensure a proper legal mandate within which to engage. In exploring the respective duties to inquire and 'keying' into the principal terms helps practitioners to decide which duty has priority.
To apply the key terms to the case:

- As she has a mental disorder, one should explore the 2003 Act duty to inquire (s33) and its operative terms (the terms pertinent in Lesley's case underlined), i.e.: 'where it appears: a person is aged 16 or over has mental disorder … living in the community… may be or may have been … subject, or exposed… to ill treatment … neglect … some other deficiency in care or treatment …; property at risk or has suffered loss or damage … living alone or without care … unable to look after property or financial affairs ... safety of some other person may be at risk'.

  Therefore, it should appear to the local authority, because it has information to suggest so, that Lesley is an adult (aged 16 or over) and has a mental disorder. She is living in the community and may be or may have been subject, or exposed, at her house, to ill-treatment or neglect, and there may be a deficiency in her care or treatment. Her property appears to be at risk or has suffered loss or damage, and she may be unable to look after her property or financial affairs. Therefore, a duty to inquire under section 33 (2003 Act) is indicated.

• As Lesley has a learning disability, and as many adults with a learning disability are incapable because of their mental disorder, one should explore the 2000 Act duty to inquire (s10), i.e.: 'to investigate any circumstances made known to a local authority… personal welfare of an adult … (potentially with impaired capacity [with a mental disorder] … seems to be at risk … need to take action to safeguard the personal welfare of the adult'.

   The local authority may be informed here and, therefore, know that there are circumstances in which the personal welfare of Lesley, where she is potentially incapable because of her learning disability, appears to be at risk, and potentially it may need to take action to safeguard the personal welfare of Lesley. Therefore, a duty to inquire under section 10 is indicated.

• Lesley appears to be at risk living in her house with Tom, and appears to be an adult at risk, so one should explore the 2007 Act duty to inquire (s4) (the terms pertinent in Lesley's case underlined), i.e.: the Council 'knows or believes the adult is at risk (of harm) … intervention might be necessary to intervene to protect the adult's well-being, property or financial affairs. An adult at risk is an adult who is (a) unable to safeguard her/his own well-being … property, rights or other interest; (b) is at risk of harm: i.e. harm includes all harmful conduct … in particular conduct which causes physical harm … conduct which causes psychological harm (e.g. causing fear, alarm or distress) … unlawful conduct which appropriates or adversely affects property, rights of interests (e.g. theft, fraud, embezzlement or extortion) … conduct which causes self-harm , and (c) because he/she is affected by … disability … mental disorder … illness … physical or mental infirmity … is more vulnerable to being harmed than adults who are not so affected. Where (i) another person's conduct is causing (or likely to cause) the adult's harm … or (ii) the adult is engaging … (or likely to engage) … in conduct which causes … (or likely to cause)… self-harm'.

Therefore, the council may appear to believe, because there is information available to suggest this from the fire officer and the hospital staff, and it is aware that Tom assaulted a care worker, and that Lesley may be an adult at risk and it might need to intervene to protect her well-being and property. She appears unable to safeguard her own well-being, property, rights and other interests. Inquiry would establish whether she is indeed an adult at risk of harm: i.e. there is harmful conduct here, in particular conduct that causes physical harm or conduct that causes psychological harm (e.g. causing fear, alarm or distress). She appears, because she is affected by mental disorder, to be more vulnerable to being harmed than adults who are not so affected; and that Tom's conduct is causing (or likely to cause) the adult harm. Therefore, the duty to inquire under section 4 (2007 Act) may be primarily indicated.

So which duty of inquiry has priority? Well, they all have! So the local authority may conduct an inquiry in any or all of the Acts, and obtain the authority and mandate from within any of them. Here local procedures, however, may suggest 'going through' the 2007 Act as a 'gateway' into the other Acts; and, after all, it is designed to protect adults at risk of harm, which is the most prominent aspect of Lesley's case. So, in Lesley's case, the 2007 Act may appear the most favoured legal mandate for inquiry (see Table 6.1 for a full exploration).

However, the 2000 and 2003 Acts also have some significance. If Lesley's need for treatment for mental disorder is an important aspect of her care and support, especially where the powers therein would authorise this, e.g. compulsory treatment in hospital or in the community, then the 2003 Act may appear the most favoured mandate; and, in her case, an important aspect is that she is manifesting symptoms of mental illness (i.e. talking to herself and withdrawn), where she may need treatment in hospital for mental illness. However, if her predominant needs and risks are 'welfare related', which arise from an incapacity caused by mental disorder, the local authority might view the 2000 Act as providing the correct mandate, especially if the powers and provisions within the Act, e.g. welfare guardianship, appear most closely related and most responsive to the adult's welfare risks and needs.

So, in Lesley's case, in determining the most appropriate duty to inquire, and because her needs and risks relate more to protection from harm, the 2007 Act might have precedence (for inquiry) over others. Following inquiry, however, when her risks and needs have been assessed, there would be a more accurate direction taken towards the most suitable Act and powers and provisions therein, which might take Lesley's case from initially being addressed within the 2007 Act, to then moving towards the 2000 Act, potentially to seek powers and provisions therein, e.g. welfare guardianship (see Table 6.1).

Other case examples, where inquiry under the 2003 Act (s33) appears necessary, i.e. 'where it appears' that the individuals concerned have mental disorder, indicating the 2003 Act (s33), are:

- Walter (3), where he is 'living alone and unable to look after himself'; and
- Wilma (5), where she is 'exposed to deficiency of care and is living alone, and is unable to look after herself'.

However, both adults are at risk of harm from others, which would prompt the consideration of inquiry under the 2007 Act (s4), and potentially affected by incapacity under the 2000 Act, where their personal welfare is at risk; thereby promoting consideration of inquiry under the 2000 Act (s10). What duty to inquire, therefore, has precedence in these cases: the 2007, 2003 or 2000 Act? Again, as discussed earlier in the Lesley case, the predominant risk they are exposed to relates more to protection from harm from others, i.e. Walter from his brother and 'his drinking friends' and Wilma from her young 'friend', which confirms that the 2007 Act and its duty to inquire (s4) are strongly indicated. Notwithstanding this, the 2003 Act would also be indicated, in particular because it has a range of corresponding powers, e.g. warrant for entry and medical examination, which may be pertinent in the Walter and Wilma cases.

In the Lesley case, in assessing and confirming the appropriateness of each Act, it is useful to apply the terms of respective duties to inquire in each of the Acts and match these with Lesley's circumstances and risks (see Table 6.1).

Table 6.1.: Assessing for the appropriate duty to inquire mandate (Lesley case)

2003 Act (s33)	2000 Act (s10)	2007 Act (s4)
"where it appears: person is aged 16 or over ... has mental disorder ... living in the community ... may be or may have been ... subject, or exposed ... to ill treatment ... neglect ... some other deficiency in care or treatment ...; property at risk or has suffered loss or damage ... living alone or without care ... unable to look after property or financial affairs ... safety of some other person may be at risk."	"circumstances made known to local authority ... personal welfare of an adult ... impaired capacity (mental disorder) ... seems to be at risk ... need to take action to safeguard the personal welfare of the adult."	"known or believed ... adult is at risk of harm ... intervention may be necessary to protect ...; adult is unable to safeguard her/his own well-being ... property ... rights ... other interests ... where another person's conduct is causing the adult's harm ... or likely to ... adult is engaging ... likely to ... in conduct which causes ... self-harm ... harm includes ... all harmful conduct ... conduct which causes physical harm ... conduct which causes psychological harm ... fear, alarm or distress ... unlawful conduct which appropriates or adversely affects property, rights of interests ... theft, fraud, embezzlement or extortion ... conduct which causes self-harm ... affected by disability ... mental disorder ... illness ... physical or mental infirmity ... more vulnerable to being harmed than adults who are not so affected."

Case Example 4: Lesley (to illustrate the assessment of relative duties to inquire):

Lesley (34) is affected by learning disability and mental illness. She resides with **Tom** (54) who abuses alcohol. Neither of them wishes to receive any support or services. He is known to be aggressively dominant of her. There was a serious fire in the house, caused by an overfull chip pan, which had been left on by Tom. This is the third time this has happened, although on previous occasions there was no serious outcome. The fire service extinguished the fire, which caused damage to the kitchen of the flat, and windows were broken. The following day, a fire prevention officer called to see Tom and Leslie. He was concerned that the couple neither understood nor was coping with the seriousness of the situation. He reported that the flat was no longer weather tight (it being winter), the wiring in the kitchen was unsafe, and the house was in a deplorable condition: there being little furniture, it being extremely cold, there being piles of papers lying around, and no evidence of food or provisions. Tom is known to be aggressively dominant of Lesley. Lesley suffered burns while trying to put out the fire. On speaking to Lesley, the fire officer found her withdrawn and talking to herself. Tom resented certain questions in respect of his concerns and told the fire officer to 'get out and leave them alone' that *he* is the master of this house *and* Lesley. Lesley agreed to go to the Accident and Emergency department, where her burns were treated; and, although she was well enough to go home, hospital staff was seriously concerned about her safety and welfare. A GP had seen Tom and Lesley recently, however he refused to divulge information on them and felt they were just naturally responding to a crisis which they would "get over", and they should be allowed to get on with their lives and their right of confidentiality protected. The fire officer has referred their case to the local authority highlighting his concerns.

In applying the respective duties to inquire criteria in respect of the Lesley case scenario:

2003 Act	2000 Act	2007 Act
Lesley is over 16 and has a mental disorder. She is living in the community, where her property is at risk and has suffered damage. She/they appear unable to look after this property and there appears a risk to the safety of other person (in the flats). Lesley appears exposed to a deficiency in care or treatment.	Lesley's circumstances are known to the local authority (after referral), where she appears to be affected by impaired capacity; where the personal welfare of Lesley seems to be at risk; and the local authority needs to take action to safeguard her personal welfare.	Lesley, is known or believed to be an adult at risk of harm, where intervention may be necessary to protect her, where Lesley may be unable to safeguard own well-being, property, rights, or other interests; where Tom's conduct is causing harm, or likely to; where harm includes conduct which causes physical harm, potentially of psychological harm, e.g. fear / distress; and where she is affected by mental disorder and is more vulnerable to being harmed than adults who are not so affected.

In addition, the combined application of Acts here may be necessary to meet the range of the needs arising for that person, eg. an adult with incapacity, because of dementia, living alone, at risk of exploitation or harm from others, with major risks to her/his welfare, has a need for care and treatment, and there is a need to protect her/his property of finances. An assessment of needs would help confirm the respective and combined application of the relative legislative frameworks, regarding commensurate duties of the local authority, e.g. section 25 of the 2003 Act (care/support services) or sect 6 of the 2007 Act (advocacy/other services).

Investigation

The practice and formality of investigation may be found across the Acts in the form of:

- the duty to inquire;
- The respective duties on other bodies (and persons and office holders) to cooperate with the inquiry;
- The visit and relative powers to facilitate and expedite the inquiry, e.g. assessment, power of access, power to obtain entry, obtaining records, conducting a medical examination of an adult at risk; and
- The applied sanctions should there be offences against obstruction or non-compliance with a requirement (e.g. giving up records).

An investigation has two elements:

- inquiry or 'enquiry', i.e. gathering information, screening, confirming grounds (or not), deciding on initial action, deciding on whether to visit or not, allocation of a key manager, allocation of key practitioners who should go out, when, how, etc.; and
- investigation, the practical application of inquiry, comprising: the visit, the assessment of risk and need, etc. including medical examination (also for incapacity), and if necessary (a) seeking facilitative powers, e.g. power of entry, assessment, access to records, etc. and/or (b) taking urgent action, e.g. removal to a place of safety or emergency admission to a hospital.

When expediting an inquiry, there is a corresponding duty on other 'persons' to 'assist', i.e.:

- Under section 34 of the 2003 Act, where the local authority has established that there is a duty to inquire (s33), there is a corresponding duty on other 'persons to assist' with the inquiry, and the person 'shall comply' with this request. Those 'persons' are the Mental Welfare Commission, the Public Guardian, the Scottish Commission for the Regulation of Care, and the local NHS Board and service.
- Under section 5 of the 2007 Act, public bodies and office holders, so far as consistent with the proper exercise of their functions, 'must cooperate' with a council making an inquiry under section 4 and with each other, where such cooperation is likely to 'enable or assist' the council making the inquiry. Public bodies include all councils, the commissions stated above, the Public Guardian, chief constables of the police force and relevant Health Board.
- Under the 2000 Act, although there is no statutory obligation to co-operate with the local authority in respect of inquiry under the 2000 Act, there is a responsibility on councils, the commissions and the Office of the Public Guardian (OPG), to consult and co-operate in certain cases, e.g. respective inquiries. The OPG may be contacted and asked to carry out an investigation into circumstances where the person's financial affairs or property appear to be at risk; or into a complaint against a proxy with powers over property and financial affairs. The same bodies need to co-operate and exchange information when investigations of complaints are being carried out that involve matters in both the welfare and financial fields (2000 Act, Explanatory Notes).

*

Significantly, the 2007 Act confirms the reporting of an adult at risk to the local authority and the sharing of information, i.e., where a public body or office-holder to which this section applies 'knows or believes' (a) that a person is an adult at risk and (b) that action needs to be taken (under Part I or otherwise) in order to protect that person from harm, the public body or office-holder must report the facts and circumstances of the case to the council for the area in which it considers the person to be.

In the context of investigation, cooperation ensures collaborative and joint working, as most investigations into the risk (and harm) of adults with mental disorder require a joint health and social care perspective and response. The respective COP give additional guidance on the delivery of inquiry.

An investigation under the 2003 Act should be delivered in the context of a local inquiry protocol. Investigating officers should consider a wide range of voluntary and compulsory interventions, e.g. care and support under the 1968 Act on an informal basis, and intervention under the 2000 and/or the 2007 Acts if necessary. If intervention under the 2003 Act is required, they may consider a removal order, or an emergency or short-term detention certificate, or even an application for a CTO. If it is decided that no further action is required under the 2003 Act, MHOs should provide reports on the inquiries (Scottish Executive, 2005b).

In the 2000 Act, the duty of a local authority to investigate circumstances where the personal welfare of an adult appears to be at risk is a statutory function. In cases which indicate that urgent action is needed to protect the person from harm then action may be taken under the 2003 or the 2007 Act as appropriate. An investigation under the 2000 Act, as well as considering risk and mental disorder, also has the additional aspect of incapacity to consider, so risk and medical examination here goes hand in hand in determining incapacity and the problems arising from this. Here, investigating officers need to make sure that the assessment and care management functions of local authorities are brought into play, and in cases which indicate that urgent action is needed to protect the person from harm, then action may be taken under the 2003 or the 2007 Act as appropriate. Although the 2000 Act does not expressly provide for urgent action, the investigating officers may consider that an intervention order or interim guardianship should immediately be sought.

The local authority needs to ascertain whether there is any need to take action either under the 2000 Act or otherwise to safeguard the personal welfare of the adult. This responds to situations where the adult is found to have impaired capacity. Where an adult lacks capacity due to mental disorder, an intervention under the 2003 Act may also be appropriate. The duty social worker should assess the most appropriate route. Another important purpose of investigation is to investigate any complaints about the exercise of functions relating to the personal welfare of an adult made in relation to welfare attorneys, guardians or persons authorised under intervention orders. The investigation of complaints is a matter for local procedure (see Scottish Government, 2008b).

If the adult has capacity, however, and is at immediate risk, the 2000 Act does not assist. The investigating officer should consider what other social work or medical interventions can be offered and should follow local procedures with regard to adults in need of support and protection, i.e. the use of the 2003 or 2007 Act. In cases where the 2003 Act appears to be relevant, the investigating officer should consult a MHO if he/she is not one, and liaise with appropriate medical practitioners.

The investigating officer should prepare a report with recommendations, which should cover prescribed topics (in Annex 3 of the Local Authority Code of Practice, 2000 Act), and whether a criminal offence should be reported to the police. This will normally form part of local authority care management procedures. The officer should report the outcome of the inquiry to the MWC, copying the report and implementation plan to the MWC, where the adult's incapacity is due to mental disorder.

The 2007 Act authorises a council officer to enter any place for the purpose of enabling or assisting a council conducting an inquiry under section 4; to decide whether it needs to do anything (by performing functions under this Part or otherwise) in order to protect an adult at risk from harm (s7). A council officer, and any person accompanying the officer, may interview, in private, any adult found in a place being visited under section 7(s8). Where (a) a council officer finds a person whom the officer knows or believes to be an adult at risk in a place being visited under section 7 and (b) the officer, or any person accompanying the officer, is a health professional, that health professional may conduct a private medical examination of the person (s9). This may be to establish physical or sexual harm, or assess the adult's medical needs, or to obtain medical evidence of harm to inform any action. It may also include an assessment of capacity and/or mental state. Additionally, a council officer may require any person holding health, financial or other records relating to an individual whom the officer knows or believes to be an adult at risk to give the records, or copies of them, to the officer. Such a requirement may be made during a visit or at any other time. Requirements made at such other times must be made in writing (s10).

If no action is taken, practitioners should (a) ensure the individual has been spoken to alone, (b) the individual's accommodation has been visited, (c) the views of all relevant professionals have been sought and considered and (d) there is evidence that the individual's welfare will be safeguarded and promoted in future. This should include the involvement of a wide range of voluntary or statutory interventions. The 'need to intervene' may also be met by using appropriate provisions contained in other legislation or by taking action on a non-statutory basis.

See Appendix 11 for detail of investigations across the Acts.

Case example (Lesley)

Following the confirmation of a duty to inquire (and the appropriate Act to conduct this inquiry; in the Lesley case the 2007 Act was viewed as potentially the most appropriate), the local authority needs to consider the respective duties to cooperate and involve the appropriate public bodies and practitioners in the investigation.

In the inquiry, there should be allocated an appropriate manager and appropriately trained and experienced staff, e.g. given the 2007 Act is the agreed legal framework for the investigation, a council officer might be a MHO, because Lesley has mental disorder; and, instead of a GP, an approved medical practitioner (AMP) could provide a medical assessment. Cooperation would be in line with section 5 of the 2007 Act, which would allow the council officer to obtain the support of a GP or an AMP, or indeed the police.

The investigation would comprise the visit, where the practitioners would wish to see Lesley (in private) to assess her risk and need, and to carry out a medical examination (also for incapacity). The practitioners would have to bear in mind the need to seek relative powers, e.g. a warrant of entry (s37), e.g. where Tom prevents access, and/or the need to access records (s10). An assessment order (s11) may be necessary to remove Lesley to a place where a medical examination could occur, especially if Tom is not allowing this to happen at home. There also may be a need to take urgent action, e.g. an urgent removal to a specified place (s40 1a: 2007 Act) or a place or safety (s293/s294, 2003 Act), or an emergency admission to hospital (s36, 2003 Act), depending on whether Lesley can consent or whether she needs detention in the place of safety to protect her, or admission to hospital for treatment is required. At this stage, the practitioners need to consider 'crossing the Acts' to seek relative and necessary powers.

Offences across the Acts

Abuse, assault and/or neglect of adults with mental disorder are to be treated seriously as they may constitute criminal offences. Indication of an offence might arise from an inquiry under any of the primary Acts, or via the police or emergency services, or a report by a member of staff or the public. The MWC may also have been involved, as in the case of Ms A.
Each Act has a specific set of offences i.e.:

- The 2003 Act: ill-treatment and wilful neglect (care services); obstruction and false statements;
- The 2000 Act: ill treatment and neglect by anyone exercising powers under the Act; and
- The 2007 Act: obstruction; failing to comply with examination of records; and offences by bodies corporate.
- The 2009 (Sexual Offences (Scot) Act 2009) Act. (N.B. previously the 2003 Act held sexual offences/sexual acts against mentally disordered adults [s311-s313] which were repealed by the 2009 Act.

It would be expected that any response to concerns raised about offences of a mentally disordered person is approached on a multi-agency basis, to include local police, and in line with locally agreed vulnerable adult protection guidelines and protocols, according to professional values and principles that ensure respect for individual autonomy and rights to self-determination.

Where there are concerns about the possibility of an inappropriate sexual relationship, e.g. between care staff and service users, or potentially between service users (where there is incapacity or non-consent), or by a person exploiting or targeting a vulnerable adult affected by mental disorder, these should be reported in line with locally agreed multi-agency procedures and a multi-agency assessment of the circumstances taken forward. According to the 2003 Act code of practice (Volume 1) (Scottish Government, 2005b), this would entail a meeting of all persons involved in the care of the person to allow full information sharing and the issue of consent to be discussed, and no assumptions should be made in the consideration of this matter. Local authorities and health boards will have protection procedures in place and recourse to these should be made available to all external providers from whom services are commissioned.

In the same COP it is said that 'while respecting a mentally disordered person's rights to autonomy and self-determination, agency staff involved in the care of the person have a responsibility in accordance with locally agreed procedures and service agreements to report any concerns regarding relationships the person may have, particularly if exploitation or abuse is suspected' (Scottish Executive, 2005b, p 232).

Particular offences relate to the process of inquiry and assessment, such as obstruction (2003 and 2007 Acts) where investigation officers could be prevented from conducting the inquiry and taking steps to protect the adult. A person obstructing an inquiry may not be allowing access to the adult or may be obstructing the practitioners in the course of their inquiry. The police who accompany the investigating officers may address this potential offence with this person and potentially could arrest them.

Also, particular offences may arise from inquiry, such as where it is determined that (a) a 'relevant person' is ill-treating or wilfully neglecting a mentally disordered person, (b) a member of staff is sexually exploiting a mentally disordered person in their care or (c) there is sexual activity concerning a mentally disordered person who is non-consenting or incapable of consenting to the sexual activity.

A sensitive approach needs to be applied to the issue of sexual relations between a mentally disordered person, who may lack capacity, and another person, e.g. spouse, partner or friend. And this has to be very carefully addressed where this exists between mentally disordered persons, especially where two such persons are incapable because of mental disorder and are involved in sexual activity with each other. Again multi-disciplinary process and protocol are important here to seek solutions.

Specifically, the offences in each of the Acts are:

In the 2003 Act: Obstruction: under section 317, where obstruction occurs, i.e. 'a person' commits an offence where he/she: (a) refuses to allow a person authorised access to any premises; (b) refuses to allow access to a mentally disordered person by a person so authorised; (c) refuses to allow the interview or examination of a mentally disordered person by a person so authorised; (d) persists in being present when requested to withdraw by a person so authorised; (e) refuses to produce any document or record to a person so authorised; or (f) otherwise obstructs a person in the exercise of any functions conferred on them by virtue of this Act; and **Ill-treatment and wilful neglect**: under section 315, where a 'relevant person (who provides care or treatment on a paid or volunteer [voluntary organisation] basis)' ill-treats or wilfully neglects a mentally disordered person.

In the 2000 Act, it is an offence, under section 83, for any person exercising powers under the Act relating to personal welfare of an adult to 'ill-treat or wilfully neglect' the adult. This includes those who hold welfare 'proxy powers', i.e. a welfare attorney, a welfare intervener or a welfare guardian. Establishing this may arise from an inquiry under section 10, from direct support of the adult, where the local authority is supervising a welfare proxy (as is duty obliged under section 10) or a referral from other parties. It may be necessary as a result of the investigation to report a suspected offence under the 2000 Act or any other offence to the police. Appropriate liaison procedures with the local police force need to be in place. The local authority legal department should be informed if a suspected offence is to be reported to the police. The reporting of a suspected offence to the police should not hinder the local authority from taking any necessary action under the 2000 Act or otherwise to protect and safeguard an adult whose personal welfare may be at risk. The offence is punishable on summary conviction to a fine not exceeding £5,000, or a term of imprisonment not exceeding six months, and on indictment to a fine or a term of imprisonment not exceeding two years.

In the 2007 Act, section 49 provides an offence relating (a) to the 'prevention or obstruction of any person from doing anything they are authorised or entitled to do under the Act' or (b) to 'refuse, without reasonable excuse, to comply with a request to provide information made under section 10 (examination of records, etc.)'.However, if the adult at risk prevents or obstructs a person, or refuses to comply with a request to provide access to any records, then the adult will not have committed an offence. Where the person has a mental disorder, action under the 2000 or the 2003 Act may be appropriate, and it may be that it would be appropriate to provide care and support under the 1968 Act. In some cases, particularly those where the adult has capacity, assistance may be provided to the adult by, for example, ensuring that they have access to suitable advice and support, should they wish to access it.

The 2009 Act introduced new powers and penalties for sex offences. S17 and s46/47 which apply to mentally disordered persons, i.e. **section 17 (capacity to consent)**, says 'A mentally disordered person is incapable of consenting to conduct where, by reason of mental disorder, the person is unable to do one or more of the following (a) understand what the conduct is, (b) form a decision as to whether to engage in the conduct (or as to whether the conduct should take place), (c) communicate any such decision' and **section 46 (sexual abuse of trust of a mentally disordered person**) says 'If a person ("A") (a) intentionally engages in a sexual activity with or directed towards a mentally disordered person ("B"), and (b) is a person mentioned in subsection (2), then A commits an offence, to be known as sexual abuse of trust of a mentally disordered person. (2) Those persons are (a) a person providing care services to B, (b) a person who (i) is an individual employed in, or contracted to provide services in or to, or (ii) not being the Scottish Ministers, is a manager of, a hospital, independent health care service or state hospital where B is given medical treatment.'

*

Additionally, of course, offences under criminal justice legislation may take precedence and priority, and charges made on the accused or harmer.

*

All investigation of offences should be conducted within local adult at risk procedures, e.g. the West of Scotland Adult at Risk procedures say:

- If a crime has been suspected of being committed, as in the case of physical or sexual harm, immediate referral to the police is essential;
- The police role is then to make the necessary inquires to gather evidence to secure a conviction; and
- Social work services may also discuss and explore with the police any other legal measures that can be taken to protect the adult from further harm at this early point in the referral process if this is felt necessary. This is to ensure that the adult at risk is safe from harm.

There is, obviously, a close association between the offences contained within the 2000, 2003 and 2007 Acts and criminal justice legislation, because these offences can lead to criminal convictions and prescribed penalties being applied. This requires close collaboration between the local authority and police service. Many areas have liaison police officers who are available to consult in these circumstances and to get involved practically in applying these provisions.

Case examples

Case examples indicate the potential of offences under the primary Acts:

- **Walter** (1): Walter's brother may have been or be committing an offence of theft. He may also be financial exploiting Walter. Additionally, he acts as Walter's power of attorney (continuing [financial] and welfare) and appears to be abusing this power. He may be open to a charge of ill-treating and wilfully neglecting Walter, where he is exercising proxy powers (s83, 2000 Act). This could lead to an investigation under section 10 by the local authority (welfare) and the Office of the Public Guardian (OPG) (finances).

- **Mary** (3): Sexual offences under section 311 of the 2003 act are indicated. Where the cousin is concerned, a criminal offence of sexual exploitation may be indicated. However, Mary is also placed in a 'state of fear (s311[3])' by her aunt and uncle who may be 'aiding, abetting ...' any other person (cousin) (s311[7]). So where the cousin may be the sexual harmer here and thereby open to conviction under this section, the aunt and uncle may also be open to conviction under the same section. In addition, there may be the existence of wilful neglect and ill-treatment under the 2000 and 2003 Acts, which may also constitute an offence.

- **Ms A** (7): Section 311 of the 2003 Act is indicated, and clearly of course criminal justice legislation. Section 311 was specifically mentioned in the MWC (2008a) report, where there may have been a different basis for pursuing convictions of the men who raped her. If a successful conviction had been obtained, these men, as is available in this section, may have been imprisoned and, as this is a sexual offence for the purposes of Part 2 of the Sexual Offences Act 2003, registered thereby (Scottish Executive, 2005b).

See Table 6.2 for a fuller description of the offences 'across the Acts'.

Table 6.2 (a)

2003 Act	2000 Act	2007 Act

Ill treatment and wilful neglect of MD person (s315), where a 'relevant person' ill treats or wilfully neglects a mentally disordered person.
 	
NB. Sections 311 and 313 of the 2003 Act were repealed by the 2009 Act (Sexual Offences (Scot) Act 2009), where penalties are also indicated.
 	
Obstruction (s317), where 'a person' commits an offence where he/she: refuses to allow a person authorised access to any premises; refuses to allow access to a mentally disordered person by a person so authorised; refuses to allow the interview or examination of a mentally disordered person by a person so authorised; persists in being present when requested to withdraw by a person so authorised; refuses to produce any document or record to a person so authorised; or otherwise obstructs a person in the exercise of any functions conferred on them by virtue of this Act.
 	
The patient themselves will not have committed an offence should they do any of the above. (S37 and 07 chp15 COP vol1).
 	
Under the 2003 Act there is a range of offences against mentally disorder persons which imposes penalties on persons found guilty of the offences (NB the Ms A case (MWC)).
	Offence of ill -treatment and wilful neglect (s83)
	
	It is an offence under this section for any person exercising powers under the Act relating to personal welfare of an adult to ill treat or wilfully neglect the adult.
	
	The offence is punishable on summary conviction to a fine not exceeding £5000 or a term of imprisonment not exceeding 6 months, and on indictment to a fine or a term of imprisonment not exceeding 2 years.
	It may be necessary as a result of the investigation to report a suspected offence under the 2000 Act or any other offence to the police. Appropriate liaison procedures with the local police force will need to be put in place. The local authority legal department should be informed if a suspected offence is to be reported to the police (LA COP).
	The reporting of a suspected offence to the police should not hinder the local authority from taking any necessary action under the 2000 Act or otherwise to protect and safeguard an adult whose personal welfare may be at risk (LA COP)
		Obstruction (s49)
		
		a. It is an **offence** (without reasonable excuse) to **prevent or obstruct** any person from doing anything they are authorised or entitled to do by virtue of a
		  * Assessment order
		  * Removal order;
		  * Banning order;
		  * Temporary banning order
		  * Warrant for entry,
		    or any provision under this part of the 2007 Act;
		
		b. It is also an offence to refuse, without reasonable excuse, to comply with a request to provide information made under Section 10 (examination of records etc).
		
		NB. If the adult at risk prevents or obstructs a person, or refuses to comply with a request to provide access to any records, then the adult will not have committed an offence
		
		Where the person has a mental disorder, action under the 2003 Act may be appropriate.
		
		Where a person has impaired capacity, an order or the appointment of a proxy under the 2000 Act may be appropriate. It may be that it would be appropriate to provide care and support under the Social Work (Scotland) Act 1968. In some cases, particularly in those where the adult has capacity, assistance may be provided to the adult by, for example, ensuring that he/she have access to suitable advice and support, should they wish this. (10 ch4 COP).

Table 2 (continued): Crossing the Acts: Offences

In crossing the Acts to pursue appropriate offences, key terms are apparent, i.e. sexual offences, ill-treatment and obstruction, and thereby key Acts are indicated, e.g.

Sexual Offences	Ill treatment and wilful neglect	Obstruction
The 2009 Act introduced new powers and penalties for sex offences. S17 and s46/47 applies to mentally disorderly persons. **Section 17 (capacity to consent)**, says 'A mentally disordered person is incapable of consenting to conduct where, by reason of mental disorder, the person is unable to do one or more of the following (a) understand what the conduct is, (b) form a decision as to whether to engage in the conduct (or as to whether the conduct should take place), (c) communicate any such decision. **Section 46 (sexual abuse of trust of a mentally disordered person)** says 'If a person ("A") (a) intentionally engages in a sexual activity with or directed towards a mentally disordered person ("B"), and (b) is a person mentioned in subsection (2), then A commits an offence, to be known as sexual abuse of trust of a mentally disordered person. (2) Those persons are (a) a person providing care services to B, (b) a person who (i) is an individual employed in, or contracted to provide services in or to, or (ii) not being the Scottish Ministers, is a manager of, a hospital, independent health care service or state hospital where B is given medical treatment.	**Ill-treatment and wilful neglect of MD person (s315, 2003 Act)** of a mentally disordered person by a relevant person, e.g. a paid carer. **Ill-treatment and wilful neglect (s83, 2000 Act)** of an adult incapable because of mental disorder by a welfare proxy. If a mentally disordered person is being ill-treated or wilfully neglected by a formal / paid carer then the 2003 Act is indicated, whereas if the adult (incapable) is being ill-treated or wilfully neglected by a person with proxy powers under the 2000 Act, then the 2000 Act is indicated.	**Obstruction (s317, 2003 Act)**, in the exercise of duties. **Obstruction (s49, 2007 Act)**, i.e.: (s49[1]) To obstruct any person from doing anything they are authorised or entitled to under any powers or provision; (s49 [2]) To refuse, without reasonable excuse, to comply with a request to provide information made under Section 10 (examination of records etc). If a MHO or an investigating officer conducting an inquiry under the 2003 Act is obstructed then s317 of that Act is indicated. Whereas if the inquiry is being conducted under the 2007 Act and the council officer (or another accompanying the council officer, e.g. medical practitioner) is obstructed, then s49 (1) under that Act is indicated, and where there is refusal to comply with a request to provide health, financial or other records, then s49 (2) of that Act is indicated.

PART THREE

THE POWERS AND THEIR RELATIONSHIP

Introduction

Across the Acts, how the powers relate have:

- a linear application (down), i.e. immediate powers that may lead to short-term powers and then potentially to long-term powers, governed by the principle of the least restrictive option, where practitioners may pursue a process-based approach depending on need and risk; and

- a horizontal application (across), where powers across the Acts have to be assessed as to their suitability, and may also be applied in a simultaneous or collective way, such as is applied to some adults who may have needs that require to be addressed across the Acts and be subject to powers from more than one Act, e.g. welfare guardianship and a community-based compulsory treatment order; and

- a diagonal (or perpendicular) approach (from one point in one Act to another point in another Act), for example, a practitioner may need to move from emergency or short-term powers in one Act to long-term powers in another.

What defines the respective use of the powers and their relationship best, however, is their consistence with the principles of the Acts (see Appendix 8). For example, (a) to determine which Act and which power or provision may provide the maximum benefit to the adult, (b) which is the least restrictive and (c) what the adult's views, wishes and feelings respective of the powers and provisions are; what they think may support and protect them best.

Chapter 7

IMMEDIATE POWERS

The range of immediate powers across the Acts is:

2003 Act	2007 Act

• **Warrants for entry and assessment**
  – For entry and medical examination
  – An authorised person warrant for removing the patient
	• **A warrant for entry**

• **Urgent removal to a place of safety**
  – An urgent removal order to a place of safety
  – Removal from a public place by the police to a place of safety
	• **An urgent removal order to a specified place**

• **Emergency detention**	**NB: There are no immediate or urgent powers available in the 2000 Act**

Immediate powers are powers obtained by practitioners on an urgent basis either where there is no need to, or there would be delay in doing so, approach a Sheriff or a tribunal under normal procedures, or where key practitioners are not available, e.g. MHOs and AMPs (e.g. for short-term detentions). They are also characterised by their short timescales, e.g. hours rather than days, i.e. removal from a public place and detained for up to 24 hours in a place of safety, or an emergency detention in hospital for a maximum of 72 hours.

Warrants also have a limited timescales, e.g. three hours to assess under section s35 (4) of the 2003 Act, or, for entry under the 2007 Act, 72 hours under section 37 (the normal warrant) or 24 hours for an urgent warrant under section 40 (1b).

Warrants for entry and assessment

Often for practitioners, while supporting and protecting adults at risk with mental disorder, there is a need to obtain formal authority to enter premises to assess an adult at risk. This may be required where the adult refuses entry to their house, where potentially they lack insight into the risks they face there or where another person, third party or harmer, is preventing access to the adult.

The 2003 Act makes particular provision in relation to inquiries by providing a set of relevant warrants respective of adults with mental disorder, which can be issued by a Sheriff or a Justice of the Peace. These warrants can only be sought by a MHO, if it is thought that either (a) entry to premises, (b) access to medical records or (c) a medical examination, is necessary and access has been or is likely to be denied (s35). Each warrant needs to be applied for separately. However, this range of warrants does not authorise the removal of the person at risk to a place of safety. Therefore, practitioners need to decide whether or not (a) investigation supported by section 35 is best or (b) a removal order, to remove the adult to a place of safety, is necessary to protect the adult. Here the principles of maximum benefit and minimum restriction may be used to guide actions.

In section 35, there are three separate warrants that can be issued (referring to the 2003 Act, V1, if necessary):

- a warrant to enter premises, where it is necessary to enter premises for the purposes of pursuing the local authority's duty to inquire (s35[1]). A Sheriff or Justice of the Peace must grant a warrant 'where he/she is satisfied that it is necessary to enter the premises for the purposes of pursuing the local authority's duty to inquire and the MHO cannot obtain entry to the premises or reasonably believes that he/she will not be able to access the premises'. This authorises 'any such police constable (where necessary) to open lock fast places on the premises so specified)'. The warrant must be exercised before the expiry of 8 days; and/or
- a warrant to detain a person (in situ), for the purpose of carrying out a medical examination, for a period of up to 3 hours (s35[4]). Where an application is made on these grounds, a Sheriff or the Justice of the Peace 'must grant the warrant where he/she is satisfied that it is necessary for a medical practitioner to carry out a medical examination of the person who is the subject of the local authority's duty to inquire and the MHO cannot obtain the consent of that person to the medical examination'; and/or
- a warrant for a medical practitioner to gain access to a person's medical records (s35[7]). Where an application is made on these grounds, a Sheriff or Justice of the Peace 'must grant the warrant where he/she is satisfied that it is necessary for a medical practitioner to have access to the person's medical records and the MHO cannot obtain the consent of that person to access their medical records'.

*

A warrant is also available under section 292 of the 2003 Act, to allow an 'authorised person', a MHO or a police constable, to enter premises, where that person has already been given authority under another section of the Act or associated regulations to take (or retake) a patient to any place or into custody. An example of a situation where this warrant may be sought is where a patient subject to a CTO has absconded from a hospital and a person who is authorised to take the patient into custody or return them to a hospital requires entry to the premises where the patient is. Another example is where a hospital-based CTO (or STDC) has been made in respect of a patient and that patient must be conveyed to a hospital, or to another residence under a community-based CTO, but access cannot be gained to the premises where the patient is currently residing or has been found (Scottish Executive, 2005a, 2005b).

The 2007 Act also offers a warrant for entry that may be granted by a Sheriff (s37) where they are satisfied that a council officer has been, or reasonably expects to be, refused entry or otherwise will be unable to enter, or any attempt by a council officer to visit the place without such a warrant would defeat the object of the visit. A warrant for entry granted by a Sheriff expires 72 hours after it has been granted. Once a warrant has been executed, it cannot be used again. The warrant authorises a council officer to visit any place specified in the warrant, accompanied by a police constable.

The accompanying constable may 'do anything', using reasonable force where necessary, to fulfil the object of the visit. This may include the opening of lock-fast places. It would be expected that the council takes all reasonable steps to ensure the security of the person's premises and belongings if force has been required to enter the premises. Wherever possible, entry to premises should first be attempted without force.

An urgent case application for a warrant for entry (s40[1b]) may be made to a Justice of the Peace if it is impracticable to make the application to the Sheriff and an adult at risk is likely to be harmed if there is any delay in granting the warrant. A warrant for entry granted by a Justice of the Peace expires 12 hours after it has been granted. Once a warrant has been executed, it cannot be used again.

See Appendix 12 for an 'across the Acts' description of powers of entry and assessment.

In the context of inquiry (2007 Act), the council may make an application to a Sheriff for an assessment order to help it decide whether the person is an adult at risk or to take an adult at risk of serious harm to a more suitable place to allow a council officer or council nominee to conduct a private interview, or where a health professional may carry out a medical examination in private.

Case examples

In the Lesley case (4), it would appear that Lesley has needs for support and, potentially, protection. There are clear risks to her while living at home, where the home is in a poor condition, and, following confirmation of a duty to inquire, there is the potential of Tom preventing access to Lesley, or Lesley refusing access to her, by any practitioners who would seek to support and protect her, which may necessitate a warrant under the 2003 or the 2007 Act, depending on which Act is being used at the time and where the most appropriate mandate for involvement rests.

Earlier it was discussed that, for Lesley, the 2007 Act offered the primary framework to pursue necessary immediate powers. The range of circumstances in Lesley's case scenario matched with the grounds/criteria of the 2007 Act, which helped confirm that the warrants and removal orders under the Act appeared the best fit for the range of circumstances and risks involved. However, as the 2003 Act might also have been seen to have priority in respect of inquiry, predominantly because of the existence of mental disorder, warrants in that Act may have been viewed appropriate. If so, a MHO may need to apply for the necessary warrants. The MHO would need to establish, again balancing the risk of the adult with the least restrictive principle, whether under section 35 (1) there is, initially, a need to sanction entry into the premises to conduct the inquiry and to assess the risk to Lesley, and under section 35 (4), whether there is a need for a medical examination.

However, under the 2007 Act, a warrant for entry may also be sought for Lesley under section 37 (Sheriff), or under section 40 (Justice of the Peace) where it is not practicable to apply to a Sheriff.

Other case examples that indicate the need to consider respective and immediate warrants of entry and assessment are:

- o Walter (1): where he or his brother may refuse access; and
- o Mary (3): where her aunt and/or uncle may prevent access to her.

Urgent removal

In the 2003 Act (s294), an urgent application for a removal order may be made to a Justice of the Peace where it is impracticable to apply to a Sheriff and where any delay in obtaining a removal order is likely to be prejudicial to the person. Additionally, it should be noted that section 293 (the primary 'non-urgent') provision, which goes before the Sheriff, allows the Sheriff to dispense (s293 (7)) with the requirements under s293 (5) which confirms representation and evidence, because this may be prejudicial to the adult's safety. This basically removes the need to have a full hearing and offers a 'fast track' towards the order. This could be considered in the range of 'immediate powers', offering immediate access to a Sheriff.

Under the 2007 Act (s40 (1a)), an adult at risk (with mental disorder) may be removed urgently to a suitable place on an application by a council to a Justice of the Peace, where it is not practicable to make application to the Sheriff for a removal order (s14), and the adult at risk is likely to be harmed (note: 'harm' rather than 'serious harm', which is required for the normal removal order (s14)) if there is any delay in granting the order. The Justice of the Peace must be satisfied that the person is an adult at risk who is likely to be harmed if not moved to another place and that the adult is to be removed to a place that is suitable and available. The urgent case order also provides a warrant for entry in relation to the visit. The adult at risk must be removed within 12 hours of the grant of the removal order and the order expires after 24 hours.

Under the 2003 Act (s297), the police may take a 'relevant person' to a place of safety if the person is in a public place and appears to be mentally disordered, in immediate need of care or treatment, and where they consider that it would be in the interests of the person, or necessary for the protection of any other person, to remove the person to a place of safety. The person may be detained there for a period of up to 24 hours. The purpose of this detention is to allow a medical practitioner to examine the person and to make arrangements for their care and treatment. Arrangements should be in place to ensure that police officers can rapidly ascertain the location of designated places of safety.

Case example (Lesley)

In the Lesley case example (4) there may be a need to obtain a warrant to remove her on an urgent basis to a specified place through an urgent case removal order (s40 1a) from a Justice of the Peace, where it is not practicable to apply to a Sheriff. The council officer needs to decide if, based on her risks, this is required here, as opposed to the council applying to the Sheriff for a normal removal order (s14). Where there is an indication of serious risk to Lesley, however, there may be a need to remove her urgently to a place of safety, under the 2003 Act (s294) through a Justice of the Peace. A suitable place of safety would need to be a suitable environment for adults with learning disability. Where in the 2007 Act an urgent section 40 (1a) removal is indicated, there would need to be consent from Lesley, because this is required under this Act. Where she withholds consent, there needs to be evidence of undue pressure from Tom to prevent consent, or evidence (from a medical practitioner) to confirm that she is incapable of consent, to pursue the order; always remembering that this order does not detain the adult, and she may leave the specified place if she so wishes. In the 2003 Act, where there is an immediate need for detention in hospital, the medical practitioner, of course, could consider an emergency detention under section 36.

Practice point ▶ ▶ ▶

Looking at the Lesley case, it would appear that Lesley has needs for support and, potentially, protection. Should the risk, as assessed by the practitioners, be unable to be managed at home, there may be for the practitioners concerned a need to consider removal from her home on a temporary basis for her protection. The practitioners would need to consider (a) the correct mandate for inquiry (across the Acts), (b) the correct set of warrants that may be necessary (the 2003 or the 2007 Act?) and (c) which removal order is most suitable (the 2003 or the 2007 Act?), depending on which Act is being used at the time, where the most appropriate mandate for involvement rests, and which power is most suited to the range of risk.

See Appendix 12 for an 'across the Acts' description of powers of entry and assessment.

Emergency detention to hospital

In the 2003 Act (s36), an emergency detention to a hospital (if in the community at the time) or in hospital (if the patient is already in hospital) is available, where it is impracticable to arrange a short-term detention to hospital; for example, where an AMP is not available and there is an immediate need to admit the patient to hospital to be seen by an AMP.

The order detains a patient in hospital on an emergency basis for up to 72 hours, where a medical practitioner (GP) considers it likely that:

a.   the patient has a mental disorder;
b.   because of that mental disorder, the patient's decision-making ability with regard to medical treatment for that mental disorder is significantly impaired;
c.   it is necessary as a matter of urgency to detain the patient in hospital in order to determine what medical treatment should be provided to the patient for mental disorder;
d.   there would be a significant risk to the health, safety or welfare of the patient or to the safety of another person if the patient were not detained in hospital; and making arrangements with a view to granting a STDC would involve undesirable delay; and
e.   where the medical practitioner has consulted a MHO and s/he has consented to the detention, unless it has been impracticable to do so.

An AMP, as soon as practicable after admission, may either detain the patient under a short-term detention or revoke the detention. Protective circumstances that may require the person to be admitted on an emergency basis may include immediate risk to self, such as from self-harm, immediate risk to others, or where the patient's condition has deteriorated to the point where any delay would place them at further risk.

Practice point ► ► ►

Emergency detention should only be used if a short-term detention cannot be obtained, e.g. where an AMP or MHO is not available. Emergency detention should be expedited in the context of a local Psychiatric Emergency Plan (PEP).

Within the 2000 Act, there are no warrants for entry, removal or assessment. However, section 3 of the Act allows the Sheriff to make an interim order quickly if the situation warrants it, while taking longer to resolve in full the issue before the court. Additionally, the Sheriff may give directions to anyone acting under the Act, about how they use their powers (the 2000 Act, Explanatory Notes). The Sheriff can authorise the local authority to take such decisions or action in relation to the adult as they thinks appropriate. This procedure was suggested as a more flexible option than applying for an order under Part 6 (welfare guardianship) where none is otherwise needed (see Patrick, 2004).

Practice point ► ► ►

Section 3 of the 2000 Act appears an underused but useful provision; for example, where there are problems obtaining assessments, reports or cooperation, or where there may be a need to move quickly to protect an adult, while an application is processed through court.

Chapter 8

SHORT TERM POWERS

The range of short-term powers across the Acts is:

2000 Act	**2003 Act**	**2007 Act**
• Intervention orders • Interim guardianship orders	• Removal orders • Short-term detentions • Interim CTOs	• Removal orders • Assessment orders • Temporary banning orders

Short-term powers are powers obtained by practitioners that offer shorter timescales, e.g. days rather than months, some of which can be granted by the practitioners themselves, e.g. a short-term detention to hospital (s44, 2003 Act) or a removal order obtained for a short period of time, e.g. 7 days, or an order obtained from the Sheriff or Tribunal with earlier expiry dates.

Removal orders

Removal from a private place (s293, 2003 Act)

A removal order may be sought by a MHO to a Sheriff for the removal of an adult at risk 'from a private place' to a 'place of safety' for up to seven days, where the person is subject to, or exposed to, ill-treatment, neglect or some other deficiency in care and treatment. The need for the order may stem from a section 33 inquiry, where access to the person has been achieved in the context of local authority duties or from the use of section 35 warrants. If there is sufficient information that suggests the adult's needs and risks are such to move directly to a removal order instead of using warrants under section 35, the MHO may proceed directly to obtain this order. The removal order authorises the MHO specified in the order, any other person so specified, and any constable of the relevant police force, to remove the person at risk to a place of safety specified in the order. However, it only authorises an entry to the patient's premises and the patient's removal to a place of safety; it does not permit access to a patient's medical records, nor does it permit detention for the purpose of carrying out a medical examination.

The order has a purpose of protecting the adult from harm and providing care and treatment for mental disorder. This order also provides detention for 7 days in the place of safety.

Removal of incapable adult (2000 Act)

Although the 2000 Act does not expressly provide for urgent action to remove an incapable adult, some authorities have been able to pursue and obtain welfare guardianship orders on a fast-track basis; in some cases speedily obtaining either interim or full powers to protect an adult at risk. This requires ready access to assessments and reports, and efficient collaborative working. Interim orders and intervention orders may be used in this context of risk to remove an adult with incapacity to an alternative setting, bearing in mind that the intervention order lacks detention powers.

Place of safety (2003 Act)

In the 2003 Act, a 'place of safety' is defined as (a) a hospital; (b) premises that are used for the purpose of providing a care home service (as defined in the Regulation of Care (Scotland) Act 2001 or (c) any other suitable place (other than a police station) the occupier of which is willing temporarily to receive a mentally disordered person. This range of settings allows a degree of scope to match the adult's needs and circumstances with a suitable place of safety, which of course does not necessarily need to be a hospital.

Removal to a suitable place (s14, 2007 Act)

Within the 2007 Act, a council may apply to a Sheriff for a removal order (s14), which would authorise a council officer, or any council nominee, to move a specified person to a specified place within 72 hours of the order being made, and the council to take such reasonable steps as it thinks fit for the purpose of protecting the moved person from harm. A removal order expires 7 days (or such shorter period as may be specified in the order) after the day on which the specified person is moved in pursuance of the order. The Sheriff may grant a removal order only if they are satisfied that the person in respect of whom the order is sought is an adult at risk who is likely to be seriously harmed if not moved to another place, and as to the availability and suitability of the place to which the adult at risk is to be moved. The order provides a warrant for entry.

A removal order cannot be made by the Sheriff if the adult withholds consent, unless (a) the adult is under undue pressure to refuse consent (s35, 2007 Act) or (b) where the adult lacks capacity to consent (where evidence is provided) where the need to establish undue pressure does not apply (2007 Act, COP: Scottish Government, 2009). Removal under the 2007 Act is primarily for protection from serious harm, although medical assessment and interviews can occur there. This order, however, does not offer detention and needs the adult's consent (unless subject to undue pressure or affected by incapacity). The COP of the Act indicates that where the adult wishes to return home or to alternative premises, they should be assisted to do so, with supports offered there.

To take to a place where assessment can occur (s11, 2007 Act)

The council may make an application to a Sheriff for an assessment order (s11) to help decide whether the person is an adult at risk and to take an adult at risk of serious harm to a more suitable place to allow a council officer or council nominee to conduct a private interview, or where a health professional may carry out a medical examination in private. The order gives a warrant for entry. The Sheriff must be satisfied that the council has reasonable cause to suspect that the subject of the order is an adult at risk who is being, or is likely to be, seriously harmed. The order may be required to establish whether the person is an adult at risk who is being, or is likely to be, seriously harmed. The order is valid for up to seven days; however, it is expected that the assessment is to be carried out in the shortest possible time.

Suitable place for assessment or removal to a specified place (2007 Act)

To remove an adult to a 'specified place' may in some circumstances require written confirmation from the person who owns or manages this place that they are willing to receive the adult for assessment purposes. For example, the place could be a friend's or relative's house or a care home. The suitability of the place to conduct a private examination could also be confirmed in writing. This would be desirable, but it may not always be practicable in urgent or emergency situations (2007 Act, COP: Scottish Government, 2009, ch9).

To remove an adult through a removal order in the 2007 Act, good practice would be for the council to provide a suitability report of both the place and the person willing to care for the adult at risk and also to obtain a written agreement from the owner of the proposed specified place; where it is, for example, a private home or independent care provider, to confirm the owner's willingness to receive the adult at risk for up to 7 days. The place to which the adult should be taken will be specified in the order and the adult must only be taken to the place specified in the order; however, there may be circumstances where, before the order is executed, the adult consents to being taken to another place (2007 Act, COP: Scottish Government, 2009, ch10).

See Appendices 13 & 14 for an 'across the Acts' description and detail of powers of removal.

Case examples

In the Mary case (3), Mary is being sexually exploited and a removal order (s14, 2007 Act) may be necessary. Following an inquiry under section 4 of the 2007 Act or section 35 of the 2003 Act, the key practitioners, in risk assessing and considering whether her risk can be managed at home, may consider removing her either to a place of safety under the 2003 Act or to a specified place under the 2007 Act. This would be governed by her needs, and whether she was capable, incapable, or there was 'undue pressure' from others, by where her needs would be best met, and by where she would be best protected from risk. In her case, she may be at risk if not 'detained' in a place of safety where her aunt or uncle might try to remove her from there or where she may wish to leave herself. This would indicate that removal under the 2003 Act (ss293/294) is best, because this has a 7 day detention authority.

Other case examples where removal is indicated are:

- Walter (1), where, again, the 2003 Act (ss293/294) appears best suited because of his non-compliance and potential resistance from his welfare proxy (brother);
- Wilma (2), where the 2007 Act (s14) may be indicated if Wilma consents to move temporarily to a 'specified place', if authorised by a Sheriff or Justice of the Peace (s40, 1a), if she cannot be protected at home from this 'friend'. However, of course, if she agreed to move to a temporary place of safety on a voluntary basis, there would be no need to approach the Sheriff for an order; and
- Lesley (4), again the 2003 Act (ss293/294) is indicated, where she has needs for protection and may not wish to go to a place of safety and may be at risk from Tom.

Practice point ▶ ▶ ▶

In weighing up removal orders, the respective criteria and principles of the Acts should assist and guide. However, remember:

- Removal under the 2003 Act has a purpose of protecting the adult from 'significant harm' and may also provide care and access to treatment for the adult with mental disorder, as well as protection. This order also offers detention for the 7 days.
- Removal under the 2007 Act is primarily for protection, although social care or medical assessment, etc. can occur there. This order, however, does not offer detention and needs the adult's consent (unless subject to undue pressure or incapacity because of mental disorder). Where the adult wishes to return home or to alternative premises they should be assisted to do so, with supports offered there.

Short-term detention

Within the 2003 Act, a short-term detention (s44) to hospital is available. The order is viewed as the 'gateway order', to be used as the primary route to detain a patient. The order may detain the patient in hospital for up to 28 days (either from the community or if already in hospital). It is granted by an AMP, who has consulted and obtained consent from a MHO. The AMP has to confirm certain conditions are met, i.e.:

a. the patient has a mental disorder;
b. because of the mental disorder, the patient's ability to make decisions about the provision of medical treatment is significantly impaired;

c. it is necessary to detain the patient in hospital for the purpose of determining what medical treatment should be given or the giving of medical treatment to the patient;
d. if the patient were not detained in hospital there would be a significant risk to the health, safety or welfare of the patient or to the safety of any other person; and
e. the granting of a short-term detention certificate is necessary.

A short-term detention and treatment of a mentally disordered person may be necessary (a) to protect the person, where mental disorder has impaired the person's ability to appreciate they need medical treatment for mental disorder (e.g. clinical depression, eating disorder, schizophrenia) and because of this the person's health (including physical health), safety or welfare is at significant risk and/or (b) to protect any other person, who may be at risk because of the person's mental disorder.

Case examples

In the Lesley case (4), there may be a need to consider a short-term detention to hospital. Lesley appears to be experiencing symptoms of mental illness and may be in need of hospital treatment. However, if after medical assessment she can be treated at home or in an alternative place in the community, or if she does not met the criteria as set out in section 44(4), then the order is not suitable. In the Mr H case (6), there were problems in the assessment of capacity and his need for treatment and care. A short-term detention to remove him to hospital where full medical assessment could be carried out (in the absence of alcohol), may have established his incapacity earlier in his case and consequently confirmed his needs for treatment and care.

Intervention orders

Intervention orders are not emergency orders; however, they may be viewed as in the range of short-terms orders, because they offer authority within a finite timescale to effect the action/intervention made in the order. Intervention orders may authorise admission to hospital or to a residential setting. Once there, of course, the adult cannot be detained and is free to leave at any time.

Practice point ► ► ►

An intervention order may protect in a number of ways e.g.:
- by putting a 'freeze' on an incapable adult's bank account to prevent financial abuse; or
- by preventing the sale or giving up of an incapable adult's house; or
- by authorising an action to protect an incapable adult, such as an assessment or admission to a place where assessment can occur.

Interim CTOs, interim guardianship and temporary banning orders

Although not technically short-term orders, interim and temporary orders offer temporary Sheriff or tribunal authority while full orders are being determined. In some cases, they provide early access to powers, which can exist over weeks, and, therefore, they may be considered part of the overall repertoire of short-term powers.

The 2000 Act does not expressly provide for urgent action, an investigating officer in these circumstances may consider that an interim guardianship order should immediately be sought (see 2000 Act, Local Authority COP, Scottish Government, 2008b), and the Sheriff may make a direction under section 3 of the 2000 Act. However, interim welfare guardianship may provide powers to remove an adult with incapacity to a residential setting on a 'fast-track' basis; however, in the context of immediate risk, this might require an urgent application to the Sheriff. Interim guardianship is a short-term order, giving authority to make decisions or take actions on behalf of the adult, lasting no longer than 6 months, or until the full guardianship order is granted.

Case examples

In the Walter (1), Wilma (2), Mary (3), Lesley (4) and the Ms A (7) cases, there is an indication of incapacity and the need for early powers to protect their health and welfare, and consequently thereof interim guardianship powers may be necessary.

*

The 2003 Act offers the most substantive range of emergency and short-term provision to protect adults at risk affected by mental disorder. The Act does not rely on consent of the adult nor does the adult need to lack capacity. However, the principles of patient participation and having regard to their present and past wishes and feelings have importance.

An interim CTO (s65) may act as a short-term measure, because it exists (at the time of writing) for a maximum of 56 days (two 28-day periods) or until a full CTO is granted. Although this is not its primary purpose, it being available until full powers are determined, the MWC says that around 64% of all applications result in an interim CTO, and its statistics indicate that a proportion of patients do not progress onto full-blown CTOs: the number of interim orders that go on to full powers is 512; and the number of interim orders only that do not go on to full orders are 242. There could be a number of reasons for this, but potentially it may be because the patient's mental disorder or compliance improves during the time the application is being pursued through the tribunal, rendering the order no longer necessary.

Although the 2007 Act offers the primary framework for protecting adults at risk, it lacks robust emergency powers, especially where the adult withholds consent for action or is incapable because of mental disorder. The most substantive order within the 2007 Act is a long-term order: the banning order.

The temporary banning order (s21), however, is the banning order's temporary variant, whereby temporary powers may be granted by a Sheriff 'pending determination' of a full order being granted by the Sheriff. The temporary order ends when the application is determined, or on any specified date determined by the Sheriff, which could offer a number of weeks or longer.

Importantly, section 41 of the 2007 Act, allows the Sheriff to 'disapply the normal application procedures', i.e. to disapply the need to have a hearing, representation, or to send notifications, etc. This would certainly shorten the court process and allow the Sheriff to move quickly to grant the order where this is urgently necessary, where 'in doing so will protect the adult at risk from serious harm or will not prejudice any person affected by the application'.

Case examples

In our case examples, there may be a need for interim or temporary powers, which would protect these adults while full powers are determined, e.g.:

- in the Walter case (1), to provide temporary powers, e.g. a temporary banning order to ban his brother who exploits him financially; and, potentially, the drinkers who exploit his house; or to provide interim welfare guardianship powers to protect his health and welfare at home, and to 'trump' or overpower his brother's welfare powers, which might also include a power to require Walter not to consort with the persons mentioned; and

- in the Mary case (3), where there may be a need to seek interim powers, e.g. interim guardianship powers to transfer her to an alternative environment, where potentially she may have been removed to a place of safety, or to impose safeguards in her home; or a temporary banning order may be necessary to prevent her cousin accessing her in the house.

'Crossing the Acts': immediate and short-term powers

In 'crossing the Acts' to seek short-term powers, Table 8.1 offer a description of the Acts and the provisions 'side by side', to help practitioners to consider (and view) how the relative powers may compare and contrast.

Table 8.1.: Crossing the Acts: Immediate and short term powers

Table 8.1: Crossing the Acts: Immediate and short term powers

Careful consideration should be given to a) whether an urgent intervention is needed because of the risk to which the person is exposed, requiring consideration of the immediate and shorter measures within the primary Acts, and/or b) whether a longer term option is needed, e.g. welfare guardianship, compulsory treatment order and/or a banning order. The principles of benefit and minimum intervention have relevance here.

Immediate and short term powers		
2003 Act	**2000 Act**	**2007 Act**
	What are they in short?	

2003 Act

The short term and emergency powers of the 2003 Act include ;

a. **a short term detention** (s44) certificate (STDC) which (if it is handed to hospital managers) will detain a patient in a hospital for up to 28 days (either directly from the community or if already in hospital) and

b. an **emergency detention** (s.36) certificate (EDC) where where a short term detention cannot be pursued, which may be necessary to protect the person. The EDC detains a patient in hospital for up to 72 hours. The STDC is for the giving of medical treatment, and granted by an approved medical practitioner (AMP) who has consulted and obtained consent from a MHO.

c. **removal to a place of safety** :

□: From a private place (s293), where a **removal order** may be sought by a MHO to a Sheriff for the removal of the adult at risk 'from a private place' to a 'place of safety' for up to seven days, where the person is subject to, or exposed, to ill-treatment, neglect or some other deficiency in care and treatment; or

□: Removal from a public place (s297), where the police may take a person to a place of safety if the person is in a public place and appears to be mentally disordered, in immediate need of care or treatment, for a period of up to 24 hours; or

□: Urgent application (s294) for a removal order may be made to a justice of peace where it is impracticable to apply to a Sheriff and where any delay in obtaining a removal order is likely to be prejudicial to the person.

N.B. An interim compulsory treatment order may be sought (see above) while a full order is being determined.

A '**place of safety**' (2003 Act) is defined as: a) a hospital; b) premises which are used for the purpose of providing a care home service (as defined in section 2(3) of the Regulation of Care (Scotland) Act 2001 (asp 8)); or c) any other suitable place (other than a police station) the occupier of which is willing temporarily to receive a mentally disordered person.

2000 Act

Removal of incapable adult (2000 Act)

Although the 2000 Act does not expressly provide for urgent action to remove an incapable adult, some authorities have been able to pursue and obtain welfare guardianship orders on a fast track basis, in some cases obtaining either interim or full powers to protect an adult at risk. This requires speedy access to assessments and reports, and efficient collaborative working. Where the person has a mental disorder, the 2003 Act would allow local authorities to seek an order for the immediate removal of the adult to a place of safety for a prescribed period. Intervention orders and interim welfare guardianship powers may be used in this context.

Intervention orders

Under this provision, it is possible to apply to the Sheriff for an intervention order to deal with clearly defined, 'one -off' financial, property or personal welfare matters in relation to an adult. An Intervention Order is not an emergency provision, because it may take significant time to pursue through Court. It does, however, offer a short term power to effect an action regarding a person's welfare, health, money or property. Intervention orders can be used where the need for action is time -limited or to deal with one -off decisions or single issue concerning the adult's property, finance or personal welfare. Local authorities can be financial interveners where there is an assessed need and there is no one else to act (LA COP).

Interim guardianship may be sought while a full order is being determined

The order is not an emergency provision; however, depending on how quickly the application can be brought before a Sheriff it may provide an early response to risk to welfare, health, finances or property. Local authorities should put in place arrangements to apply for an interim guardianship order within this abbreviated timescale. This will require liaison with local medical practitioners about the urgent provision of the necessary reports of incapacity to support the application.

Intimation may not be required (shortening the period within which to obtain the interim order) where the Court considers intimation or notification would be likely to pose a serious risk to the health of the adult (s11).

2007 Act

The 2007 Act offers short term powers, i.e.:

a. **a removal order** (s14) which authorises a Council Officer or any Council nominee to move an adult at risk to a specified place to protect him/her from harm; or

b. **an 'urgent cases' removal order** (s40 1a) allows an urgent application to go before a Justice of Peace where it is not practical to approach a Sheriff and the adult is likely to be harmed by any delay caused in granting the removal order; or

c. **an assessment order** (s11) to take an adult at risk of serious harm to a more suitable place to allow a Council Officer or Council nominee to conduct a private interview or where a medical practitioner can conduct a medical examination.

A suitable place for assessment or removal to a specified place (2007 Act)

The place could be a friend's or relative's house or a care home, or a health centre or health related establishment for a medical examination. The suitability of the place to conduct a private interview should be confirmed in writing. Good practice would be that the Council provides a suitability report of both the place and the person willing to care for the adult at risk and also obtain a written agreement from the owner of the proposed specified place, for example a private home or independent care provider to confirm the owner's willingness to receive the adult at risk for up to 7 days.

N.B. A temporary banning order may be sought while a full order is being determined.

Table 8.1.: Crossing the Acts: Immediate and short term powers

What are their grounds (criteria and conditions) for adults at risk with mental disorder?		
2003 Act 'affected by mental disorder'	**2000 Act** 'adult with incapacity (mental disorder)'	**2007 Act** 'adult at risk (mental disorder)'
Removal order To grant a removal order (s293) the Sheriff must be satisfied the adult has a mental disorder, and a. that the person may be or may have been, subject, or exposed, to ill treatment, neglect or some other deficiency in care or treatment; or b. that because of mental disorder, the persons property may be, or may have suffered loss or damage, or may be, or may have been at risk of suffering loss or damage; or c. that the person may be living alone or without care, and unable to look after himself or his property or financial affairs. **Urgent application (s294)** for a **removal order** can be made to a Justice of the Peace if it is impracticable to make the application to the Sheriff and if any delay in obtaining the removal order would be prejudicial to the person who is the subject of the application. **The police may take a person to a place of safety (s297)**, if that person is in a public place appears to be mentally disordered and in immediate need of care or treatment. **For a short term detention (s44)**, where the AMP has confirmed: * the patient has a mental disorder; * because of the mental disorder, the patient's ability to make decisions about the provision of medical treatment is significantly impaired; * it is necessary to detain the patient in hospital for the purpose of determining what medical treatment should be given to the patient or giving medical treatment to the patient; * if the patient were not detained in hospital there would be a significant risk to the health, safety or welfare of the patient or to the safety of any other person; and * the granting of a short-term detention certificate is necessary (s44). **For an emergency detention (s36)**, where a GP has confirmed * the patient has a mental disorder; and * because of that mental disorder, the patient's decision-making ability with regard to medical treatment for that mental disorder is significantly impaired; and * it is necessary as a matter of urgency to detain the patient in hospital in order to determine what medical treatment should be provided to the patient for the suspected mental disorder; and * there would be a significant risk to the health, safety or welfare of the patient or to the safety of another person if the patient were not detained in hospital; and * making arrangements with a view to granting a short-term detention certificate would involve undesirable delay. (s36)	**Intervention order** The Sheriff may make an intervention order, on an application, if he is satisfied that the adult is incapable of taking the action, or is incapable in relation to the decision about his property, financial affairs or personal welfare to which the application relates. **Guardianship orders** The Sheriff he may grant an order where he is satisfied a. the adult is incapable in relation to decisions about, or of acting to safeguard or promote his interests in, his property, financial affairs or personal welfare, and is likely to continue to be so incapable; and b. no other means provided by or under this Act would be sufficient to enable the adult's interests in his property, financial affairs or personal welfare to be safeguarded or promoted. **Interim guardianship** The 2000 Act does not deal expressly with urgency. In particular, there is no provision to expedite applications for intervention orders or guardianship, including interim guardianship, in case of urgency. An application for an interim order may be heard and granted by a Sheriff within a few days if the need is very pressing, however this still requires a full summary application with reports (6.26 LA COP).	**Removal order** The Sheriff may grant a removal order only if satisfied: a. that the person in respect of whom the order is sought is an adult at risk who is likely to be seriously harmed if not moved to another place; and b. as to the availability and suitability of the place to which the adult at risk is to be moved. (s15) **Assessment order** The Sheriff may grant an assessment order only if satisfied a. that the Council has reasonable cause to suspect that the person in respect of whom the order is sought is an adult at risk who is being, or is likely to be, seriously harmed; b. that the assessment order is required in order to establish whether the person is an adult at risk who is being, or is likely to be, seriously harmed, and c. as to the availability and suitability of the place at which the person is to be interviewed and examined. **Urgent removal** A Council can apply to a Justice of the Peace of the commission area in which the adult is located, where: * it is not practicable to make application to the Sheriff; and * an adult at risk is likely to be harmed if there is any delay in granting the order. The Justice of the Peace must be satisfied that the person is an adult at risk who is likely to be seriously harmed if not moved to another place and that the adult is to be removed to a place that is suitable and available. (s40) **Consent and capacity** If the Council decides to pursue an application where the affected adult has capacity to consent and has made known their refusal to consent, then the Council must prove that the adult has been "*unduly pressurised*" to refuse to consent to the granting of an order. Where the adult does not have capacity to consent, the requirement to prove undue pressure does not apply. However evidence of lack of capacity will be required by the Sheriff. **Grounds for temporary banning order:** 'pending determination' of an application of a banning order' Same grounds and powers as the full order.

Table 8.1.: Crossing the Acts: Immediate and short term powers

	Who and what are they for?	
2003 Act	**2000 Act**	**2007 Act**
An adult 'affected by mental disorder'	An 'adult with incapacity (mental disorder)'	An 'adult at risk (mental disorder)'
Removal orders (s294) are for adults (16 years or over) who have a mental disorder in a private place (home etc), who may be subject, or exposed, to ill-treatment; or neglect; or some other deficiency in care or treatment; or living alone or without care and unable to look after property or financial affairs; and are likely to suffer significant harm if not removed to a place of safety.	**An intervention order** may (s.53) be necessary for an 'incapable adult' under the Act, where a one off action is needed to protect an adult's welfare, property or finances, e.g.:: a. Where the adult's finances or property (moveable or heritable) or tenancy is at risk and needs protection or decisions made in this regard; b. Where the adult's health or welfare is at risk and needs a protective action or a decision made in this regard.	**A removal order (s14)** is to protect an adult at risk, to assess the adult's situation and to support and protect. A removal order will be granted only where the Sheriff is satisfied that the adult is likely to be seriously harmed if not moved to another place and that there is a suitable place available to remove the adult to. The order is primarily for protection and not for a Council interview or a medical examination. It permits the person named in the order to be moved from any place to protect them from harm. For example, the place the adult at risk actually lives may however be a contributory factor in the harm and the move may provide "breathing space" for the specified person.
Removal from public place (s297) is for a 'relevant person' who a police constable 'reasonably suspects' has a mental disorder and that the relevant person is in immediate need of care or treatment in public place; and the constable considers that it would be in the interests of the person, or necessary for the protection of any other person, to remove the relevant person to a place of safety.	In respect of adults at risk, an intervention order could be suitable for a. freezing an adult's assets or funds in order to protect them while suspicions of exploitation are investigated by the Public Guardian; b. taking legal action to protect the adult's interests; and c. requiring the adult to attend hospital for specific medical treatment or assessment (other than for mental disorder). (5.2 LA COP)	**An assessment order (s11)** may be viewed in the context of investigation as a means to assess (also medically) and confirm an adult at risk, and to consider steps to protect the adult. This will establish whether the person is an adult at risk who is being, or is likely to be, seriously harmed, and will be used only if it is not practicable (due to a lack of privacy or otherwise) to interview the person under a normal interview or to conduct a medical examination of the adult during a normal investigation visit (s8).
A short term detention (s44) is for persons with a mental disorder (mental illness, learning disability, personality disorder) as assessed by an AMP, where the criteria (below exists). The order is for detention and determining what treatment should be given to the patient or the giving of medical treatment. The order may be necessary to a) protect the person, where mental disorder has impaired the person's ability to see s/he needs medical treatment for mental disorder, e.g. clinical depression, eating disorder, schizophrenia, and because of this the person's health (including physical health), safety or welfare (health, happiness, prosperity) is at significant risk; or b) to protect any other person, who may be at risk because of the person's mental disorder.	An intervention order is to deal with clearly defined, one-off, financial, property or personal welfare matters and may be sought via the Sheriff. This order, although short term as it lasts only as long as it takes for the action to be taken, may take weeks (sometimes longer) to progress through the Sheriff Court, thereby reducing its effectiveness in protecting adults on a short term or immediate basis. For this reason it is best to consider this to be an order which would benefit the adult over a lengthy period of time. Hillary Patrick (Authorising significant intervention for adults who lack capacity, 2004) says 'sometimes the Court may be satisfied that an intervention order will suffice (an intervention order should always be considered as a less restrictive option). [This may be] an early intervention where 'there are situations where the use of guardianship or an intervention order at an early stage can be seen as a less restrictive option'.	
An emergency detention (s36) is for persons who need to be admitted on an emergency basis to be assessed by an AMP 'as soon as practicable' in hospital. Reasons for the detention may included immediate risk, such as from self harm, immediate risk to others, or where the patient's condition has deteriorated to the point where any delay would place them in further risk.	**Interim guardianship** may be necessary to protect an adult at risk, where there is a need for long term powers, but early steps need to be taken to protect the adult's welfare or finances or property, where a full order is being determined. Pursuing a set of powers 'pro tem', may help to provide a framework of care or protection, until the full set of power are obtained.	

Table 8.1.: Crossing the Acts: Immediate and short term powers

How may the powers be used (imaginatively) to protect adults at risk with mental disorder?		
2003 Act	**2000 Act**	**2007 Act**
Removal orders are available to respond to adult at risk matters, i.e. the adult is subject or exposed to ill-treatment; or neglect; or some other deficiency in care or treatment; or living alone or without care and unable to look after property or financial affairs; and are likely to suffer significant harm if not removed to a place of safety. Adult at risk scenarios which would prompt a removal order include the adult withdrawing for services or to prevent access to him/her at home; or where, after gaining access to the adult perhaps through a warrant of entry, that the adult should be moved to a place of safety. There are no statistics on how the order is used; but, from the writer's experience and from anecdotal information, adults with mental illness such as bipolar disorder and dementia have been protected through the use of removal orders. It is in the protection of adults with learning disability they are less indicated, presumably because most adults with learning disability don't live alone, are more likely to be living within family groups or in supported living arrangements. However, as adults may be open to 'ill-treatment', 'neglect' and open to 'significant harm' from others the removal order may be used to remove such an adult to a place of safety. The location of the 'place of safety' offers room for creativity, especially when protecting an adult who doesn't necessarily need to go to hospital for treatment (either physical or mental health), e.g. an older person with dementia, who may be admitted to a non hospital setting, such as a residential setting, or another house, potentially to live with another relative, friend or neighbour. **Removal from public place also seeks to protect adults at risk,** i.e. in immediate need of care or treatment in public place, in the interests of the person, or necessary for the protection of any other person, to remove the relevant person to a place of safety. Here also anecdotal information suggests that adults acting 'strangely' e.g. with hallucinations, delusions, etc., come to the attention of the police or older people where it is clear they are confused or disorientated, or adults affected by drug or alcohol where there indication of mental disorder. However, other adults with less positive symptoms or apparent signs may be missed, e.g. adults with negative symptoms (with schizophrenia) or adults with alcohol related brain damage with memory deficits, or adult with personality disorder creating a commotion. Again, as above, a more flexible use of the place of safety needs exploration, avoiding hospital admission where not needed. **A short term detention** may be used to protect adults at risk, where there is a need for treatment and 98% of people admitted are affected by mental illness. In certain circumstances adults with learning disability and personality disorder may need also access to treatment, or to determine what treatment should be given to the patients or the giving of medical treatment. Adults at risk from self harm may be indicated or where there is risk to others, e.g. children; however, where the adult's welfare is at risk, e.g. of homelessness, to relationships, a STD may be indicated. Equally, where the adult lacks ability to self care, detention to provide medical treatment may be needed, which may provide care, rehabilitation (e.g. addressing independent living skills or educational deficits), psychological or other forms of treatment as determined by section 329. **An emergency detention** would certainly be an option to protect an adult with mental disorder at risk, especially where the adult is at risk of self harm or is posing risk to others, and again information suggest that it is used more exclusively for adults with mental illness. It may be best used, however, to get the adult before an AMP for assessment, after hours and in crisis, for example an older person living alone, unable to self care.	**An intervention order** may be pursued to protect an adult at risk, incapable because of mental disorder, thereby protecting the adult's welfare, property or finances. An adult may be at risk from financial exploitation or abuse, their welfare may be in jeopardy, because of others or their property may be at risk. The order may be used to obtain the care and treatment the adult needs to remove them from risk, e.g. assessment in a general hospital or in a residential care establishment, or indeed to authorise a community care assessment or a benefits check. **A welfare intervention order** may be appropriate where the adult's health is at risk, e.g. where they are is unable to give consent to significant medical, dental or other treatments, or operations; or where the adult may require to attend hospital for specific medical treatment or assessment (with restrictions). **A financial intervention order** may be needed to either freeze an adult's assets or funds in order to protect them while suspicions of exploitation are investigated by the Public Guardian, or to protect the adult's home. It may also be used to protect the adult's finances by operating or closing an account held by the adult or to set up a trust. **An interim welfare guardianship order** may protect the adult at risk by making decisions on where the adult should live on a temporary basis until a long term option is agreed. This may allow the local authority to prepare a community care assessment or an adult protection plan, or to authorise respective services thereof, and may decide (temporarily) with whom the adult should or should not consent, until full powers are obtained. **An interim financial guardianship order** may protect the adult's finances or property while full and long term powers are pursued through Court. A relative set of powers could be put in place pro tem, e.g. to manage the adult's funds and/or accounts; claim and receive pensions or benefits; obtain and pay for any goods or services of benefit to the adult; or to have access to relevant confidential information.	**A removal order** may protect an adult at risk with mental disorder by removing the adult to a relative specified place, e.g. a hospital or a residential care establishment to support and protect him/her there. For a stressed carer looking after an adult with mental illness, e.g. with dementia this may provide 'respite' for the specified person. It may also give period of time to allow the adult to consider options for future care and protection. Significantly, it can offer key practitioners time to assess and prepare a care and protection plan. The removal order does not have the facility of detention, however, which may pose problems in respect of an adult with florid mental illness. Notwithstanding this, adults with mental disorder, who may not resist the transfer, may be protected through this order. **An assessment order** may protect an adult with mental disorder by providing an opportunity to assess the adult's mental state, care needs, risk, etc.; where it is not practicable (due to a lack of privacy or otherwise) to interview the person under a normal interview or conduct a medical examination of the person during a visit under a normal investigation visit. This may be particularly important where the adult is incapable because of mental disorder, where confirmation of this may be required by the Sheriff in the pursuit of another order, e.g. a removal or banning order. **A temporary banning order** may protect the adult 'pro-tem' while a full order goes through the Court. This may be necessary where there is opposition in Court thereby protracting the process or where there is a need for further evidence or reports, or legal representation. **Disapplying the normal application procedures may assist,** where under section 41 the sheriff can 'disapply' the application procedures, i.e. disapplying the need to arrange a hearing, allowing representation, and to send notifications. This would certainly shorten the process and allow the sheriff to move quickly to grant the order where this is urgently necessary.

Table 8.1.: Crossing the Acts: Immediate and short term powers

2003 Act	2000 Act	2007 Act
What are their timescales?		
Removal order (s293/294): (exercised within 72 hours) effective for up to 7 days. **Removal order (public place) (s297):** for up to 24 hours. **Short term detentions (s44):** (exercised within 3 days of certificate) for up to 28 days. **Emergency detention (s36):** removal within 72 hours; effective for up to 72 hours in which AMP should assess and consider short term detention 'as soon as practicable' after admission.	**Intervention orders** should be actioned after being granted, however, some orders relate to matters which may take some time to effect, e.g. preparing a community care assessment or adult protection plan or selling a house to invest into care. **Interim guardianship** can exist for up to six months until full powers are obtain.	**Removal order (s14)** authorises the removal of the adult within 24 hours and, although effective for a maximum of seven days, it is envisaged that it will not be required to last that long in the majority of cases. **An assessment order (s11)** is effective for 7 days, however, it is envisaged that assessment will occur as quickly as possible and the adult would return home as soon as possible.
How do you get them, and what are the practical arrangements and the roles of the key practitioners?		
Removal order (from a private place): for this, a MHO would apply to a Sheriff (s293), or to a Justice of the Peace (s294) where impractical to obtain the order from a Sheriff. The order authorises the MHO specified in the order, any other persons so specified, and any constable of the police force maintained for the area in which the premises are situated, before the expiry of the period of 72 hours beginning with the granting of the order, to enter any premises so specified; authorising any such constable, before the expiry of that period, for the purpose of exercising the power, to open lockfast places on premises so specified and authorising the removal of the person to a place of safety specified in the order (not a police station); and the detention of that person in that place for such period, not exceeding 7 days, as may be specified in the order. **Removal order, from a public place (s297):** this is actioned by a police constable, where the person would be taken from a public place to a place of safety (normally a designated hospital or another place. If no place of safety is available the adult may be taken to a police station, but for only as long as it takes to obtain the services of a medical practitioner who would transfer to the adult to a more appropriate place of safety, e.g. a hospital. **Short term detention (s44):** this is granted by an AMP who obtains the consent of an MHO. The person would be transferred to hospital within 3 days of the certificate being signed by the AMP, normally by nurse escort. **Emergency detention (s36):** certified by a medical practitioner (GP) who would obtain consent from a MHO (unless impracticable to do so) and the person would be transferred to hospital within 72 hours of the certificate being signed by the GP, normally by nurse escort (in the context of the local psychiatric emergency plan (PEP).	**Intervention and interim guardianship orders** would be sought by the local authority or a private person, both would need two medical reports (one from an AMP) and where there are welfare matters, a report by the MHO on the appropriateness of the order and where the applicant is a private person their suitability to act as intervener or guardian. The application would be submitted to the Sheriff Court; However, it can take months to obtain, after two or three or even four hearings. A safeguarder may be allocated and/or a curator ad litem. Independent medical and social work reports may be requested. An independent advocacy worker is entitled to appear in Court.	**An application for a removal order** (s14) would be made by the Council; normally by the legal section of the Council. Normally it would require assessment and a report by the council officer and where there is a mental disorder, this may involve a MHO. **An application for an assessment order** (s11) would be actioned by a council officer or any council nominee, and may involve a MHO where there is mental disorder. The medical examination would be conducted by medical practitioner such as a general practitioner, or in the case of an adult with mental disorder, a consultant psychiatrist.
How do they relate to other relative powers?		
The 2003 Act with the 2000 and 2007 Acts.	**The 2000 Act with the 2003 and 2007 Acts.**	**The 2007 Act with the 2003 and the 2000 Acts.**
A removal order (2003 Act) alongside the pursuit of a welfare guardianship order (fast track if necessary) (2000 Act), thereby giving some time (up to 7 days) in which to pursue the order (perhaps seeking interim guardianship), or * A **banning order (2007 Act)** (fast track if necessary) to protect the adult from harm from another (perhaps seeing a temporary banning order). * A **short term detention (2007 or the 2003 Act) alongside an intervention order (2000 Act)**, thereby providing treatment in hospital alongside an intervention related to the adult's health, welfare or finances.	**An intervention order or interim guardianship** could be applied alongside provisions in other Acts, e.g. * A **banning order (2007 Act)**, thereby providing a framework to protect adult's welfare and finances while being protected from a hammer; or * A **removal order (2007 or the 2003 Act)** to place the adult in a place of safety of specified place while intervention order or interim guardianship is pursued.	A **removal order (2007 Act)** may provide time and assessment to consider the suitability of other provisions in other Acts, e.g. * **Offences under the 2003 Act,** or * **Welfare guardianship (2000 Act).** **An assessment order (2007 Act)** may allow assessment which may indicate that another Act would be better suited to protect the adult, e.g. * **A removal order (2003 Act)** or * **A short term detention (2003 Act)** (or indeed an emergency detention), or * **A guardianship order (2000 Act),** either a fast track or interim order, or the full order.

Chapter 9

LONG TERM POWERS

The range of long-term powers across the Acts is:

2003 Act	**2000 Act**	2007 Act
Compulsory Treatment Orders	**Guardianship Orders**	**Banning Orders**
• Hospital-based powers	• Welfare powers	• Banning a subject from an adult's premises
• Community-based powers 2000 Act	• Financial powers	• Banning a subject from an area
	• Welfare and financial powers	• Other measures and conditions

Compulsory Treatment Orders (2003 Act)

Compulsory treatment orders offer long-term powers to provide compulsory treatment and care of a person with mental disorder. The order can be expedited either:

• in hospital (as the majority of them are), offering detention and treatment under compulsion (CTO); or
• in the community, offering a range of compulsory measures, such as attendance with a view of receiving mental treatment and/or community care services, residing at a specified place, or allowing access to the resident medical officer (RMO), MHO, etc. (CCTO).

This range of measures could be used constructively to support and protect an adult with mental disorder who meets the grounds for the order. These powers are comprehensive and may be useful to help an individual remain safe and well in the community, and to prevent cyclical admissions. The orders are also available to manage risk relative to adults with mental disorders, such as learning disability, dementia and personality disorder, and could be used imaginatively to manage risk. For example, where an adult is at risk of losing their home because of problem behaviour associated with mental disorder, the CCTO could provide a framework to allow access to the adult by key professionals, attendance for care and treatment, and even transfer of the adult to an alternative, more suitable, residence.

The order initially lasts for six months and then can be renewed for another 6 months, thereafter to be renewed on a twelve monthly basis. The order is made by the Mental Health Tribunal for Scotland (MHTS) at a tribunal hearing following an application by a MHO, which contains two medical reports (one from an AMP) and a proposed care plan.

Although CTOs are predominantly used to provide compulsory treatment in a hospital, they have application in the community thereby applying measures on the patient there to ensure treatment and care, and their use there is growing (MWC stats). Their application in the area of support and protection of adults at risk with mental disorder, however, appears relatively rare, where an adult may meet the grounds for the order and the order responds to the risk to which the adult is exposed in the community. Notwithstanding this, the order may provide a 'framework of support', which may protect such an adult from self-harm or lack of self-care, where their treatment is in jeopardy because of others, or where their mental disorder puts their welfare, health or safety at risk, or where there needs to be access to them to offer support and protection, or where they may need to reside somewhere to provide treatment and care or where they may pose a risk to others; basically, where the powers and measures manage and respond to the range of risk in the community.

From the author's experience, the most common measures applied in the context of community-based CTOs (CCTOs) appear to be (no statistics are available at the MHTS): attendance for treatment, access to RMOs, MHOs, etc. and, sometimes, residence. However, the patient may also be required to attend for community care services, relevant services, or any treatment, care or services, and be required to obtain the permission of the MHO to change residence.

Measures for an adult at risk with mental disorder might include:

- to attend a place to receive medical treatment, e.g. nursing, care or psychological therapies, which could include counselling, cognitive-behavioural therapy, etc.; or
- to attend a place to receive community care services, relevant services or any treatment, care or service, e.g. a day centre, which might help manage risk; or
- to reside at a specified place, e.g. respite or a place of safety, or residential environment; or
- to allow the MHO, RMO or any person responsible for providing medical treatment and community care services to visit the adult at their residence.

For example, a CCTO might be a useful provision in the case of an adult with incapacity, e.g. affected by ARBD or learning disability, thereby ensuring access to a RMO and MHO or others, where medical treatment (including care) could be provided; and, if necessary, to be transferred to another setting where their need for treatment requires this.

Equally, a CCTO may be useful in the case of adults with personality disorder, a much marginalised group in legal terms, by providing a framework of treatment and care, providing treatment that can include nursing, care, psychological interventions and rehabilitation.

However, as regards an adult affected by personality disorder, e.g. borderline personality disorder, there may be an argument against their being subject to a CCTO because of non-compliance and the thorny matter of 'treatability', where it may be viewed that treatment may not provide benefit (or not be available) to them. However, as the range of treatment is outwith 'pharmaceutical': drugs, etc., to include psychological therapies and care, these may provide major benefits and may assist the management of risk, for example, reducing the incidence of self-harming behaviour and diverting such adults away from the criminal justice system. The power of access and an assertive approach of the powers, potentially in the context of the care programme approach (CPA), to overcome non-compliance, may provide a crucial framework of treatment, care and protection.

The order may also offer the facility, through variation, to transfer individuals from hospital to the community or from community to hospital, and the powers may also be suspended, i.e. a) the detention measure in hospital, thereby allowing individuals to return to the community, or b) in the community, where either the measures of attendance, residence, visiting, approval and informing MHOs of any change of address could be suspended. A CCTO, therefore, can be used constructively to provide a much-needed framework of treatment, care and protection for an adult at risk with mental disorder.

Case example

In the case of John (5): John has a learning disability and asperger's syndrome and poses a risk to others. He is subject to a CCTO and a welfare guardianship. The CCTO provides a structured framework, which requires him to allow access to his RMO and MHO, and for him to attend an adult learning centre/resource centre, thereby managing risk to others.

Guardianship Orders (2000 Act)

Guardianship orders provide a suite of powers to respond to the problems associated with an adult's incapacity across welfare (and medical treatment), financial and property matters (or a combination of these), including specific risks thereof. The orders are granted by a Sheriff in the Sheriff Court and can exist for any substantive period of time. Although the default period is three years, more orders are being granted on an indefinite basis. They are provided in three forms: singular welfare orders, financial orders or combined welfare/financial orders. The application may be made by a local authority or by a private person, either a relative or a person acting on behalf of the adult or relative, e.g. solicitor. The protective suite of relative powers may be necessary to support and protect an adult with impaired capacity at risk living at home. It could provide an important framework to manage risk and maintain the adult's health, welfare and safety in the community.
For the local authority, the orders offer:

- Welfare guardianship, where the local authority may apply for and act as welfare guardian; or

- Financial guardianship, where the local authority cannot act as a financial guardian, but may need to apply for the order and locate an appropriate financial guardian; or
- Combined welfare and financial guardianship, where the local authority may act as welfare guardian in conjunction with a non-local authority financial guardian; or
- Private/relative application and the exercise of private welfare guardian powers, which would be supervised by the local authority.

Practice point ▶▶▶

Guardianship is the primary long-term statutory provision for adults affected by mental incapacity as a result of mental disorder. It can provide a substantive framework of care and support in the community to manage the risk of an adult with incapacity.

Welfare guardianship powers should be assessed and sought based on the adult's need and risks, and their incapacity respective of the powers. A range of powers, respective of risk, could include:

- to decide what care and support services may be appropriate for the adult;
- to assist the adult in attending to their medical, dental and nursing needs;
- to consent or withhold consent to medical treatment or procedures on behalf of the adult;
- to assist or take decisions of behalf of the adult in all aspects of personal care, including washing, dressing and personal appearance, diet, hygiene and toileting;
- to allow access to the adult in their place of residence, by any person or body on any matter concerning the health and personal welfare of the adult;
- to authorise the use of Tele-care equipment, to protect the adult's health, safety and welfare;
- to decide with whom the adult should or should not consort; and
- to remove the adult to a residential or nursing home setting should this be required to protect their welfare and safety.

Case examples

- In the Walter case (1), Walter could be a candidate for welfare guardianship, where powers could (a) authorise his range of treatment (although if he is non-compliant here powers within the 2003 Act may be necessary), (b) ensure that he receives care and support at home, (c) ensures access to him by the practitioners and support staff concerned and (d) impart some control over the person(s) who is/are exploiting him. However, if the power to decide with whom he should not consort is either unsuitable or untenable to protect him, a banning order in the 2007 Act may be necessary.
- Equally, Wilma (2) may also be a candidate with similar needs.

- In Mary's case (3), she may also benefit from being on a welfare guardianship order where decisions could be made on her behalf ensuring her welfare and safety, with powers of access and to make decisions regarding her long-term accommodation, which might ensure that she achieves optimum independence and development.
- In John's case (5), a combined CCTO and welfare guardianship is applied: the CCTO to authorize compulsory treatment and care and the welfare guardianship to make decisions and take actions respective of his incapacity.

Banning Orders (2007 Act)

A banning order may ban a subject of the order from being in an adult's premises (and, if necessary, an area of residence) for up to six months, which may include a range of conditions applied on the subject and a power of arrest. The order is made by a Sheriff in the Sheriff Court, following an application made 'only by or on behalf of' an adult or any other person who is entitled to occupy the place concerned, or the council. If the council decides to pursue an application where the affected adult has capacity to consent and has made known their refusal to consent, then the council must present evidence that the adult has been unduly pressurised to refuse consent to the granting of an order. Where the adult does not have capacity to consent, the requirement to prove undue pressure does not apply; however, evidence of lack of capacity will be required by the Sheriff.

A banning order bans the subject of the order from being in a specified place, e.g. the adult's house or residence; and, if necessary, a specified area, e.g. the area surrounding the adult's residence, and other specified conditions, e.g. supervised contact.

In detail, a banning order would:

a. ban the subject of the order from being in a specified place;
and may also
b. ban the subject from being in a specified area in the vicinity of the specified place;
c. authorise the summary ejection of the subject from the specified place and specified area;
d. prohibit the subject from moving any specified thing from the specified place;
e. direct any specified person to take specified measures to preserve any moveable property owned or controlled by the subject, which remains in the specified place while the order has effect;
f. be made subject to any specified conditions; or
g. require or authorise any person to do, or to refrain from doing, anything else that the Sheriff thinks necessary for the proper enforcement of the order.

A condition specified in a banning order may, in particular, authorise the subject to be in the place or area from which the subject is banned in specified circumstances (for example, while being supervised by another person or during specified times).

In the case of an adult at risk with mental disorder, the powers of the banning order could be tailored, e.g.:

- to ban the harmer of the adult at risk from being in the adult's house, care environment, or any other specified place the adult may be in or visiting; and
- ban the harmer from being in an area in the vicinity of this place, and, if necessary, to authorise the removal of the harmer thereof; it may also
- stop the harmer from taking anything from this place belonging to the adult;
- apply specified conditions to the order, which could apply to the harmer, e.g. dealing with abusing behaviour or alcohol abuse, agreeing to treatment or supervised contact; or
- require any person to stop facilitating the harm of the adult; or
- authorise any person to take necessary steps to protect the adult.

Case examples

- In the case of Walter (1), there may be a need to pursue a banning order to prevent the exploitation, in particular, of his finances (his brother) and his home (his 'friends').
- The Wilma case (2) indicates a need (to be confirmed) to prevent the 'male friend' who may be exploiting her sexually from accessing her.
- In the Mary case (3) the banning order may ban the harmers from her premises. However, this does not appear feasible given that it is their accommodation. It may be best, therefore, to consider her moving from there, thereby achieving independence.
- In the case of Ms A (7), (had it been available) it may have been useful to consider a banning order that would have banned the harmers (should they have been known) from her house and her area of residence; an issue in her case where it was not safe for her to enter the locality where the harmers were.

Multiple orders

Inevitably, while protecting an adult with mental disorder at risk, a range of powers across the primary Acts may be necessary, in particular, for an adult with severe and enduring mental disorder, living in the community, with risk across health, welfare, finances and safety, who requires non-voluntary care and treatment in the community, and is affected by incapacity arising from mental disorder. Here the 2000 and 2003 Acts would require consideration, in particular the long-term powers of community-based compulsory treatment and welfare guardianship: multiple powers. Add the existence of significant harm from others, and the 2007 Act may be added to the repertoire of Acts, powers and provisions; to offer, in particular, a banning order.

Across the orders, there are multiple powers available (also see Appendix 15), e.g. to:

CCTO	• attend a place to receive medical treatment, e.g. nursing, care or psychological therapies; or • attend a place to receive community care services, relevant services or any treatment, care or service, e.g. a day centre; or • reside at a specified place, e.g. respite or a place of safety, or residential environment; or • allow the MHO, RMO; or any person responsible for providing medical treatment and community care services to visit the adult in his/her residence.
WG	• decide what care and support services for the adult; • assist the adult in attending to his/her medical, dental and nursing needs; • consent or withhold consent to medical treatment or procedures on behalf of the said adult; • assist and take decisions of behalf of the said adult in all aspects of her personal care, including washing, dressing and personal appearance, diet, hygiene and toileting; • allow access the said adult in his/her place of residence, by any person or body on any matter concerning the health and personal welfare of the said adult; • authorise the use of telecare equipment, which would protect the said adult's health, safety and welfare; • decide with whom the adult should or should not consort; and/or • remove the said adult to a residential or nursing home setting should this be required to protect his/her welfare and safety.
BO	• ban the harmer of the adult at risk from being in the adult's house, care environment, or any other specified place the adult may be or visiting; and to ban the harmer from being in a area in the vicinity of this place, and, if necessary; to authorise the removal of the harmer thereof; • stop the harmers from taking anything from this place belonging to the adult; • apply specified conditions to the order, which could apply to the harmer, e.g. dealing with abusing behaviour, alcohol abuse or agreeing to treatment, or arranging for supervised contact; • require any person to do stop facilitating the harm of the adult; and • authorise any person to do take steps to protect the adult.

It may also be necessary to seek powers to protect an adult's finances and property, in particular if they are incapable of managing and making decisions in this respect. To assist, there are supportive provisions (mentioned earlier) including Part 2 of the 2000 Act (continuing power of attorney), where an adult with capacity may grant the authority to a person or others to manage their finances on their behalf (which would continue where the adult loses capacity), and Part 3 of the 2000 Act, where the adult is incapable in this respect and needs a person or body (including the local authority) to manage their accounts and funds, and more 'informal provisions' such as a Department for Work and Pensions (DWP) appointee arrangement. However, where the adult is incapable across a range of financial and property based matters, and these are of serious significance, i.e. the adult has substantial amounts of money and heritable property, which are at risk and need to be managed, then financial guardianship may need to be brought into the mix of long-term powers and provisions.

Financial guardianship (Part 6) may be necessary to protect and secure the finances and property of the adult (with incapacity), which may be open to risk, exploitation, misappropriation, or theft, i.e. to protect and manage: any heritable property (and land); any account of the adult's pensions, benefits, allowances, services, etc.; investments; the adult's estate and any business belonging to the adult. This may involve taking legal action in respect of the adult's funds or property and/or obtaining and paying for any goods or services of benefit to the adult, and having access to confidential information.

Powers across the long-term orders

The application of multiple powers across the primary long-term orders may offer a comprehensive range of measures, across risk to health, welfare, safety, finance and property.

See Appendix 15 for the range of powers in, and grounds for, long-term orders.

Putting all of these measures and powers together may be viewed as a restrictive range of powers; however, as with John (5) there may be a need to have a substantive range of powers applied, in his case the parallel application of a CCTO and a welfare guardianship order. Here the RMO and the MHO expedite the powers of the CCTO and his father acts as his welfare guardian. Additionally, Part 3 of the 2000 Act allows his father to access and manage his funds, i.e.:

Community based CTO, with powers to:	Welfare guardianship, with powers to:
1. Give medical treatment. 2. Require attendance for medical treatment. 3. Require attendance for community care services. 4. Require adult to reside in specified place. 5. Allow visits by RMO, MHO, etc. 6. Obtain approval of MHO to change address.	1. Decide on care and accommodation. 2. Decide on contact with others. 3. Consent to medical treatment. 4. Decide on social, leisure and educational activities. 5. Supervise, accompany and support the adult on a 24 hour basis.
Supportive provisions	
Part 3 (2000): to manage funds and accounts.	Care and support services (s25, 2003 Act) Independent advocacy services
• local adult at risk procedures, i.e. risk management (HCR 20 etc) and adult protection planning; and • local care management and care programme approach	

Combining these powers in a managed care and support system, may meet the objective of supporting and protecting adults in the community, and to ensure the protection of others; in John's case, women, from his risk behaviour. Although a comprehensive, and some may say, restrictive range of powers, this needs to be balanced with an alternative scenario where some adults with the need for this framework might be detained in hospital on a long-term basis; or, where without controls applied, risk-related behaviour results in such adults being convicted of offences, with the potential of being transferred to a secure setting.

Table 9.1 offers an 'across the Acts' description of the long-term powers in application, their grounds and criteria, provision, timescales, non-compliance, etc. This is to prompt the reader to 'think across the Acts' and not just of an individual Act, or in a linear way.

Table 9.1.: Crossing the Acts: Long Term Powers

	What happens if there is non compliance?		
Compulsory Treatment Orders	**Guardianship Orders**		**Banning Order**

The Act provides for two sets of powers where a patient does not comply with community-based compulsory measures.
 	
1) as described in sections 113 to 115 of the Act, relates to a lack of compliance with any community-based compulsory measures;
 	
2) and described in section 112 of the Act, can be exercised with respect to a lack of compliance with the "attendance requirement" alone. All reasonable steps must be taken to ensure the person complies with the order (assertive outreach?).
 	
112 may be used for non attendance for treatment, where a RMO authorises detention for 6 hours in hospital for medical treatment. This requires MHO consent.
 	
S113 may be used for general non compliance, where the RMO Authorises detention in hospital for 72 hours if person does not comply with other aspects of the order (AMP exam), and
 	
S114 where the RMO can detain the person in hospital for a further 28 days if required. If there is a need for further treatment or variance of the order. This requires MHO consent.
	On non-compliance with decisions of guardian with welfare power (s70), where any decision of a guardian with powers relating to the personal welfare of the adult is not complied with by the adult or by any other person, and the adult or other person might reasonably be expected to comply with the decision, the Sheriff may, on an application by the guardian:
	
	a. make an order ordaining the adult or any person named in the order to implement the decision of the guardian;
	
	b. where the non-compliance relates to a decision of the guardian as to the place of residence of the adult, grant a warrant authorising a constable
	
	  * to enter any premises where the adult is, or is reasonably supposed to be;
	
	  * to apprehend the adult and to remove him to such place as the guardian may direct.
	
	c. where any decision of a guardian with powers relating to the personal welfare of the adult is not complied with by any person other than the adult, and that person might reasonably be expected to comply with the decision, the Sheriff may, on an application by the guardian make an order ordaining the person named in the order to implement the decision of the guardian.
			The Sheriff, at the time of granting the banning order, may attach a power of arrest (s25).
			
			Evidence for arrest would be based on the likelihood of the subject breaching the banning order or or any of the conditions attached to the banning order.
			
			If any of these conditions were breached the subject may be arrested without warrant if a constable reasonably suspects them to be in breach of the order and that they are likely to breach the order again if not arrested.

	What are the roles of the key practitioners?		
The mental health officer a) prepares and submits the application, b) prepares the MHO report and c) the proposed care plan, d) makes the application; and e) leads the evidence at the Tribunal. The MHO must identify the patient's named person, notify certain parties that the application is being made (the patient; the patient's named person; and the Commission); must inform the patient of his/her rights; and must interview the patient. Two medical examination need to be carried out within 5 days of each other. One of the medical practitioners needs to be approved (an approved medical practitioner) by the local authority health board (or state hospital). The AMP (RMO) carries out the primary medical examination and prepares the medical report. Another medical practitioner carries out a medical examinations and submit a medical reports (this can be the person's GP) Following the granting of the order a RMO (normally the AMP) prepares the 'working care plan' and manages the order (and recorded measures), thereby applying non compliance, etc.	The MHO may provide a guardianship assessment which may be presented to a local authority case conference to consider guardianship. Where an application is made to the Sheriff Court, where there are welfare powers requested an MHO needs to prepare report on the appropriateness of the order and, if the proposed guardian is a private individual, e.g. a relative, on the suitability of the person. The MHO may be requested to attend Court to explain his/her findings. An AMP would prepare one of the medical reports to accompany the application; a GP or another AMP would prepared the second medical report.		A Council Officer assessment would be central to the making of an application for a banning order to the Sheriff Court. The Council (local authority) would most commonly make the application, although others can make the application (see above). A Council Officer may be a MHO where the adult has mental disorder, who might provide a vital bridge to the 2003 and 2000 Acts. A GP or AMP may confirm the adult to be incapable in respect of being able to consent to the order (as is required) as indicated by the amended code of practice.

Table 9.1.: Crossing the Acts: Long Term Powers

What are their criteria in respect of adults at risk?

Compulsory Treatment Orders	Guardianship Orders	Banning Order

Where the Tribunal confirms
 	
1. the adult has a mental disorder which poses risk to self or others, or places the adult in a situation of risk from others, or from self, or to others;
 	
2. that medical treatment which would assist the management of risk by preventing the mental disorder worsening or by alleviating any of the symptoms, or effects, of the disorder, is available for the adult;
 	
3. that if the adult were not provided with such medical treatment there would be a significant risk to the health, safety or welfare of the adult; or to the safety of any other person;
 	
4. that because of the mental disorder the adult's ability to make decisions about the provision of such medical treatment is significantly impaired; and
 	
5. that the making of a compulsory treatment order is necessary to manage and respond to risk
 	
Before recommending that community-based compulsory measures be applied for, the medical practitioner would be expected to demonstrate in the mental health report that issues such as those listed above, in addition to any others relevant to the patient's case, have been fully taken into consideration. In doing so, it will be important to demonstrate that consideration has been given to the potential impact of these community-based compulsory measures on any carers or other persons who live with and/or care for the patient (2003 Act, V2 COP).
	Where the Sheriff confirms
	
	1. an 'adult with incapacity' is at risk to their welfare, finances or property;
	
	2. the order is necessary and appropriate (and there are no other means under the Act) and the proposed guardian is suitable (except local authority) to protect the adult's welfare, finances, or property; and
	
	3. the principles apply; e.g. management of risk is a benefit to the adult and is of the least restrictive option in relation to the freedom of the adult.
	
	An "adult with incapacity" means a person who has attained the age of 16 years; "incapable" means incapable of
	
	a. acting (to protect themselves from risk to their welfare, finances or property); or
	
	b. making decisions (where the lack of decision making capacity places the adult's welfare, finances or property at risk); or
	
	c. communicating decisions (where the lack of ability to communicate decisions places the adult's welfare, finances or property at risk); or
	
	d. understanding decisions (where the lack of ability to understand decisions places the adult's welfare, finances or property at risk); or
	
	e. retaining the memory of decisions (where the lack of retention of memory of decisions places the adult's welfare, finances or property at risk).
	
	as mentioned in any provision of this Act, by reason of mental disorder; and "incapacity" shall be construed accordingly.
		Where the Sheriff is satisfied
		
		1. that an adult (with mental illness, learning disability, or personality disorder) is at risk is being, or is likely to be, seriously harmed by another person,
		
		2. that the adult (as above) at risk's well-being or property would be better safeguarded by banning another person from a place occupied by the adult than it would be by moving the adult from that place, and
		
		3. that either
		  a. the adult (as above) at risk is entitled, or permitted by a third party, or
		  b. neither the adult at risk nor the subject is entitled, or permitted by a third party,
		to occupy the place from which the subject is to be banned
		
		"Adults at risk" are adults (with mental illness, learning disability, or personality disorder) who
		a. are unable to safeguard their own well-being, property, rights or other interests,
		b. are at risk of harm, and
		c. because they are affected by mental disorder (mental illness, learning disability, or personality disorder) are more vulnerable to being harmed than adults who are not so affected.
		
		An adult is at risk of harm if
		a. another person's conduct is causing (or is likely to cause) the adult to be harmed, or
		b. the adult is engaging (or is likely to engage) in conduct which causes (or is likely to cause) self-harm

Table 9.1.: Crossing the Acts: Long Term Powers

What are they for and what do they provide?

Compulsory Treatment Orders	Guardianship Orders	Banning Order
1. Compulsory treatment in hospital (a hospital CTO) may be used where it is not possible to treat an individual in the community and where the risk to the person's health, welfare or safety would be in jeopardy should they not receive treatment there in hospital. 2. Community based compulsory treatment (a community based CTO [a CCTO]) may be used (for an adult at risk) where: * community-based powers would provide a safe and viable alternative to compulsory hospitalisation (e.g. where welfare risk in the community); * a patient has previously relapsed whilst off medication in the community, and as a result, has presented a risk to themselves and/or others (e.g. where a framework of care and treatment can maintain medication compliance and prevent the risk posed happening); * all other means of trying to negotiate with the patient and maintain them in the community without compulsion have been tried and have failed (e.g. where the person has a history of non compliance with medication and this has caused major risk to the person's life); and * alternative, less restrictive approaches to secure and adequate adherence with necessary treatments have been shown to be impracticable (e.g. where an informal framework has not provided a framework of safety).	They may be used to protect a vulnerable adult with mental disorder with impaired capacity, where a range of actions are required, which may have to be sustained over a period of time, such as three to five years, or of which may be indefinite. This may include adults exposed to welfare, sexual, and/or financial exploitation, neglect or harm by others; and may include particular powers, e.g. to decide where the adult should live, to apply for a community care assessment, for the adult or receive community care services, or to decide with whom the adult should or should not consort. Generally, they provide powers to a. to deal with such particular matters in relation to the property, financial affairs or personal welfare of the adult; b. power to deal with all aspects of the personal welfare of the adult; c. power to pursue or defend an action of declarator of nullity of marriage, or of divorce or separation in the name of the adult; d. power to manage the property or financial affairs of the adult, or such parts of them as may be specified in the order; e. power to authorise the adult to carry out such transactions or categories of transactions as the guardian may specify.	Banning orders will only be granted where the adult at risk is in danger of being seriously harmed, and where banning the subject of the order from a specified place is likely to safeguard the adult's well -being and property more effectively than would the removal of the adult at risk (COP). The banning order bans the subject of the order from being in a specified place (e.g. the adult house or residence) or specified area (e.g. the area surrounding the adult's residence), and other specified conditions (e.g. supervised contact). 1. A banning order bans the subject of the order from being in a specified place. 2. A banning order may also a. ban the subject from being in a specified area in the vicinity of the specified place, b. authorise the summary ejection of the subject from the specified place and the specified area, c. prohibit the subject from moving any specified thing from the specified place, d. direct any specified person to take specified measures to preserve any moveable property owned or controlled by the subject which remains in the specified place while the order has effect, e. be made subject to any specified conditions, f. require or authorise any person to do, or to refrain from doing, anything else which the Sheriff thinks necessary for the proper enforcement of the order.
The orders may 1. detain the patient in hospital and give medical treatment; or 2. impose requirements in the community on the patient, i.e. a) the imposition of a requirement on the patient to attend: on specified or directed dates; or at specified or directed intervals, specified or directed places with a view to receiving medical treatment; b) the imposition of a requirement on the patient to attend: on specified or directed dates; or at specified or directed intervals, specified or directed places with a view to receiving community care services, relevant services or any treatment, care or service; c) the imposition of a requirement on the patient to reside at a specified place; d) the imposition of a requirement on the patient to allow (i) MHO; (ii) RMO; or (iii) any person responsible for providing medical treatment, community care services, relevant services or any treatment, care or service to the patient who is authorised by the RMO, to visit the patient in the place where the patient resides; e) the imposition of a requirement on the patient to obtain the approval of the mental health officer to any proposed change of address; and f) the imposition of a requirement on the patient to inform the mental health officer of any change of address before the change takes effect. (s66: 2003 Act).	Welfare guardianship powers may include powers to: 1. decide where the adult should live 2. apply for a community care assessment for the adult; 3. consent to community care services; 4. apply to receive and manage self -directed support (direct payments) from the social work department; 5. have access to personal information concerning the adult,; 6. consent or withhold consent to medical treatment for the adult; 7. arrange for the adult to undertake work, education or training; 8. take the adult on holiday or authorise someone else to do so; 9. provide access to the adult for medical treatment, dentistry etc. 10. make decisions on the adult's dress, diet, personal appearance; 11. make decisions on the adult's social and cultural activities; 12. pursue, defend or compromise any legal action on behalf of the adult involving his or her personal welfare; or to 13. decide with whom the adult should or should not consort.	A condition specified in a banning order may, in particular, authorise the subject to be in the place or area from which the subject is banned in specified circumstances (for example, while being supervised by another person or during specified times).

Table 9.1.: Crossing the Acts: Long Term Powers

How may the powers be used to protect adults at risk with mental disorder?

Changing the emphasis of the powers available through the Acts to focus on risk may change the nature of the powers applied a nd provide a more tailored set of powers respective of the adult's risks, i.e.

Community based CTO to	Welfare guardianship to	Banning order to

☐ require the adult to attend (specified / directed dates; or at specified / directed intervals) places (specified / directed) with a view to receiving medical treatment, which would respond to risk, e.g. health centres, resource centres, day hospitals, etc.;
 	
☐ require the adult to attend (on specified / directed dates; or at specified / directed intervals) places (specified / directed) with a view to receiving community care services, relevant services or any treatment, care or service, which would assist the protection and support of an adult (with mental disorder) at risk;
 	
☐ require the adult to reside at a specified place, e.g. a residential setting, where this would provide treatment and care, which would support and protect an adult at risk;
 	
☐ require the adult to allow a MHO, RMO; or any person responsible for providing medical treatment, community care services, relevant services or any treatment, care or service (including support and protection services) to the adult who is authorised by the RMO, to visit the adult in the place where the patient resides;
 	
☐ require the adult to obtain the approval of the MHO to any proposed change of address to inform the MHO of any change of address before the change takes effect , where this relates to the support and protection of the adult at risk because of mental disorder.
	☐ remove the adult to a safer place and have them reside there;
	☐ apply for a risk assessment for the adult;
	☐ consent to adult protection services;
	☐ apply to receive and manage support and protection funding;
	☐ have access to risk management information on the adult;
	☐ consent or withhold consent to medical assessment or treatment concerning risk to the adult's health, welfare or personal safety;
	☐ arrange for the adult to undertake education or training which would assist protection and management of welfare risk;
	☐ deter or take the adult away from environments or situations which poses risk to personal welfare;
	☐ access the adult to provide support and protection of welfare;
	☐ make decisions on the safety and protection of adult's welfare;
	☐ make decisions on the adult's social and cultural activities which promote the adult's welfare and safety;
	☐ pursue, defend or compromise any legal action on behalf of the adult involving risk to his or her personal welfare; and
	☐ decide with whom the adult should or should not consort.
		☐ ban the subject of the order from being in a specified place where the adult with mental disorder may be;
		☐ ban the subject from being in a specified area in the vicinity of the place where the adult resides or spends their time;
		☐ authorise the summary ejection of the subject from the specified place and the specified area;
		☐ prohibit the subject from moving any specified thing from the specified place,
		☐ direct any specified person to take specified measures to preserve any moveable property owned or controlled by the subject which remains in the specified place while the order has effect,
		☐ be made subject to any specified conditions, relating to the protection of an adult with mental disorder, e.g.
		  * not preventing the adult's treatment of mental disorder;
		  * not assisting the adult's self harm; or
		  * not restricting the liberty or independence of the adult;
		☐ require or authorise any person to do, or to refrain from doing, anything else which the Sheriff thinks necessary for the proper enforcement of the order; e.g.:
		  * not preventing the adult's treatment of mental disorder;
		  * not assisting the adult's self harm;
		  * not restricting the liberty or independence of the adult; or
		  * not assisting any harmer's access to the adult.

The adult: a. to attend a place to receive medical treatment, e.g. nursing, care or psychological therapies; or b. to attend a place to receive community care services, relevant services or any treatment, care or service, e.g. a day centre; or c. to reside at a specified place, e.g. respite or a place of safety, or residential environment; or d. to allow the MHO, RMO; or any person responsible for providing medical treatment and community care services to visit the adult in his/her residence.	**Example of specific powers** **The welfare guardian:** to decide what care and support services for the adult; a. to assist the adult in attending to his/her medical, dental and nursing needs; b. to consent or withhold consent to medical treatment or procedures on behalf of the said adult; c. to assist and take decisions of behalf of the said adult in all aspects of her personal care, including washing, dressing and personal appearance, diet, hygiene and toileting; d. to allow access the said adult in his/her place of residence, by any person or body on any matter concerning the health and personal welfare of the said adult; e. to authorise the use of tele -care equipment, which would protect the said adult's health, safety and welfare; f. to decide with whom the adult should or should not consort; and g. to remove the said adult to a residential or nursing home setting should this be required to protect his/her welfare and safety.	**The order:** a. bans the harmer of the adult at risk from being in the adult's house, care environment; or any other specified place the adult may be or visiting; and to ban the harmer from being in a area in the vicinity of this place, and, if necessary; to authorise the removal of the harmer thereof; b. stops the harmers from taking anything from this place belonging to the adult; c. applies specified conditions to the order, which could apply to the harmer, e.g. dealing with abusing behaviour, alcohol abuse or agreeing to treatment, or arranging for supervised contact; or d. requires any person to do stop facilitating the harm of the adult, or e. authorises any person or person to do take steps to protect the adult.

Table 9.1.: Crossing the Acts: Long Term Powers

What are their timescales?

Compulsory Treatment Orders	Guardianship Orders	Banning Order
If granted, the order would be authorised (by the tribunal) for the period of 6 months beginning with the day on which the order is made, such of the measures mentioned in section 66(1) of the Act, as may be specified in the order (s64(4)). Where a determination (to extend) is made in respect of the first review, the period of 6 months beginning with the day on which the compulsory treatment order will cease. Where a determination is made in respect of the first further review, the period of 12 months beginning with the expiry of the period mentioned. Where a determination is made in respect of a subsequent further review, the period of 12 months beginning with the expiry of the period of 12 months for which the order is extended as a result of the immediately preceding further review.	A default term for guardianship may be three to five years. In exceptional circumstances indefinite powers may be granted, e.g. where the adult has permanent incapacity and there is no possibility of improved capacity (MWC 2009).	1. A banning order can last for any period up to a maximum of six months; 2. The applicant should consider what would be the shortest period possible in line with the general principles of the adult at risk's wishes and what would be beneficial to the adult; 3. The period for a banning order will be specified by the Sheriff; and 4. A banning order may be recalled or varied.

How do you get them and what does an application consist of?

Compulsory Treatment Orders	Guardianship Orders	Banning Order
A mental health officer shall apply to the Tribunal (s63) for a CTO in respect of that patient, where two medical practitioners (one a AMP) carry out medical examinations of the patient in accordance with s58. The mental health officer shall make the application before the expiry of the period of 14 days beginning with a) in the case where each of the mental health reports specifies the same date (or dates), that date (or the later, or latest, of those dates); or (b) in the case where each of those reports specifies for those purposes a different date (or different dates), the later (or latest) of those dates. An application for a CTO consists of: a) two mental health reports prepared by the medical practitioners (one a AMP) (s57); b) the mental health officer's report (s61); and c) the proposed care plan produced by the MHO (s62).	An application may be made by any person claiming an interest in the property, financial affairs or personal welfare of an adult to the Sheriff for an order appointing an individual or office holder as guardian in relation to the adult's property, financial affairs or personal welfare. Where it appears to the local authority that the conditions /criteria mentioned (s58(1)(a/b) apply to the adult; and no application has been made or is likely to be made for an order under this section; and a guardianship order is necessary for the protection of the property, financial affairs or personal welfare of the adult, the local authority shall apply under this section for an order. There shall be lodged in court along with an application under this section: a. reports, in prescribed form, of an examination and assessment of the adult carried out not more than 30 days before the lodging of the application by at least two medical practitioners one of whom, in a case where the incapacity is by reason of mental disorder, must be a medical practitioner approved for the purposes of section 22 of the 2003 Act; b. where the application relates to the personal welfare of the adult, a report, in prescribed form, from the MHO of the appropriateness of the order sought, based on an interview and assessment of the adult carried out not more than 30 days before the lodging of the application; and the suitability of the individual nominated in the application to be appointed guardian; and c. where the application relates only to the property or financial affairs of the adult, a report, in prescribed form, based on an interview and assessment of the adult carried out not more than 30 days before the lodging of the application, by a person who has sufficient knowledge to make such a report.	An application for a banning order may be made to the Sheriff by or on behalf of: 1. an adult whose well-being or property would be safeguarded by the order; or 2. any other person who is entitled to occupy the place concerned; or 3. a Council, where nobody else is likely to apply and no other proceedings to eject or ban the person concerned from the place concerned are pending before a court.

Table 9.1.: Crossing the Acts: Long Term Powers

How do the powers relate?		
Compulsory Treatment Orders	**Guardianship Orders**	**Banning Order**
The long term powers of the 2003 Act offer a flexible and long term framework for treating serious mental illnesses such as schizophrenia and bipolar disorder, but not so much for the need for care arising from the effect of permanent and incapacitating conditions such as dementia or alcohol related brain damage. Notwithstanding the use of the 2003 Act as discussed above, this may be where a MHO may consider stepping out of the 2003 Act into the 2000 Act or indeed the 2007 Act. In many circumstances, however, it will be appropriate for the local authority to use its powers under the 1968 Act to provide services to an adult with mental disorder, providing non compulsory provisions. The 2000 Act also offers provisions to protect welfare, finances and property, where the adult is incapable due to mental disorder, and provides authority to treat under section 47, but does not offer compulsory powers in this regard, remembering certain medical treatments are out-with the scope of the 2000 Act, in particular those specified in the 2003 Act. Moreover, there is an important interrelationship between the 2003 and the 2007 Act, in particular where there is harm from others, and where the provisions of the 2003 Act do not assist.	The use of powers (in welfare guardianship) to require the adult not to consort with another person, potentially a harmer, should be treated with caution. The power which may be sought to create a barrier between an adult at risk from a person posing risk; however, the requirement is on the adult and not on the other person. In some cases a banning order (2007 Act) may be more appropriate because the requirement there is on the harmer and not the adult. Generally, in many circumstances it will be appropriate for the local authority to use its powers under the 1968 Act to provide services to an adult who lacks capacity to consent to receiving services. The 2000 Act lacks emergency powers e.g. warrants for entry and removal, where consideration needs to be given to the 2003 and 2007 Acts, and certain medical treatments are also out-with the scope of the 2000 Act, in particular those specified in the 2003 Act.	In many circumstances it will be appropriate for the local authority to use its powers under the 1968 Act to provide services to an adult with mental disorder. The 2000 Act also offers provisions to protect welfare, finances and property, where the adult is incapable due to mental disorder, and provides authority to treat under section 47 but does not offer compulsory powers in this regard, and certain medical treatments are also out-with the scope of the 2000 Act, in particular those specified in the 2003 Act. There is an important inter-relationship between the 2003 and the 2007 Act, in particular where there is harm from others, and where the provisions of the 2003 Act do not assist.

Summary of Part 3

Applying this range of measures, i.e.:

- confirming a mandate for inquiry;
- considering immediate powers;
- confirming the need for short-term powers;
- exploring the need for long-term powers; and
- applying supportive provisions,

requires a flexible and creative approach and needs to be applied in a synchronised and planned way.

Practitioners, however, need to be 'fleet of foot' in traversing or stepping across the chasms between the Acts, or assailing or climbing up and down the Acts, or going from one corner of one Act to another. All of these mandates, powers and provisions, however, taken together across the Acts, provide a wide range of measures, but also an extensive array of interrelationships.

To assist understanding (and the practical application of the Acts):

- Appendix 16 offers a linear description of the above Acts' 'protective parts' (as in the list above), giving types (e.g. inquiry, power or provision, such as to cause inquiry to be made), the Act (e.g. 2003), the section (e.g. section 33), who obtains (e.g. the local authority) and who grants (e.g. the local authority);
- Appendix 17 describes the links across the Acts; and
- Appendix 18 describes the interrelationships and links across the Acts' powers and provisions, giving an indication of the need to work across and up and down the Acts.

Working 'across the Acts', therefore, cannot be applied in a 'linear' or 'step one, step two' process, it requires 'a step across, from side to side, up and down, from one corner to another' across the range of provisions, i.e.:

- A leap across and down, e.g.:

  - an investigating officer, investigating an adult's circumstances under section 10 of the 2000 Act, may see the need to traverse the Acts, e.g. to the 2007 Act and then to reach deep into the Act, e.g. to obtain a long-term order, such as a banning order. This is quite a leap from inquiry under the 2000 Act to a banning order under the 2007 Act, but this may be necessary to access the correct and suitable provision respective of the adult's risk; or
  - the conclusion of an inquiry under the 2007 Act, which arrives at the need for welfare guardianship to support and protect the adult; or

-   the conclusion of an inquiry under the 2003 Act, which arrives at the need for a banning order to support and protect the adult.

•   A leap back up the Acts (and across) may also be necessary, e.g.:

-   from welfare guardianship to inquiry, i.e. to section 10 (2000 Act): a supervising officer (of a private welfare guardianship), or an investigating officer who is investigating a complaint against a private welfare guardian neglecting or harming the adult's welfare would obtain their mandate under section 10 (2000 Act) to investigate, or indeed under section 4 (2007 Act) where there is a confirmation of an 'adult at risk' or under section 33 (2003 Act), where an adult with mental disorder is being ill-treated, etc.; or
-   from a community based compulsory treatment order back to inquiry, or to immediate or short-term powers, for example where an adult has not 'breached' the order, and where non-compliance (Chapter 5, 2003 Act) cannot return the adult to hospital, and where the community-based measures granted by the tribunal do not assist, a RMO may have to consider a short-term detention, or where an AMP is not available, a GP may have to admit through emergency detention. Equally, there may be a need for a MHO to remove the adult to a place of safety (s293/4), where the adult does not need to go to hospital for treatment. One can also envisage the possibility of an adult on a CCTO who is, or becomes, an adult at risk, i.e. is being harmed by another, where an investigation under section 4 (2007 Act) may need to be made, or where the adult is incapable and their welfare is at risk a section 10 investigation may be necessary; or
-   an adult on a banning order, where the banning order does not protect the adult and immediate powers are necessary, for example, where the subject of the order (the harmer) has breached the order, invoking the power of arrest provision, or where the adult (with mental disorder) needs to be removed to a place of safety under the 2003 Act, or emergency or short-term detention to a hospital (2003 Act), where there is a need for treatment, or indeed to a general hospital for treatment for physical illness/injury of an incapable adult under an intervention order (2000 Act), or to seeking provision under the 2000 Act to protect or manage the adult's finances (Part 3 or Part 6).

In summary, it would be a difficult task to explain all the connections up and down and across and from side to side in and across the Acts. Properly, practitioners themselves will establish the connections, links and interrelationships, as risk and need determine. Practitioners may wish to view the three Acts and their provisions as a palette of protection and support, adding individual provisions (colours) to the overall legislative and protection plan as is necessary; thereby, creating an overall picture of power and provision across the Acts.

PART FOUR

PRACTICAL APPLICATION

Chapter 10

APPLYING THE POWERS

The powers and provisions in the Acts are static, they are confirmed in law; and, failing legislative amendment, they are what practitioners have available to assist them support and protect adults with mental disorder. How they are used, however, has more pertinence in a practical sense. This chapter explores the practical application of the powers across the Acts.

(1) Ensure the adult's centrality

For adults at risk with mental disorder, drawn into a legal context with a wide range of laws and powers, in the context of local procedures and provisions of services, this can be a daunting and intimidating experience (see Appendix 42). Key practitioners, therefore, need to help adults understand that the legislation can be empowering and supportive, and not restrictive or disempowering.

Legislation, however, has rightly so over the years moved from a 'do to and do for' position to a 'do with and do alongside' philosophy and practice. This is demonstrated practically across the legislations, with the application of the principles of participation, empowerment and ensuring access to advocacy services. The 'personalisation policy', however, should be espoused practically in a collaborative way with service users, ensuring 'choice' and 'control' where legislative options are pursued.

The adult needs to be central to any legislative response and this has to be the primary objective of any support and protection plan. Indeed, the 2007 Act is predicated on consent and empowerment, where there are no compulsory powers in the Act, and where the adult needs to consent and co-operate with any proposed action, for example where it is confirmed under section 22 that an application for a banning order may be made 'only by or on behalf of an adult ..., etc.'. The Council, however, can make an application where 'nobody else is likely to apply ..., etc.'.

Occasionally, adult centrality is not possible, i.e. because of mental disorder, incapacity and/or the degree of risk, protective action may be taken outwith the adult's consent, occasionally to save the adult's life. However, even when using formal powers in this way, the adult should feel part of what is going on, central and involved. This takes skill, however, and a good explanation to the adult of the benefits of formal powers against the dangers to the adult's health, safety or welfare, of not pursuing formal protection, reinforced after the event; and later when the adult, following the protective measure or treatment, has gained insight or then appreciates the benefits of the measure.

The allocation of an independent advocacy worker would help ensure the adult's central position, and the need for legal advocacy should be identified early in any formal intervention, to protect the adult's human and legal rights and, if necessary, assist the adult in appealing or challenging any legislative intervention.

Therefore, rightly so, the adult should have a central place in the application of protective powers; however, they also should have a primary involvement in the preparation of both assessment and plans. Adult centrality is demonstrated practically (and formally) where a MHO (or RMO) involves an adult in the preparation of a care plan (including CTO proposed and working care plans), thereby ensuring active participation, and jointly designing the plan as a vehicle to recovery, accessing recreational, social and spiritual supports (MWC, 2009b). However, it is in the preparation of risk assessment the adult's involvement and participation is essential.

Wherever possible, the adult should contribute here, where the assessor can explore with the adult the primary risks to their health, welfare and safety, and, in particular, risk from others and risk of self-harm, and discuss potential strategies to deal with this risk; in particular, wherever possible, to how the adult can be empowered to take necessary actions.

(2) Ensure the 'only where necessary' approach

The primary 'only where necessary' approach to pursuing formal intervention is espoused in the principles of minimum intervention and the least restrictive approach endorsed across the Acts. Indeed, as indicated earlier, practice under the 2007 Act is more about 'support' on a voluntary and consensual basis, than 'protection' on a formal basis. Indeed, any formal action needs to rule out the potential of voluntary and informal interventions. Only when it is not possible to support and protect the adult in this way should formal steps be taken. Again, as with adult centrality, independent advocacy is strongly indicated in this respect across the Acts.

Key practitioners, such as MHOs, need to demonstrate 'necessity' in court and tribunals, and GPs need to confirm 'urgent necessity' when pursuing emergency detentions. However, the 'where necessary' approach begins way before practitioners engage with an adult at risk; where, even before visiting or interviewing an adult, thought would be given to how formal intervention may be avoided wherever possible. This may be by considering the range of care and support services available and the need for a community care or single shared assessment, in the context of local adult at risk procedures.

'Only where necessary', however, includes taking affirmative action 'where necessary'. Practitioners have a duty of care and protection under the Acts, and action to protect the adult's safety should be taken 'where necessary'. Practitioners have been criticised in inquiries for not taking assertive action or using formal powers to remove an adult from risk.

(3) Avoid the pitfalls

Some significant pitfalls, in protecting adults with mental disorder, are well described in major MWC deficiency in care inquiries, in particular the Borders case (SWSI, 2004), i.e. failure to consider appropriate powers, a lack of collaborative working, poor sharing of information, poor care planning, a lack of risk assessments and a lack of compliance with adult protection procedures. Practitioners need to have these failings firmly in mind as they engage in any case of support and protection of an adult at risk with mental disorder.

Additionally, many adults may be placed in ongoing risk where social work and health services close the case on those adults, where there is a need for continuity of care, such as is confirmed in the 2003 Act in respect of the designated (and continued) MHO role.

In the same way that community care should be delivered relative to need, adult protection should be provided relative to risk. One of the pitfalls community care has, however, is where delivery of care is predicated on available resources, thereby fitting the person's needs to the resource, whether the resource fully meets the person's needs or not. In the same way, a pitfall of adult protection is to apply the provision or power, because it is expedient or convenient for the services to do so, unreflective of individual needs or risk. Assessed risk, therefore, has to govern protective action.

Another pitfall is to follow a set course, i.e. (a) to decide on protective action, (b) to get evidence to obtain this and (c) to pursue and deliver the provision. While this may be necessary and appropriate, such as in child protection, where there is parental consent or where the Panel or Sheriff's authority is required, adults have a right of consent and not to cooperate if they do not wish to. Adults have a right to say "Go away, this is my life, this is my risk, don't call me, I'll call you." So, empowerment, self-determination and partnership are the name of the game. However, where consent and compliance are not available, and the adult is at risk, then formal provision should be considered to protect the adult from others, and sometimes from themselves.

Additionally, another pitfall is where practitioners operate outwith adequate managerial support and guidance. Many practitioners are left 'to get on with it', e.g. trying to access legal advice, finding (or designing) the appropriate forms, doing all the background work while visiting and assessing adults, appearing at meetings/case conferences/hearings, etc., while trying to comply with local procedures. Key practitioners need to be able to 'get on with the practice', while the administration and management of the case, and the process, are coordinated and facilitated by a manager, or a suitably allocated officer, with legal support where necessary.

(4) Be inventive *and* pragmatic

In protecting adults at risk, practitioners need to be creative in support and protection planning. Without invention, thereby attempting new creative ways to protect, adult protection practice will not develop, and some adults at risk may be either poorly protected or overly protected. New ways of working and applying new orders in imaginative ways need to be explored. Only then will practitioners learn about what works well.

The area of adult protection is relatively new, outwith the use of the mental health legislation, which has been around in an operational sense since the 1984 Act. High-profile cases that have gone wrong can lead practitioners and agencies to become risk averse, where a safe option is sought. However, promoting adult self-determination and assisting adults to develop strengths and abilities to protect themselves, requires a degree of risk taking. David Carson and Susan Clift, at a British Association of Social Workers (BASW) forensic social work special interest group annual study day in 2009 (written up in Professional Social Work, 2010, p 24), pointed out that 'risk cannot be entirely eliminated; indeed that professionals have a duty to take risks; and that risk taking is about the management of uncertainty'. Therefore, key practitioners have to challenge risk and find creative ways of dealing with this risk.

Practitioners need to balance risk to the adult with the adult's right of liberty and, sometimes, while promoting self-determination, adults may be exposed to risk. This should, however, as best can be done in the circumstances, be achieved in a risk-managed and planned way, offering reliable safeguards and crisis contingency.

Additionally, invention and creativity needs to match an increasing degree of difficulty posed by adults at risk with complex needs. Applying a suite of powers and provisions across the Acts, and across a range of risk to and from an adult with mental disorder, is becoming more commonplace and indeed necessary. Having a range of Acts and provisions now allows a varied and comprehensive response to need and risk, albeit it is a challenging proposition to ensure a good match between risk and the provisions that both support and protect.

As mentioned, applying powers across the legislations is certainly becoming more apparent. There are cases of joint welfare guardianship and CTOs; for example, an adult with learning disability needing care and treatment on a compulsory basis in the community who also, because he lacks capacity in this regard, needs a welfare guardian to make necessary decisions about health and welfare (see John: case example 5). However, the application of this requires a creative approach by the key practitioners and a robust care plan to ensure that it works.

Invention, however, needs to be balanced by pragmatism and a need to take a sensible approach. 'In a perfect world', deciding which power or provision is needed would be based on scientific analysis, and one would settle on the power or provision that best matches the range of risk or need of an adult at risk. However, life and adult protection is not a perfect world. Adult protection practice is predicated on a range of dynamics, in particular judgement, available personnel and resources, and skill, knowledge and abilities. Achieving a perfect response is not always possible and a 'best fit' approach is often employed based on available staff and resources, and knowledge and information available.

The contemporary use of powers highlights this. One only has to look at the use of short-term and emergency detentions, where short-term detentions are utilised during office hours and emergency detention after working hours, presumably because AMPs are not so readily available after hours. So, emergency detentions have become an after-hours provision rather than a general provision available should a short-term detention not be available. In island communities, short-term detentions are only used when there is an AMP available, e.g. in Orkney, an AMP or consultant psychiatrist (because he does not live on the islands) arrives on prescribed days each week or may travel on request of the health board to see patients. Also 'in a perfect world' a Sheriff would be available at all times to consider a warrant for entry or a removal order (either in the 2003 or 2007 Act); but again, in some rural and island communities, Sheriffs are not always available, of course, and practitioners may have to rely on a Justice of the Peace to obtain these orders as a matter of course.

Practitioners, therefore, especially in an emergency or where there is an immediate need, do not operate in a perfect world and, therefore, any application of the Acts or across the Acts needs to allow for a degree of pragmatism in order to protect adults at risk with mental disorder. Not quite a 'needs must' approach, but where there is a serious and immediate need practitioners have to, in the best interests of the adult, do what is necessary at the time, based on what they know about the adult, available resources and their relative knowledge and experience. However, for long-term powers this should not be the case as much, because there should be available a range of key practitioners, such as AMPs, MHOs and council officers, with relevant knowledge of the provisions, and there should be sufficient access to courts and tribunals to obtain orders.

In exploring powers and provisions, moreover, practitioners may be guided by what they have used in the past to protect adults with mental disorder; MHOs may be more comfortable pursuing orders under the 2003 Act, and, for adults with incapacity, welfare guardianship. Council officers, however, may feel more competent operating in the context of the 2007 Act. For some practitioners, i.e. GPs, AMPs, and MHOs who act as council officers, working across the Acts has gained more significance and the range of provision more comprehensive. A 'real world' approach now transcends the Acts.

A pragmatic approach also has to be taken relative to available services and resources. In island and rural communities access to suitable places of safety may be limited because of a lack of psychiatric inpatient facilities. A place of safety may be a local general hospital or a residential environment, until a more appropriate placement becomes or is made available. Although precluded within the 2003 Act, a place of safety, following a removal order (s293/4), should not be a police station; but what if there is no other option to protect the adult?

Additionally, while this is not a perfect world, adults with mental disorder cannot be expected to 'toe the line' while living in the community. Where compulsory powers can be delivered ably in a safe and secure setting, such as a psychiatric ward with highly-trained nursing staff to exercise such powers, staff supporting and protecting such adults living in the community, in their own house or other accommodation where structures and 'strictures' are not 'as solid' as in-house or inpatient services, need to possess a range of pertinent skills and abilities. Adults with mental disorder will, of course, live their lives and do what they wish to do, whether powers are applied on them to do otherwise or not. In a sense, authorised power is only appreciated practically based on skilled exercise and the quality of a trusting relationship between those who hold the powers and the adults who are subject to the powers, and, within this, pragmatism (and a degree of latitude) is certainly required.

(5) Consider what works (and what doesn't)

Practitioners should be guided by what is viewed to work well, as case law and practice develop, setting precedence and best practice. Deficiency in care cases describe what doesn't work well. Advice and statistics (and guidance) from the MWC can help decide what is appropriate, what is best practice, and how powers and provisions should be applied, e.g. the use of short-term detentions over emergency detentions, and the use of welfare guardianship at home.

What works, because we know this, is good collaborative working. What legislative options work well is less clearly defined, mainly because agencies are not so good at outcome measurement, confirming how the provisions affect the adult and their lives, and their family's lives, over time. Health outcomes can be viewed as recovery and/or symptom management; however, social care is less clearly defined, although better quality of life comes to mind. For adult protection, on a pragmatic scale, this could be the removal or management of risk. So, applying legislative options can be tested against some outcomes, but this is rather crude; other measurements such as greater control for such adults, and choice and empowerment in one's life, may offer more sensitive, and potentially more meaningful, outcome measurements. However, applying a formal option may remove risk and give greater control, where applying a formal option in the context of longer-term engagement through adult protection management may help the adult gain more control of their lives; after all, if a formal option doesn't ultimately lead to the adult being 'more able' to protect themselves, to take actions themselves and to recognise the risk factors that need them to take action, then a paternalistic approach may occur. For these reasons, what works needs to be considered in both the immediate, by way of removing the adult from risk, but also in the long term, where long-term benefits may be determined.

Short-term powers may be predicated by need (for care and treatment) and immediate powers by risk; however, what works for one group may not work for others. An adult incapable because of learning disability or dementia might not be a suitable candidate for an emergency or short-term detention to hospital (unless they need treatment for their mental disorder) where they have primary needs for support and protection. An informal transfer to a safe place, or a removal order to a place of safety (2003 Act) or specified place (2007 Act), is often more appropriate.

Additionally, where an emergency or short-term detention requires GP or AMP involvement, removal orders are within the scope and authority of the local authority, i.e. MHOs under the 2003 Act and the council (or the council officer) under the 2007 Act, giving the local authority a degree of control over the process. This may be an important factor in determining whether the intervention needs a health or social care led response. A practitioner would need to be clear whether detention is required because the removal order of the 2007 Act does not permit the detention of the adult, requiring the consent of the adult, whereas the 2003 Act does.

Furthermore, long-term orders, such as CCTOs, may not be very suitable if the adult is incapable of complying with the treatment plan, which may prompt continual non-compliance measures. Conversely, a CCTO may provide essential measures to ensure the adult's residence, access and attendance to community care services, etc. An adult with fluctuating mental illness such as a bipolar disorder may not be very suitable for welfare guardianship if it doesn't respond to their changing need (for treatment) or risk. Conversely, however, guardianship may provide a vital framework and structure of care, to assist the management of risk.

Guardianship may be more suitable where clear powers are needed to take decisions such as where an adult with incapacity should live. It may also provide a framework of care which may be the determining factor to allow an adult to live at home with supports, albeit to be governed by good care management. However, where there is non-compliance with the directions of the guardian; for example, where the adult refuses to allow access to the named guardian, this may render the order unworkable, leading the guardian to seek non-compliance powers, which may result in the adult being transferred into a residential care environment.

Other orders that may be appropriate include a banning order to ban a harmer from an adult's home. This may work because it should prevent the harmer accessing the adult. However, what happens where the adult allows the harmer into the house or where the police are not able to exercise a power of arrest? Then the order may not work.

Therefore, an important aspect in determining whether an order will work (or which order will work) is to expose the order to the problems of non-compliance, which might affect its success; for example, by establishing 'back-up plans or crisis contingency' to decide where the adult's needs, under those circumstances, would be best met, e.g. an adult with a learning disability may be best cared for in a more supportive environment, rather than being moved to hospital. So, non-compliance under welfare guardianship may be the best option, promoting welfare guardianship, because it may deliver this, contrary to a CCTO, which may lead to a hospital detention.

Certain Acts and respective orders work best for certain groups affected by mental disorder, and this is the way they are applied (see the statistics earlier): e.g. the 2003 Act for adults with mental illnesses, such as schizophrenia and bipolar disorder; the 2000 Act for adults with dementia and learning disability; and the 2007 Act for adults able to consent and be involved in the delivery of the provision. However, what about adults with personality disorder at risk from self and others, adults with serious self-care issues and adults with serious multiple conditions (co-morbidity), e.g. adults with learning disability and mental illness, and those abusing alcohol and affected by ARBD, those posing a risk to others and those at risk of falling into the criminal justice system? What works best for these groups and what works less well?

Here, there may be a distinction introduced between care and treatment on the one hand and support and protection on the other. While this work promotes the use of the primary Acts, and their powers, where necessary, to both support and protect, the use of the Acts, in particular the 2003 Act, to provide, and sometimes impose, care and treatment, may be promoted, as is one of the Act's primary purposes, i.e. to protect persons with mental disorder who need access (sometimes assertively) to care and treatment, often more treatment than care, and, where necessary (and by exception), on a compulsory basis.

(6) Explore the options

Legislative options, of course, need to be based on need and, in particular, in relation to adults with mental disorder, risk. Therefore, a confirmation of power or provision has to be based on an assessment of risk and the power's ability to manage the risk. In the same way that individual powers within a welfare guardianship are predicated (or should be predicated) on the confirmation of incapacity respective of the power, individual powers that respond to risk need to be based on the confirmation of the particular risk itself. Therefore, a confirmation of neglect of an adult affected by incapacity would take the practitioner towards a direct power to protect the adult from this risk, e.g. a removal order under the 2003 Act and/or welfare guardianship under the 2000 Act.

Particular Acts and their relative powers, therefore, respond to particular needs and risks, e.g. the 2007 Act, and its response to harm from others, allows practitioners to concentrate efforts in the use of this Act and its protection orders and powers. Similarly, other Acts have precedence over respective Acts, e.g. the 2003 Act has provisions dedicated to supporting and protecting adults with mental disorder, e.g. a duty to inquire, removal orders, etc. Therefore, exploring primary legislative frameworks within which to operate is important for practitioners as they are planning interventions, and it is useful to consider their primary application respective of certain risks.

Table 10.1 breaks down the range and types of harm relative to the key Acts and attempts to delineate typical risk associated with the Acts, thereby placing these respectively with Acts designed to meet these risks. For example, risk to personal welfare and property and finances may be responded to appropriately by the 2000 Act (if the adult has incapacity in this respect), whereas assault may be responded to within the provisions of the 2007 Act, and so on. From the table, however, one may see that one or more of the primary Acts may be viewed as the predominant or first option Act and others as secondary, e.g. the 2007 Act for abuse from others, the 2003 Act for self-harming or lack of treatment or care and the 2000 Act for incapacity to manage finances.

Confirming a primary Act, respective of the adult's risk, risk assessed and detailed, allows practitioners to more accurately choose the most suitable Act to explore its relative provision, e.g. 2007 Act and protection orders or the 2000 Act and its financial powers. Exploring secondary Acts in the same way, e.g. the 2003 Act and an emergency provision, allows parallel (or secondary) provisions to be considered alongside the primary provision, which also allows a degree of contingency planning, e.g. pursuing a removal order under the 2007 Act, thereby seeking consent (or compliance if the adult is incapable) and fitting with the principle of the least restrictive approach, and having a removal order under the 2003 Act (which allows detention) in mind where the adult withholds consent or becomes non-compliant with transferring to a safe (specified) place.

Table 10.1 indicates the range and type of risk, giving examples, and highlights the respective primary or predominant Acts, and secondary or parallel Acts (in brackets). One can see, for example, that the 2007 Act may have a primary application to sexual harm and offences (outwith criminal justice legislation) caused by a harmer. However, the 2003 Act also has a range of offences, which are designed to protect mentally disordered adults from a sexual offence, which may be applied in a primary, parallel or simultaneous way.

So, therefore, practitioners also need to look outside the primary (predominant) options (Acts) to have a wide perspective of the Acts available, in their primary, secondary and parallel forms, respective of risk. In this respect, one can also determine primary, secondary and parallel powers, and a similar exercise can be applied here. By adding primary, secondary and parallel powers, an extensive range of options may be seen (Table 10.2).

Table 10.1.: The range and types of harm relative to the key Acts

Risk	Type	Examples	Primary (Acts) options (and secondary Acts)
from others	abuse / harm	targeted abuse	2007
	assault	physical, sexual, financial, psychological harm	2007
	offences	sexual offences, etc	2007 (2003)
	neglect	not providing care	2007 (2003)
	deficiency in care / omissions to act	not acting to protect or safeguard a person with mental disorder	2007 (2003)
from self	self-neglect or lack of care	lack of hygiene, not eating appropriately;	2003 (2007)
	behaviour (incapacity)	disinhibition, scratching, head hitting	2000
	self-harming	taking pills, cutting, parasuicide / suicide attempts	2003
to personal welfare	unable to self-care	not looking after self, house, finances	2003 (2000)
	living alone without care	not looking after self, house, finances	2003 (2000)
	deficiency in care and treatment	poor or inadequate treatment or care provision	2003
	incapable in respect of welfare	lack of capacity to act or make decisions about person welfare	2000 (2003)
to health	lack of treatment	medication /assessment / detention	2003 (2000)
to property and finances	not paying bills	lack of ability or capacity to manage finances	2000 (if incapable) (2003)
	financial abuse	theft, extortion, fraud, misappropriation of funds, etc	2007 (2000 if incapable)
to others	from behaviour	harming carers	2000 (if incapable) (2003)
	Assault of others	posing harm to others	2003 (2000 if incapable)

Table 10.2.: Range and types of harm relative to the key Acts and their Powers

Risk	Type	Predominant Acts (secondary Acts)	Primary Powers (secondary or parallel powers)
from others	abuse / harm	2007 (2003)	Banning order (2007 Act) (Duty to inquire / Removal orders)
	assault	2007 (2003)	Banning order (2007 Act) (Duty to inquire/Removal orders/Offences:2003 Act)
	offences	2007 (2003)	Banning order (2007 Act) (Offences under Part 21: 2003 Act)
	neglect	2007 (2003)	Assessment or Removal Order (2007 Act) (Powers of access or removal: 2003 Act)
	deficiency in care / omissions to act	2007 (2003)	Inquiry / Investigation (2007 Act) (Inquiry / powers of entry (2003 Act)
from self	self-neglect or lack of care	2003 (2007)	Inquiry / powers of entry, etc. (2003 Act) (Inquiry / Investigation: 2007 Act)
	Behaviour (incapacity)	2000	Welfare Guardianship (2000 Act)
	Self-harming	2003	Short term / emergency detention (2003 Act)
to personal welfare	unable to self-care	2003 (2000)	Inquiry / powers of entry, etc. (2003 Act) (Welfare Guardianship: 2000 Act)
	living alone without care	2003 (2000)	Inquiry / powers of entry, etc. (2003 Act) (Welfare Guardianship: 2000 Act)
	deficiency in care and treatment	2003 (2000)	Inquiry / powers of entry, etc. (2003 Act) (Welfare Guardianship: 2000 Act)
	incapable in respect of	2003 (2000)	Inquiry / powers of entry, etc. (2003 Act) (Welfare Guardianship: 2000 Act)
to health (physical)	lack of treatment	2003 (2000)	Removal (place of safety: gen hospital) (2003 Act) (Intervention Order or W Guardianship: 2000 Act)
to health (mental)	lack of treatment	2003 (2000)	Short term / emergency detention (2003 Act) (s47 or Welfare Guardianship: 2000 Act)
to property and finances	not paying bills	2000 (if incapable) (2003)	Part 3 or Financial Guardianship (2000 Act) (Inquiry, etc.: 2003 Act)
	financial abuse	2007 (2000 if incapable)	Inquiry / Investigation (2007 Act) (Part 3 or Financial Guardianship: 2000 Act)
to others	from behaviour	2000 (if incapable) (2003)	Welfare Guardianship (2000 Act) Compulsory Treatment order: 2003 Act)
	Assault of others	2003 (2000 if incapable)	Short term / emergency detention (2003 Act) (Welfare Guardianship: 2000 Act)

Applying the powers of the 2000 and 2003 Acts individually or together (as indicated in Table 10.2) and their long-term provision (simultaneously), therefore, offers an extensive framework to protect adults with mental disorder, who may or may not be affected by impaired capacity, and their health, welfare, safety, property and finances. Add the 2007 Act and its appropriate powers against harmers, and a general vulnerable adult protective framework, and a wide and parallel range of provision is available. In determining this, a weighing and balancing exercise might help practitioners to decide what could be primary and secondary options. To ponder the parallel application of long-term powers, one can see particular multiple frameworks emerging, e.g.:

- Guardianship (welfare or/and financial) and community based compulsory treatment orders;
- Guardianship (welfare or/and financial) and banning orders;
- Community based compulsory treatment orders and banning orders; and
- Guardianship (welfare or/and financial) and community based compulsory treatment orders and banning order.

Adding the powers of the banning order to the powers available within a compulsory treatment order and/or guardianship order may offer a comprehensive, but perhaps restrictive, range of protective measures for certain groups, e.g.:

- a compulsory treatment order and a banning order, e.g. for an adult with mental illness needing treatment on a compulsory basis, living at home, being harmed by a harmer coming into their house; or
- welfare guardianship and a banning order, e.g. for an adult with learning disability or dementia incapable in respect of major welfare matters, living at home, being harmed by a person in, or going into, their home; or
- financial guardianship and a banning order, e.g. for an adult with learning disability or dementia, incapable in respect of major financial matters, living at home, being harmed (financially) by a person in, or going into, their home.

Employing such an extensive range of powers for an adult at risk, however, must be balanced by the principles in the Acts, in particular to ensure that it benefits the adult and it is confirmed as the least restrictive option/approach available.

In arriving at a legislative design, key practitioners need to explore the legislative option relative to risk. Assessment and confirmation of risk should lead to the confirmation of power and provision, and should clarify the objective of seeking the power and provision, giving the legislative design validity and integrity.

See Appendix 19 for preparing a legislative design.

In exploring legislative options, as well as moving up and down the options (i.e. inquiry to immediate powers, to short-term powers, etc.) from side to side (straddling or traversing) across the Acts and the options, practitioners may also need to 'step' in a perpendicular (or triangular) way, e.g. from inquiry in the 2003 Act to welfare guardianship in the 2000 Act, thereby avoiding a prescriptive approach and offering a flexible and creative approach.

See Appendices 17 and 18 for charts indicating links across the Acts/provisions.

(7) Assess powers and provisions against risk

Across the extensive range of powers and provisions a 'best fit' approach may be pursued respective of the needs and risks of adults affected by mental disorder. However, as can be seen from the risk landscape (Appendix 1), risks associated with mental disorder are multiple and varied. Accurately applying powers and provisions to meet and match the range of risk is essential; where assessment of risk is vital, not only to confirm the range of risk, but also to clarify the degree of risk with which the adult is faced, i.e. to health, welfare, safety, finances, property, social circumstances, family life, etc. Thereafter, to match these risks to powers, thereby matching the adult's needs and risks with what the relative provisions can offer, is required: an assessment (or analysis) of match. This is also essential in determining the potential success of the order, power or provision.

In seeking the most appropriate provision, an essential 'test' of powers and provisions available across the Acts to meet risk would be governed by the principles of the Acts, in particular ensuring maximum benefit and the least restrictive approach; thereby weighing up the relative benefits of each potentially suitable provision against the person's risks and needs and agreeing the least restrictive option that meets the needs and matches the risks.

Applying the principles of least restrictiveness, maximum benefit, and taking account of the adult's views, wishes and feelings, while ensuring the provision will meet the adult's needs and risks, will assist in determining the most suitable power or provision.
Sometimes, however, key practitioners may need to strike a balance between the support and protection of the adult and protection of their rights to liberty and freedom.

(8) Use the principles

In their practical application, the principles govern all legislative actions and should inform the substantive assessment for and granting of applications (i.e. a guardianship, a CTO or a banning order) made to court or the tribunal, and the granting of short-term and emergency detention, assessment and removals orders, and provisions such as accounts and funds, i.e. a) the assessment of and the application for the provision or power and b) the determination of orders or provision by the key practitioners, the court, tribunal or OPG.

Principles such as 'benefit' and the ensuring 'minimum restriction' have critical importance in a) deciding to make an application for an order and b) the granting of an order; indeed, why would orders be granted unless the applicant can confirm that there will be a benefit to the adult and this would affect their lives in the least restrictive way? Indeed, even before any application is made, a case conference should explore the application of the principles while exploring the provisions across the Acts to ensure the correct provision to pursue, e.g. where the provisions' principles are applied to the range of options, what is the least restrictive option, which provides the most (or maximum) benefit?

(9) Ask the questions (to get the answers)

In protecting adults at risk with mental disorder, key practitioners need to ask the questions to get the answers. Some crucial and pertinent questions are, of course:

- Does the adult have a mental disorder? This is needed to take the adult into the realms of the primary Acts, or indeed the powers of the 2003 Act, e.g. emergency or short-term detention; or where 'it appears' (for duty to inquire (s33) or one (police constable) 'reasonably suspects' (as is in s297) or there is an indication or belief (for duty to inquire under s4, 2007 Act) that the adult is an adult at risk (affected by mental disorder).
- Is the adult, affected by mental disorder, an adult at risk? That is necessary to satisfy section 4 of the 2007 Act (the 3-point test) or 'exposed to ill-treatment, neglect, or some deficiency in care; or living alone without care and unable to look after himself ...', to invoke the duty to inquire under section 33 of the 2003 Act.
- What is the level and degree of risk or harm? Is it 'serious', as required for protection orders under the 2007 Act; or is it 'significant', as required for orders under the 2003 Act?
- Is the order 'necessary'? It is a requirement to confirm 'necessity' when applying for orders (intervention and guardianship) under the 2000 Act, or where under the 2003 Act a short-term detention or a compulsory treatment order is sought. Or where it is 'a matter of urgency' where it is 'urgently necessary' to pursue emergency detention under the 2003 Act.
- Is there a need for emergency (or immediate), short-term, or long-term powers? How may the adult be supported and protected until full risk assessment may determine the need for long-term powers?
- One of the most important questions is: 'will this work?'. If an order will not work, why would practitioners pursue it? If an order is bound to fail, is there another order which will succeed?
- Others?

(10) Compare and contrast the legislative options

Deciding which legislative option has most merit in responding to an adult's risk is necessary given the range of provision offered across the Acts, some having similar but also distinct application, e.g. welfare guardianship and CCTOs. Both seek to ensure care and protection in the community and both have some common elements, (e.g. residence powers) but both also have distinctly different ways of being applied (e.g. welfare guardianship at home to protect welfare and a CCTO to provide treatment).

Deciding the most appropriate legislative design, relative to a given set of circumstances, benefits from an exploration of the strengths and weaknesses of each of the orders related to the adult's needs and risks, e.g.:

- welfare guardianship:

    - strengths: local authority control over application; flexible and long term timescales; relatives may apply; a tailored range of powers;
    - weaknesses: complexity; potentially a long time going through court; ambivalence over use; not easy to change; weak non-compliance powers;

- community based compulsory treatment order:

    - strengths: speed of process; flexibility (variance); may be used preventatively; ongoing RMO and MHO involvement; reciprocity; care planning; responsive non-compliance powers;
    - weaknesses: complexity of application and reports; static powers; poor response to emergency; (sometimes) the patient's poor perception of it.

An important way of comparing and contrasting these two orders (and an important determinant of a successful outcome) applied in the community, is to consider the potential of non-compliance by the adult, respective of the compulsory provision, set in the context of risk assessing and contingency planning. For example, (a) non-compliance with guardianship powers may prompt the guardian to proceed through the 2000 Act (s70) towards a residential option, whereas (b) non-compliance in a CTO may prompt the RMO to consider treatment under section 112, or to move the person to hospital under sections 113 and 114, or other formal options in the 2003 Act. Therefore, if a contingency plan suggests a care option (e.g. residential care) as a response to non-compliance then welfare guardianship may be indicated, whereas if treatment in hospital may be necessary, then a CTO may be preferred.

Using the principles of the Acts, while comparing and contrasting the powers, may help practitioners decide on a suitable legislative design: for example, comparing a guardianship order, e.g. to take decisions as to which persons the adult may consort with, whether on a supervised or unsupervised basis (welfare guardianship) and to take decisions regarding the access and management of the adult's benefits and accounts (financial guardianship); with the powers of a banning order, i.e. to ban the subject from being in a specified place and a specified area and to be made subject to specified measures.

Consequently, the relative principles of each need to be applied and certain questions asked; e.g. Is it less restrictive to the adult at risk to have the harmer banned from accessing the adult than the adult required not to consort with the harmer? What are the adult's wishes and feelings about contact with the harmer? Do they fear the potential damage to their relationship? In addition, as above, the application of non-compliance measures should be considered here, i.e. what happens if the adult consorts with the harmer? Is the next step to move the adult into a residential care home using section 70 of the 2000 Act? Is this the least restrictive option? Alternatively, is it best that the harmer is arrested (presuming a power of arrest has been requested in the banning order court proceedings) and taken into custody?

(11) Confirm criteria and grounds, together

When provisions are identified and confirmed as meeting risks as assessed, and viewed to be principles compliant, then the grounds and the criteria of the orders need to be confirmed before they are pursued.

Appendix 20 describes the conditions (criteria) required to pursue the long-term provisions of CTOs, welfare guardianship and banning orders. This requires a detailed confirmation of each of the criteria against the adult's circumstances. Where criteria cannot be met, the order cannot be sought, thereby ruling out this order (or orders) from the legislative design or ruling in the order(s) that does (or do). However, let us look at the common or universal criteria 'across the Acts'.

The first 'general' criterion that spans the 2000, 2003 and 2007 Acts is 'mental disorder', which also spans their relative provisions, which may impact on a person's health, welfare, safety, finances and property: a range of matters that may be responded to across the Acts.

A second criterion relates to an adult's ability, impaired by mental disorder, i.e. inability to take decisions about treatment under the 2003 Act; made incapable under the 2000 Act; and being unable to safeguard themselves and property, etc. under the 2007 Act.

A third criterion involves risk, i.e. under the 2003 Act: significant risk to health, safety or welfare; under the 2000 Act: risk to welfare, property or finances; or under the 2007 Act: at risk of harm, and serious harm (as defined in the Act), for orders, has to be established.

A forth criterion is one of necessity, i.e. under the 2003 Act, where it has to be necessary to detain or compel a patient to receive treatment; or where the guardianship order is necessary, as confirmed by a Sheriff under the 2000 Act, or where a Sheriff is satisfied that the order is necessary under the 2007 Act. This includes the 'no order' principle, which should be applied, ensuring that an informal, voluntary approach is always available.

A fifth criterion may be based on the principles of each Act, where common principles of the least restrictive or minimal intervention, and benefit or maximum benefit, have particular significance in the seeking of powers.

Appendix 21 offers a checklist, which may be used in assessing and confirming criteria relative to the provision or power. Indeed, by approaching the assessment based on the adult's needs and risks, the checklist can point to the most appropriate formal option.

Deciding which power or provision, while spanning the Acts, avoiding the pitfalls, and applying powers in a real world, are necessary. However, how this is done or how this should be done can only be achieved collectively across agencies and key practitioners. It should be a rare occurrence that a key practitioner acts on their own, when protecting mentally disordered adults at risk. Even emergency detentions should involve two key practitioners, i.e. a GP and a MHO (unless it is impracticable to do so). Having two or more trained (and hopefully experienced) professionals involved in a shared health and social care approach, thereby applying the 'two (or more) heads are better than one' theory, would at least allow for discussion over the range of provisions, balancing one against the other, etc., to point them towards a preferred, and hopefully defensible, action.

Applying formal powers across the legislative framework for adults at risk in a collaborative vacuum is not safe practice, whereas applying formal provisions (and underpinning principles) in the context of effective joint working is.

(12) Obtain appropriate authority

Key practitioners must have authority to engage and act to protect adults at risk with mental disorder. 'Authority' has a number of aspects, i.e. (a) legal authority to engage and act, which is available within section 4 of the 2007 Act or section 33 of the 2003 Act; (b) personal and professional authority, which is gained by knowledge, skill, experience and use of self of the practitioner; (c) that which may be ascribed (or empowered) by the agency or the adult themselves; and (d) the power obtained by granting bodies such as the Sheriff or tribunal, or granted by certain practitioners with 'authority' to grant (or certify) such powers, e.g. GPs and AMPs. For initial and immediate intervention (a), (b) and (c) is necessary; and, without this range of authority, practitioners can be inhibited, insecure, and hesitant in engaging and protecting an adult at risk; and for formal actions (d) is, of course, required to provide the power(s) to take steps or act to protect the adult; (a), (b) and (c) 'empower' the practitioners; whereas (d) gives power to their actions.

If a practitioner finds themselves feeling insecure while visiting or interviewing an adult at risk or any potential harmer, then there is a problem with (a), (b) or (c). If in applying formal powers (d) the practitioner is having difficulty exercising the granted powers, then there may also be a problem with (a), (b) or (c). After all, as said earlier, the certificate, order or measure applied on some adults can be seen to be no more than 'a piece of paper', especially if the adult lacks capacity to understand the nature of the order or lacks insight into their predicament; it is how this is exercised by practitioners that matters. How it is exercised is governed, mandated and ascribed, by personal and professional 'authority'.

Summary

In summary, to safely and effectively 'apply' the powers:

1. Ensure adult centrality.
2. Ensure the 'only where necessary approach'.
3. Avoid the pitfalls.
4. Be inventive (and take calculated risk) and be pragmatic.
5. Consider what works (and what doesn't).
6. Explore primary and secondary options.
7. Assess powers (and provisions) against risk.
8. Use the principles.
9. Ask the questions (to get the answers).
10. Compare and contrast the legislative options.
11. Confirm criteria and grounds, together.
12. Acquire appropriate authority.

Case example

Applying the above 12-point application to the Walter case (1):

1. Practitioners would ensure that Walter has an active involvement in his support and protection plan; where, in his case, the need to engage him and build a relationship, to maximise his co-operation, would appear to be necessary, indeed an independent advocacy worker is indicated.
2. Practitioners would ensure that all informal and voluntary options are explored and exhausted before formal action is considered.
3. Practitioners should be minded to avoid the pitfalls highlighted by the Mr H case and ensure an appropriate assessment of capacity.
4. Practitioners should be inventive about the framework of care he needs, e.g. welfare guardianship at home to protect him and ensure his health and welfare. However, they should also see his case 'in the real world', by being pragmatic and realising that Walter is most likely to continue drinking and is likely to access alcohol, he is unlikely to fully co-operate with the services and with the powers applied, or to get on with staff supporting and protecting him, he may be likely to continue to seek contact with his 'friends' and he is likely to maintain contact and a relationship with his brother. His 'adult protection plan', therefore, needs to build in a degree of latitude and flexibility.
5. In considering what works and what doesn't with scenarios such as Walter's, it would be frugal to consider that welfare guardianship has worked in such cases; however, applying a CCTO in this type of scenario where there are clear indications that he may not comply with the measures therein (perhaps prompting continued exercise of non-compliance measures), may not.
6. In exploring the protective (and formal) options, it would appear that welfare guardianship is a primary option, and a CCTO may be a secondary option; however, given the concerns relating to non-compliance in Walter's case perhaps, a secondary or parallel option may be a banning order.
7. In matching his risk with powers, this should rule in the most appropriate options and rule out the least appropriate options (immediate, short-term, and long-term).
8. By using the principles, this may indicate that welfare guardianship may be less restrictive than a CCTO (to be confirmed by criteria).
9. Ask the questions, e.g. will this work?
10. Compare and contrast the powers, one against the other to decide the most appropriate.
11. Confirm the criteria of grounds of each provision sought, to ensure that the powers are appropriate; involving a MHO and an AMP, to confirm grounds (and to prepare and expedite a legislative design and plan).
12. Acquire authority; through adequate and correct mandate (and 'authority') to engage, and have the necessary powers to protect.

Chapter 11

ADULT PROTECTION/RISK MANAGEMENT FRAMEWORKS

Just as the lead responsibility of child protection rests with the local authority, so does adult protection. However, the overall management of an adult protection framework and the implementation of adult at risk procedures rests with the local authority in partnership with other public bodies, overseen by a local Adult Protection Committee (APC). Delivery of adult protection is, of course, placed firmly in the context of interagency planning, working and collaboration.

Risk management

This work emphasises the place of risk assessment in the area of protection of adults with mental disorder who may be at risk. The corollary of this is the need to put in place robust and responsive risk management systems and plans for individuals. No more so in relation to the key groups mentioned, i.e. adults with serious mental disorder, adults who may be incapable because of mental disorder, and adults who may be open to self-harm.

For obvious reasons, all formal and legislative responses need to be delivered in the context of robust and practical interdisciplinary assessment and planning. Primarily, adult protection frameworks have parallels with care management, a well-known and accepted way of delivering care. In the same way care management is about managing care, adult protection should be about managing risk, and in the same way delivery of care is set in a care management system, adult protection should be set in an adult protection/risk management system. Each can be applied individually and each may be mutually exclusive.

However, both can exist side by side, and indeed often would, i.e. delivery of care – protection of adult at risk. Both systems have a number of components, one stemming from the other, and all parts are essential in the overall delivery of care and protection (see Table 11.1).

Table 11.1 Care and risk management

care management	risk management
a) Screening and determining the level of assessment; b) Assessing need; c) Care planning; d) Implementing the care plan; and e) Monitoring and reviewing.	a) Screening and determining the initial action(s); b) Assessing risk; c) Adult protection planning; d) Implementing the protection plan; and e) Monitoring and reviewing.

In exploring care management, Nocon and Qureshi (1996), however, use a 'domain' approach when illustrating the assessment of community care needs, i.e. creating care domains, which give focus to particular aspects as they relate to particular groups, e.g. people with learning disability: independent functioning, socialisation, etc. Therefore, they ensure that crucial areas of an individual's life are assessed and, even more importantly, outcomes of the assessment may be evaluated over time.

In the same way that domains may assist care management, they may also assist risk management, where risk domains, relating to adults with mental disorder at risk, can ensure that critical areas of harm are assessed and addressed, e.g. financial harm, welfare harm, sexual harm, etc (see Appendix 3).

However, many care assessments arrive at a list of needs, sometimes indicating resources, which of course are not needs, rather than an assessment of need, which arrives at a professional and, in respect of mentally disordered adults at risk, a specialist assessment of need. In assessing risk, as it relates to adults at risk with a mental disorder, an assessor needs to consider not just a list or risks, or risk profiling, they also need to assess how and why these risk affect an adult's life, encapsulating crucial aspects such as safety, welfare, health, property and finances. Only when this is known should a risk management plan be devised.

In a formal sense, how these risks may be addressed across the primary Acts also needs assessment, such are the risks to adults with mental disorder, e.g. because of mental disorder they could lose or destroy their lives. This requires consideration (and assessment) of protective legislation with their respective powers. Such an assessment may be carried out by a MHO, because this officer is a pivotal practitioner (in respect of mental disorder) across the Acts; or, if not available, a social worker trained in risk assessing across the Acts.

Practitioners need to consider available risk assessment tools and explore their adequacy, and to deliver risk assessment which relates to the risk with which adults with mental disorder may be exposed. In protecting adults at risk, a risk assessment needs to have a consistent format across the agencies, and adult protection plans need to have relative content with an emphasis towards protection and management of risk, and delivery of duties and powers.

Any risk or adult protection framework needs to respond to the concerns highlighted by the MWC (in its deficiency of care inquiries), that it is not the availability of legislation that is the problem in protecting adults with mental disorder, it is practitioners' knowledge of the Acts and their practical application in the community. The framework employed should ensure that consideration of the relative laws is inbuilt within adult protection/risk management, as they concern adults with mental disorder at risk in the community.

Adult protection/risk management frameworks

Joint Implementation Team formats

The introduction of risk assessment and protection plan formats produced by the Joint Improvement Team (JIT) was a welcome innovation in the support and protection of adults at risk. It introduced consistent, nationwide assessment and planning tools to a disparate and vacant adult at risk (format) context. They are, however, predicated in protecting adults across the adult care spectrum, not only those with mental disorder and do not refer to the crossing of legislation.

The JIT risk assessment and adult protection plan formats (see Appendix 22) were implemented to coincide with the implementation of the 2007 Act and the development of local adult protection procedures (JIT, 2008), and prescribe what risk assessments and protection plans should include, i.e.

- Core information/data, which should be carried out where an assessment is carried out under adult at risk procedures;
- Communication requirements, which identifies who is to be involved in the risk assessment and informed of the outcomes;
- Risk assessment; and
- The adult protection plan, where an adult protection case conference views this to be necessary.

The JIT protection plan formats cover details such as chronology and patterns of risk, obtaining views of all, listing, detailing and describing risk; providing the who, what, why, where and when; and the protective factors, recommendations, conclusions with immediate and long-term needs and notification to all involved.

Nationally, the JIT adult protection plan provides the basic structure for managing and responding to risk. The plan would follow the case conference, can stand alone or alongside care plans, confirms lead workers and a core group, confirms details of support and protection support, and the roles of each professional, and ensures the active engagement of service user and carers. It defines actions and roles, ensures information sharing, contains a contingency agreement and confirms review dates. It recommends an alert on local databases indicating a plan is in operation and it records distribution. It covers support and treatment, control measures (including any legal actions), direct contact with the person, risk management with the perpetrator, information-sharing arrangements, and risk management coordination. Table 11.2 indicates the adult protection plan structure offered by JIT in its actions section.

Table 11.2 JIT adult protection plan

Actions and Roles	Responsibility	Timescales/ deadlines	Intended outcomes
a) support, treatment, therapy (specify services)			
b) control measures (including legal actions)			
c) direct contact with person			
d) risk management with perpetrator			
e) information sharing arrangements			
f) risk management coordination			
g) other actions			

The JIT plan offers a comprehensive and detailed exploration of actions necessary, and has legal actions delineated.

Adult protection frameworks for adults with mental disorder

Adults at risk with mental disorder have a range of risks that other adults at risk (or vulnerable adults) may not have, and may need protection across a range of legislations. This requires risk management able to span these risks and the range of primary Acts and the provisions available within these Acts. It would appear necessary, therefore, to apply a framework that can respond to relevant risk areas, i.e. 'risk domains', where each domain has individual actions (giving consideration of formal options across the Acts), objectives, roles and responsibilities, and timescales for actions.

This work, and its recommended formats and approach, is informed by the JIT work; however, it expands its focus on management of risk as it relates to the risks of adults with mental disorder. It is relative to adults with mental disorder, highlighting particular risks and responding to the failings in practice and service systems highlighted in some MWC deficiency in care inquiries, e.g. failure to consider statutory intervention. The approach offered here, however, can be used simultaneously ('in sync') with the JIT formats, especially where there is an existence of mental disorder, and a need to assess across a range of risk, commensurate with the range of legislation with which to address this range of risk.

> *See Appendix 22 for JIT risk assessment and adult protection plans;*
> *Appendices 23 and 32 for an assessment of risk format and form;*
> *and Appendices 24 and 33 for an adult protection plan and form.*

Adult protection process explored and developed

Screening and initial action(s)

Initially, the local authority, on receiving a referral or on having knowledge of an adult at risk, would explore and discuss with the referrer or the member of staff raising the concern. Then local agreement would be reached over the basis for action, engagement and/or investigation.

A primary task for a local authority officer (sometimes in conjunction with health colleagues) is to confirm (or not) whether the adult referred is considered to be an 'adult at risk' using the definition offered in the 2007 Act (the '3-point test'). Thereafter, the local authority needs to consider a mandate for involvement and whether a duty to inquire, under the 2007 (or under the other primary Acts) exists.

A crucial aspect of screening, however, is to confirm whether initial or immediate action is required or not to protect the adult, and, if so, whether formal action is indicated to provide temporary support and protection of the adult, e.g. a warrant for entry or removal to a place of safety, while full assessment of risk is made. Informal actions with the full consent of the adult would, of course, take precedence in any action.

Appropriate duty to inquire needs to be confirmed because this forms the basis of seeking appropriate initial action and ensures that practitioners have a proper and adequate mandate for investigation, as discussed in Chapter 5. Thereafter, key practitioners need to ensure that relative immediate powers are explored and confirmed, weighing and balancing, as necessary (or comparing and contrasting) as discussed in Chapter 10, to ensure that immediate formal actions are appropriate to the risk and circumstances of the adult at risk. Therefore, initially, for adults with mental disorder at risk, there appears a need to have a two-stage screening and initial action process: a) to confirm an adult at risk (using the definition offered in the 2007 Act) and b) if mental disorder exists, to confirm a relative duty to inquire.

'Duty to inquire' is a legal duty for local authorities (across the primary Acts and not just the 2007 Act), albeit applied in a collaborative way and in recognition of other agency duties, e.g. to cooperate; and other agencies need to know that adults with mental disorder at risk (who may fit the duty of inquiry of the 2003 and 2000 Acts) should be referred.

However, confirming a relative duty to inquire across the three Acts is necessary, because some mentally disordered people (and their risk) may be missed if practitioners only comply with the 2007 Act criteria, e.g. 'a council must make inquiries about a person's well-being, property or financial affairs if it knows or believes (a) that the person is an adult at risk (of harm)', (see definition in Appendix 9 [2007 Act]). Applying the 2000 Act (s10) criteria refers to risk to the 'personal welfare of an adult (who may be incapable)', and the 2003 Act (s33) refers to 'some deficiency in care and treatment', and 'where the adult may be living alone without care' (see Appendix 9). While these matters, for some, appear similar; however, for others, they may address different matters; and an assessment of 'fit' is required to establish the correct mandate to inquire (see Appendix 10).

An exploration of which Act offers the most appropriate formal framework appears necessary at the early stage of an investigation, which would ensure that practitioners are operating within the correct legal mandate. In this respect, on some occasions, practitioners (social work) may operate within a 'duty of care' as found in section 12 of the 1968 Act.

A commensurate or parallel initial task is to consider the form, training and experience of the visiting team, which preferably should, again because of the nature of mental disorder, offer a shared health and social care perspective, where generally two appropriately trained and experienced officers/practitioners should be allocated. Relative to the needs and risks of adults with mental disorder, this may be a MHO and an AMP, thereby, offering this shared health and social care perspective.

This co-working is needed to ensure, because of the nature of mental disorder, access to a medical practitioner, and, potentially, depending on the needs of the adult, an AMP, who could provide a suitable medical examination, and the skill and experience of the social work officer (acting as council officer) to ensure adequate assessment and consideration of respective legislative frameworks, i.e. the 2003 and 2000 Acts. The most appropriate social work practitioner, in this respect, may be a MHO.

Where an investigation is considered necessary, in respect of an adult with mental disorder at risk, either by a case conference or by the agencies concerned, the investigation needs to respond to and reflect the needs and risks of the adults.

Suitable allocated key practitioners should have the experience and knowledge to provide a suitable risk assessment and, if necessary, span the Acts. Where an allocated council officer does not have necessary knowledge and experience, then they should have access to specialist practitioners to receive guidance and support. MHOs and AMPs transcend the Acts and the powers necessary to protect an adult with mental disorder. So, if a warrant of entry is required under the 2003 Act, this can be sought, and where a short term detention is necessary, these practitioners can respond.

Having access to a MHO opens up the 2003 Act where warrants are available within section 35 of the 2003 Act, and can only be sought by an MHO, i.e. entry, medical examination and access to medical records, which may offer a more appropriate framework for an adult with mental disorder, especially where the adult lacks insight (or capacity). In addition, the removal order (s293) under the 2003 Act may be more suitable where the adult is unable to cooperate with the action; as is required for a removal order (urgent or otherwise) under the 2007 Act (unless there is undue pressure or incapacity).

Assessment of risk

Unless action is considered unnecessary, during or after initial engagement and/or action, assessment of risk needs to be considered and completed where necessary. In preparing an assessment of risk, specific risk domains may assist (see Appendices 2 and 3), which are drawn from the primary range of risk with which adults with mental disorder may be exposed (see Appendix 1); for example, financial harm: a lack of cash yet there are sufficient state benefits, may prompt the assessor to assess where the adult's money is going; and sexual harm: where there is inappropriate behaviour by the adult, to explore why this is occurring. Equally, however, risk assessment may rule out abuse or harm, and therefore the inquiry/investigation duty may be met, although the application of care management and care and support services may be necessary to meet need.

Assessment of risk should have a twofold approach: (a) risk profiling (risk description, including history and likelihood of harm) and (b) risk assessment (assessment of risk). Furthermore, for adults with mental disorder, assessment of risk needs to encompass a range of particular risk areas, e.g. risk from others, from self, to personal welfare, to health, to property and finances, and to others. Assessment, however, also needs to consider a range of needs and circumstances, including (a) the need to refer for a community care assessment, which may include financial, accommodation and benefits assessment, (b) specialist assessment, such as assessing capacity and confirming mental disorder and relative legislative and treatment options and (c) carers' views, where available, where risk history and family concerns should be inbuilt within the overall risk assessment.

Application of the primary Acts, in particular, demands both risk assessment and adult protection planning, taking account of their principles and definitions, and involving the adult at risk and others at all stages, responding to communication needs and capacity. Risk assessment would weigh up the advantages/disadvantages, gains/losses to the adult's quality of life, or freedom, or independence, which might result from actions, within defined comprehensive plans for support and actions, with clearly defined roles, responsibilities, timescales/deadlines and intended outcomes.

In many cases, in applying the 2003 Act, MHOs are risk assessing or obtaining a risk assessment of the person and their circumstances, which could be of self harm (or suicidal ideation or actions), or where there are risks posed to others (such as caused by mental disorder), or regarding deprivation of liberty, or considering immediate, deteriorating and long-term risk, or identifying risk to children, families and carers.

Primarily, however, respective of adults with mental disorder, risk assessment needs to inform legislative action across the Acts, especially where key practitioners are pursuing formal powers or measures, e.g.:

- the 2000 Act: assessing risk to personal welfare, finances and property;
- the 2003 Act: assessing risk to health, safety and welfare; ill-treatment, neglect, deficiency in care, risk to property, offences e.g. risk of sexual assault, etc.;
- the 2007 Act: assessing risk of harm, etc.; and
- confirming grounds or criteria for applications to courts under the 1995, 2000 or 2007 Acts and applications to the Mental Health Tribunal under the 2003 Act.

Available risk assessment formats, in particular the JIT formats (see Appendix 22), are mindful of the need to give attention to (a) history of significant events, (b) the need to make a comprehensive assessment of all possible risks and risk factors and (c) promoting a 'balanced view between risk and protective factors'. These formats, as described, are the primary means by which adult protection conferences may be fully informed, to reach the right conclusions.

This work positively regards the work carried out by the JIT in designing and implementing risk assessment and adult protection plans, and in its review (also literature review) of risk assessment practice and models across Scotland. The JIT risk assessment format rightly includes (a) capacity, (b) chronology of significant events, (c) current risk or concerns, (d) current risk description, then (e) the risk assessment and lastly (f) recommendations and actions, which may include prompting an adult protection case conference and the taking of legal actions.

Certain caveats exist here, however; for example, an assessment of capacity should be specifically related to the matters in hand and commensurate to need. For example: financial problems (e.g. memory problems/forgetting to pay bills) may lead to an assessment of capacity relating to these financial problems, which may confirm incapacity in relation to these problems and confirm a need for a financial power based on impaired capacity; and financial powers sought to respond to the financial problems, such as Part 3 (2000 Act) Accounts and Funds to open a bank account or to arrange a direct debit set-up to pay bills. Recent guidance on capacity assessment amends practice to ensure assessment relates to an adult's condition and circumstances (Scottish Government, 2008).

The JIT assessment, however, apart from considering aspects of capacity/incapacity, is not a relative risk assessment tool for adults with mental disorder; it is a generic assessment tool across the legally defined range of adult at risk groups, which of course the 2007 Act covers. No assessment, however, should be overly prescribed, but it should allow specific risk to inform relative protective and formal actions; in particular, where there is a need to seek powers across the primary Acts for those with mental disorder. Risk assessment, therefore, needs to be mindful of the particular risks associated with the effect of mental disorder on an adult so affected and the kind of risks with which such adults may be exposed.

Additionally, an assessment of the risk to welfare would appear to be necessary, which obviously has primary significance while working within the 2000 Act, as it relates to an adult incapable because of mental disorder. Assessment of welfare, however, also concerns adults with mental disorder across the Acts, considering aspects of welfare such as relationships, employment, housing, etc. (and is an aspect of the criteria required for compulsory treatment under the 2003 Act, i.e. significant risk to health, safety or welfare). An assessment of welfare risk should consider what welfare decisions may be needed on a longer term basis where the adult lacks the capacity to make such decisions for themselves, which may prompt the need for welfare guardianship. A suite of powers, therefore, reflective of needs, risks, and impaired capacity in these matters, may then (if necessary) be sought from a Sheriff; also being mindful of an assessment of deprivation of liberty, when considering the use of section 13ZA of the 1968 Act. An assessment of welfare may be drawn from the 'domain approach', where welfare would have its own specific area to be risk assessed.

Another caveat identified, is that the JIT assessment in its generic approach leaves the assessor open to assessing the apparent risks, e.g. physical harm, and therefore more subjective risks relative to mental disorder, e.g. welfare or emotional or right's harm, which are not so apparent, may be missed. Additionally, should the assessor not take account of mental disorder, they may assume that the adult has ability, capacity, understanding and insight, and is consenting to or accepting the risk/harm, thereby exercising choice, which of course should be respected, leading to no action being taken and the harm prevailing.

The approach offered by this work (see Appendix 23 [a risk assessment format]) seeks to respond specifically to the risk associated with adults with mental disorder.

Also see Appendix 31 for a risk assessment form.

Adult protection plans

An adult protection plan should highlight and confirm risk taken from the assessment of risk and not, initially, focus on support or resources. Only when risk is assessed and confirmed, will the assessor (or a case conference) be in a position to consider the response to this by way of management, provision and support. A plan should relate to and be reflective of the risk with which an adult with mental disorder may be faced. In designing a plan, which would confirm the protective actions relative to the main areas (the domains) of risk and individual aspects, a format/framework within which practitioners can operate practically is required. The JIT formats provide this and this is the recommended national framework offered. However, this work (see Table 11.3 and Appendix 24) offers a specifically related adult protection plan framework derived from the exploration of risk associated with mental disorder.

The format for adult protection/risk management offered here follows the approach taken earlier, respective of assessing risk and employing a risk domain approach, which prompts practitioners to be clear of what formal or informal protective action responds to particular areas of risk, e.g. financial harm (risk domain) leading to financial guardianship (formal protective action). This approach can be laid out clearly in an adult protection/risk management plan, as illustrated in Table 11.3.

Table 11.3 Adult protection/risk management plan

Risk (domains and aspects), e.g.:	Protection actions (informal and formal)	Objectives	Roles and Responsibilities	Timescales
Sexual:				
Financial:				
Psychological:				
Welfare:				

In confirming (a) the relevant risk domains, (b) the informal and formal protective actions required within each domain, (c) the objectives of the action(s), i.e. why the action is needed and long-term outcomes of the intervention, (d) the roles and responsibilities of the key practitioners in delivering the plan and (e) the timescales required to deliver the objectives and actions, this would inform key practitioners well of the area of risk and the legislative mandate within which to deal with this risk, and the purpose behind the action.
This adult protection/risk management plan could be triggered by the adult protection case conference, necessary to deliver the powers/provision and to ensure the long-term protection of the adult.

See Appendix 25 for an example of an adult protection plan in the Mary case (3)
and also Appendix 32 for an adult protection/risk management plan form.

Adult protection legislative design (plan)

Where formal powers and provisions are indicted, and it is agreed that these should be pursued, a legislative design and plan should be prepared. Having completed (a) assessment of risk, thereby delineating the type and degree of risk, and assessing this risk (b) a match with appropriate powers and provisions and (c) a determination of how these powers and provisions would meet with criteria and the principles of the Acts (see Chapter 10), key practitioners should be clear which powers to pursue and should be able to prepare a legislative design that encapsulates the application of an appropriate formal provision in a practical way; thereafter, to plan a process to ensure the application has every chance of success in court or tribunal. After the order is granted, this formal framework needs to be set in the context of an interagency and multidisciplinary care plan, adult protection plan or care programme, relative to the person's needs and risk; also, of course, being mindful of the carer's needs, ensuring assessment and support thereof.

At the point where long-term provisions are being considered, all the relative provisions across the Acts need to be 'weighed' against the adult's risks. As a long-term provision can take some time to pursue, e.g. welfare guardianship through the Sheriff Court, the quicker this can be done the better, to get an application under way, in the knowledge that there are no powers outwith 7 days (unless the adult is admitted to hospital for treatment under a short-term detention). Assessing the provisions, therefore, as discussed in Chapter 9 is necessary at this stage.

Plan and process should confirm how the adult would be protected throughout the application process, which in some cases may take many months. This may involve the use of short-term or immediate orders, or interim or temporary orders. The plan needs to consider the immediate involvement and protection of the adult on the short-term and then in the long term. As discussed, one of the most important tasks initially is determining the duty or mandate for inquiry, and which investigating (inquiry) mandate is most appropriate, i.e. section 10 (2000 Act), section 33 (2003 Act) or section 4 (2007 Act); for the investigation will be based on this, thereby authorising the investigating officers in the practical exercise of the investigation. Confirming who has statutory tasks and responsibilities here is essential, clarifying the report writers, applicants and who needs to be involved in informing and giving evidence on the application.

Case example: Walter (1)

In Walter's case, a legislative plan approach could be as follows:

(1)   Apply in the context of local adult at risk procedures, i.e. assessment of risk and assessment of capacity, adult protection plan, etc.

(2)   Confirm the most appropriate mandate for initial involvement, i.e. duty to inquire under the 2000, 2003 or 2007 Act.

(3)   Under the 2000 Act:

    a. Consider inquiry under section 10 (and expedite if appropriate):

            i.personal welfare at risk; and

            ii.the exercise of the attorney's proxy powers.

    b. Alert the Office of the Public Guardian to allow investigation there (of continuing power of attorney exercise of powers (s6)).

    c. Assess for offences of ill-treatment and neglect (s83).

    d. Assess for welfare guardianship (interim and full powers);.

    e. Assess for Part 3 (Accounts and Funds).

    f. Obtain authority to provide treatment under Part 5 (s47) medical treatment (physical problems).

(4)   Under the 2003 Act:

    a. Based on investigation visit, establish the need for section 35 warrants (e.g. for entry and medical examination).

    b. Based on investigation visit, establish the need for a removal order (s293/4).

    c. Assess for medical treatment for mental disorder, potentially under compulsion.

    d. Assess for offences of ill-treatment and neglect (s311 to s317).

    e. Assess for care and support services (s25).

(5)   Under the 2007 Act:

    a. Consider inquiry (s4) and expedite if appropriate.

    b. Assess for protection orders, i.e. banning order (s17).

(6)   Under the 1990 Act and 1968 Act, assess and access care and support services.

(7)   Confirm legislative design and pursue provision(s).

(8)   Prepare an adult protection/risk management plan for Walter.

See Appendix 19: preparing a legislative design.

Adult protection plan implementation

Following the adult protection plan, it is necessary, again mirroring the care management system, to prepare an implementation plan; and, again, primarily because the particular risks of an adult with mental disorder need this. The implementation plan would be completed after the protection plan is agreed and endorsed by all services and the key practitioners concerned, thereby confirming a care group who would take the plan forward.

The plan is necessary to ensure delivery of the powers/provisions and to discharge the long-term protection of the adult. Initially, it would confirm the identity of the named adult protection officer, e.g. a council officer (who could be a MHO), who may pursue immediate/short-term provisions and prepare the adult protection plan.

The implementation plan would provide the 'who does what, when and how, and the ands ...', in the context of the adult protection/risk management plan (see Table 11.4).

Table 11.4: Implementation plan

Why	i.e. names, locations and contact details of all the core group involved; and key formal players, e.g. named welfare guardian;
How	e.g. communication and information needs;
What	e.g. details of protection powers and provisions;
When	i.e. frequency, purpose and sites of reviews (in particular detailing when orders and powers need reviewed, in anticipation of expiry, to prepare for application for extension or renewal); and
And	e.g. arrangements for discharge of powers and provisions, where no longer necessary and alternative care or protection arrangements agreed.

The pursuit of powers explored

Many adults at risk require an early response to protect them on an immediate or short-term basis, by pursuing action such as obtaining warrants for entry or removal to a place of safety, before the need for longer-term powers has been established. Indeed, long-term powers need careful assessment to establish their need, and an assessment of risk, as discussed earlier, may take days or weeks to prepare.

An adult protection case conference may be convened to consider longer term actions and may prompt the need for such powers; thereafter, to allocate practitioners, such as a MHO, to pursue such orders. This may require additional assessment of the need for such provision, e.g. welfare guardianship, and in some areas a case conference to consider the need for guardianship. Longer term powers can take weeks, sometimes months, to obtain.

For many adults with a mental disorder, there is a need to protect the adult on an immediate or short-term basis, to protect the adult initially in the early crisis stage, and then in the long-term, offering ways of supporting and protecting the adult over time (see Table 11.5).

Therefore, short actions pursued may exist outwith an adult protection plan; however, long-term powers should exist within its context, which is required where a long-term framework is needed. Given that there may be 10 working days to prepare it (WOS procedures; see section 'Adults at risk procedures explored' below), there is no adult protection plan for immediate and short-term actions, although these may be taken in the context of local adult at risk procedures. It would seem, therefore, that a parallel approach may be taken on many occasions, sometimes moving from a short-term timeline to a long-term timeline concurrently, one task merging into the other. Sometimes parallel timelines existing simultaneously, longer-term measures being pursued while short-term measures are in place, e.g. while the adult is in a temporary place of safety or in hospital informally or on short-term detention.

Therefore, to ensure an appropriate response to risk associated with mental disorder across the legislations, a dual path approach to actions (early/short-term and long-term interventions) appears necessary (see Table 11.5).

Table 11.5 Parallel/dual response to risk

Early and short term interventions		
→ → → → → → → → → →		
e.g. inquiry/ investigation →	Short term actions e.g.: • warrant for entry ; • medical examination; ↓ e.g. removal to a place of safety or short term detention. ↓	
Assessing need for longer term powers or provisions	→ Pursuit of longer term powers and provisions (if needed)	
	→ → → → → → → → → → →	
Longer term and long term powers and provisions		

Monitoring and review of risk and applied powers

An adult protection review process should:

- monitor and respond to ongoing and changing risk, ensure ongoing management and respond to increasing (or indeed decreasing) risk, which may require review of, and amendment to, the adult protection plan. This would involve the core group, including the key practitioners and those providing support and protection, and would have an emphasis on reviewing the efficacy of the adult protection/risk management plan applied over time, thereby offering a facility to amend or provide additional services, powers or provisions necessary to protect the adult. This could be built into the care plan or a care programme review; and
- monitor and review the ongoing application of powers and provisions. This would be guided by the practical application of the principles of the relative Acts, which may have a threefold concern, i.e.

a. the monitoring of legal and human rights of persons subject to powers, where on exercising powers the principles ensure that the adult is central to any intervention, and is an active participant involved, doing with and alongside the adult rather than doing to. Principles such as patient participation, giving regard to the adult's ascertainable wishes and feelings, both past and present, ensure this adult-centred approach; and

b. the monitoring of the exercising of powers by proxies or practitioners, where those expediting powers are governed by the principles of the particular Act in the practical exercise and delivery of its powers, thereby ensuring that the powers are applied in the most beneficial and in the least restrictive way, and ensuring the adult's active participation in their application. This provides a basis of challenge or appeal against the orders themselves and against the persons who apply the powers. Moreover, the practitioners or proxies applying the powers can be monitored (and supervised, e.g. welfare power of attorney and welfare guardianship) in the light of the exercise of powers applied, governed by the principles applied. Indeed, a local authority investigation can occur (s10, 2000 Act) where a complaint is made against a welfare proxy under the 2000 Act; and

c. the reviewing of the efficacy of the powers and provision, i.e. are they necessary to protect the adult over time? Powers no longer required should be revoked or discharged, potentially providing an informal support and protection plan and service. Again, the relative principles of the Act employed can govern this review, e.g. questioning whether the powers are proving to be overly restrictive and continue to provide benefit.

Ongoing risk monitoring and review procedures should be inbuilt, offering syntheses with any CPA or care management systems.

Crisis contingency planning

Crisis contingency planning (CCP), should respond to risk (and crisis) either not anticipated, e.g. an unforeseen crisis, or anticipated, but the risk management plan cannot or should not (at a particular time) respond. Risk anticipated would, of course, wherever possible, be included within an adult protection/risk management plan (see risk scenario planning below).

CCP should reflect an agreement (giving details) made by the core group on how to respond to particular and anticipated risk (domains and risk aspects) should the adult protection plan fail to fully protect the adult. CCP would detail identified places of safety, arrangements to transfer, and the powers necessary with which to do this. It would detail the who would respond and how, including the involvement of the police.

In particular, it should explore a number of potential crisis/risk scenarios for the adult, detailing the potential response to this. This derives from a model (HCR20: historical, clinical, risk management 20), which is offered in criminal justice work with mentally disordered offenders (see Douglas et al., undated), which has a focus towards violence by the adult, but has useful scenario planning which could help protect adults at risk. Within the model there would normally be three or more scenarios, e.g. (a) crisis scenario 1: harmer has accessed the vulnerable adult after hours, creating fear and distress in the adult and causing sexual harm, (b) a crisis management plan, e.g. i) Police to be contacted immediately by care staff or support workers and protective action taken' ii) contact with out of hours services to respond and (c) a case conference arranged within five days of an incident to consider action and a response.

See Appendix 33 for a crisis contingency plan form.

Case example: Mary (3)

As an illustration of the adult protection framework 'in action', the Mary case is explored here, i.e.

Mary is 23-years-old and is affected by learning disability, which affects her ability to make important decisions regarding her safety and welfare. She lives with her aunt and uncle. They are emotional harming her, threatening to throw her out, and financial abusing her, by using her benefits to meet their needs and not hers. She would like to leave the house and set up on her own, but is scared of being on her own, and is denied this by her domineering uncle. Her cousin is sexually abusing and exploiting her. The aunt and uncle know about this, but do not do anything to stop this, other than forcing her to take oral contraception tablets. She says she is 'scared' to a day centre officer and indicates she 'doesn't like' what is going on.

Employing the adult protection/risk management framework offered in this work, the following emerges.

Assessment of risk (Mary)

Overall risk description (using risk domains and the risk landscape): (i) sexual harm: regular harm; non-consent, or incapacity to consent, to sexual intercourse; harmer: cousin; third party aiders: uncle (maybe aunt); (ii) financial harm: misappropriation of benefits; consistent; harmers: uncle and aunt; (iii) emotional harm: fear, undue pressure, threat; consistent harm; harmers: uncle and aunt (and cousin); iv) health harm: forcible medication (oral contraceptives); consistent; harmers: uncle and aunt; and v) rights harm: choice, consent, independence; consistent; harmers: cousin, uncle and aunt.

- Assessment of the relationship between the adult's risk and the effect of mental disorder on this, i.e.: (a) she may lack capacity to understand the risk associated with this and to make decisions to protect herself from this harm; (b) she may not have developed sufficient strengths, confidence or understanding to realise that she does not have to accept either the emotional or the sexual harm; and (c) the harm exists because the cousin, aunt and uncle know the adult lacks capacity to understand she can say no to the sexual exploitation or to seek help.

- Assessment of how and why this risk occurs in the relevant risk domains, i.e.(i) the sexual harm occurs because of the inequality of power between the adult and the harmer(s) and her inability or lack of capacity to take steps to understand her predicament and to protect herself against it. It happens because her cousin has power over her, and because the aunt and uncle facilitate the harm; (ii) the financial harm happens because the adult's uncle and aunt have control of her funds; (iii) the emotional harm occurs because the harmers have excessive power and control over the adult, exercising undue pressure over her. They appear to believe they can apply emotional harm with impunity; (iv) health harm occurs because the harmers have control over her use of contraceptive medication and can impart this control over her; and (v) rights harm exists because the adult is not able/capable of exercising her rights, and there is such an imbalance of power between her and her uncle, aunt and cousin.
- Providing an overall assessment of the risks, e.g.: there is an overall, consistent and serious range of harm and abusing behaviour, against a vulnerable adult by her aunt, uncle and, in particular (respective of sexual offences under the 2003 Act) her cousin, thereby applying control and abuse, which is having a serious effect on her health, welfare, finances and safety, falling within the criteria of adult at risk of harm (2007 Act), requiring a robust and early response across social work, health, the police and department of work and pensions.

Assessment of powers and provisions (including supportive/informal) (to be included in the adult protection/risk management plan)

- as Mary lacks capacity to understand the risk associated with the harm and to make decisions to protect herself from this harm, and as her capacity appears to be permanent (to be confirmed), relating to her learning disability, formal action is indicated: to assist her to develop sufficient strengths, confidence and understanding to realise that she does not have to accept either the emotional or the sexual harm, and to assist her to leave the house safely for an independent life – advocacy and a care worker. Through investigation, to expose the harm, when the cousin, aunt and uncle know the adult lacks capacity to protect herself and make decisions, and to confirm that formal action is necessary to protect her from the sexual and emotional harm and exploitation.
- Mary has positive aspects, which need to be factored into the assessment of the need for powers and provisions; for example, she has shown independent thinking, such as wanting to leave the house and set up on her own (albeit not 'thrown out'), and she has voiced her fears to a day centre officer and indicates that she 'doesn't like what is going on'. This could be the basis to empower her and help her take the necessary steps to protect herself.
- As formal action is indicated, the primary Acts and potential provisions or powers indicated here are: (i) as she has a mental disorder, the 2003 Act is indicated: e.g.

duty of inquiry (s33); (potential): warrant of entry (s35 [1]); medical assessment (s35 [4]); removal to place of safety (s293); offences (s311); longer term: advocacy, assessment and provision of care and support services; (ii) as she may be incapable because of mental disorder (to be assessed and confirmed), the 2000 Act is indicated: e.g. short term: assessment of capacity; longer term: welfare guardianship (2000 Act), to make decisions as to where she should reside and (iii) as she is an adult at risk (after assessment), the 2007 Act is indicated: immediate/short term: duty to inquire (s4); and, based on undue pressure or incapacity, an assessment or removal order(ss11 and 14) should be considered, and in the longer term a banning order (s19), to prevent the cousin, or the aunt and uncle, from visiting her (unescorted) in her new place of residence.

An assessment of need

A community care or single shared assessment might focus on Mary's need for independence and the resources required to facilitate this. For her initial needs, however, for care, support and treatment, it is necessary to identity and confirm the range of informal, voluntary and supportive provisions necessary, which may be applied in conjunction with any formal protective measures to reduce the need for them.

An adult protection plan

Drawing from the assessment of risk (and need), an adult protection/risk management plan may be devised, e.g. see Table 11.6.

Table 11.6. An Adult Protection Plan (Mary)

Actions → Domains and Aspects ↓	Protection actions (informal and formal)	Objectives	Roles and Responsibilities	Timescales
Sexual: sexual exploitation.	Inquiry (s33 [2003 Act] or s4 [2007 Act]); (potential): 2003 Act warrants, i.e. warrant of entry (s35 [1]; medical assessment (s35 [4]; removal to place of safety (s293); offences (s311) informal: advocacy, assessment, provision of care /support services;formal: banning order (2007 Act)	Initially to assess her, remove her if necessary; to protect her from harm on the long term.	Council officer: to investigate, and pursue banning order if necessary; MHO to pursue warrants, and welfare guardianship if necessary; care manager to assess, seek care /support services.	Short term: within 7 days; long term: banning order over 6 months
Financial: misappropriation of funds; loss of money.	Welfare benefits support; Part 3 of the 2000 Act	To protect her finances	Care manager (learning disability)	Initiated over 4 weeks; to last 3 years
Emotional harm: causing fear, threat, and distress.	Informal support and counselling	To build her confidence and strengths	Support worker and counsellor (learning disability)	Continuing
Welfare (and human rights) harm: risk to welfare; opportunity, freedoms, independence.	Welfare guardianship; Provision of suitable accommodation and care package.	To protect her welfare and human rights	Mental health officer and named welfare guardian (welfare guardian); care manager (accommodation and care package).	Over 3 years

An adult protection implementation plan

Here an adult protection plan is necessary to deliver the powers/provision and to ensure the long-term protection of the adult, initially: to allocate a named adult protection officer (council officer) to pursue short-term provisions and to prepare an adult protection plan; to allocate a MHO to assess (and pursue if necessary) long-term provision, i.e. welfare guardianship; to allocate a care manager to pursue an appropriate accommodation, and a support and care package; and to deal with financial aspects (DWP/benefits) (see Table 11.7)

Table 11.7: an implementation plan (Mary)

Who	Names, locations and contact details of all the core group involved; and key formal players, e.g. Council officer, MHO, GP, AMP, advocate, care manager.
How	The adult has communication and information needs; Independent advocate to assist her communicate her fears and needs.
What	Details of protection powers.
When	Frequency, purpose and sites of reviews (in particular detailing when orders and powers need reviewed, in anticipation of expiry, to prepare for application for extension or renewal).
And	Arrangements for discharge of powers and provisions, where no longer necessary and alternative care or protection arrangements agreed.

A crisis contingency plan (Mary)

A 'Mary' CCP, multi-agency agreement, could be confirmed by the adult protection case conference and by the core group, which ensures clarity of (a) how unanticipated risk (domains and risk aspects) be met, should the adult protection plan fail to provide protection of Mary or (b) anticipated risk, but the risk management plan cannot or should not (at a particular time) respond. The CCP details the identified places of safety and arrangements to transfer, and the powers necessary with which to do this, and who would respond and how, including the involvement of the police.

In the CCP (respective of Mary's risk) a potential risk scenarios are: Risk scenario 1: (a) risk description: Mary's cousin has obtained access to her and has sexually assaulted her, creating fear and distress and causing sexual harm; (b) risk management plan: 1. Police to be contacted immediately by care staff or support workers and protective action taken. 2. To contact with out of hours services to respond. 3. A case conference arranged within five days of an incident to consider action and responses.

Adult at risk procedures explored

Local adult at risk procedures were reviewed, or more exactly recreated from vulnerable adult procedures, after recommendations made following the Borders Report (SWSI, 2004) and on implementation of the 2007 Act.

The West of Scotland (WOS) Adult Support and Protection Practice Guidance, which are endorsed by 13 partner local authorities and 5 health boards, are indicative in their structure of many procedures across Scotland. They have the following structure:

- Referral (referral procedures):
- Investigation (and risk assessment):
- Action (refusal of entry; warrants, protection orders (2007 Act);
- Adult Protection Case Conference (and protection plan); and
- Monitoring and review.

The procedures, however, are predicated on the 2007 Act and across the range of adult at risk groups. i.e. 'affected by disability, mental disorder, illness or physical or mental infirmity ...'. While this is important and necessary, thereby to protect vulnerable adult groups who have not been protected in a legislative way before, one has to recognise that adults with a mental disorder have complex needs, which may need to be met across the 2003, 2000 and 2007 Acts.

To ensure access to protective powers and provisions, there will inevitably be occasions where such adults need access to key practitioners such as MHOs and AMPs, and access to specific risk assessment and protection plans, and relative resources. This requires a dedicated approach in a procedural context.

Local procedures need to respond to the complexity and specialty required to protect adults at risk with mental disorder. Certain additional aspects, as discussed in this work, need to be inbuilt within local procedures, e.g. assessing power and provisions relative of risk, preparing a legislative design, monitoring and reviewing powers and provisions, and allocating a trained and experienced 'manager' to coordinate the process while the practitioner gets on with delivery.

Intervention for adults with mental disorder needs a particular process to ensure a relative and adequate early response. A relative process should comprise 1: the referral receipt; 2: the screening of the referral; 3: the allocation of a suitable coordination manager; 4: the allocation of a suitable investigation team or key practitioners; 5: to agree a mandate for inquiry; 6: a pre-visit meeting; 7: the investigation visit; 8: the consideration of immediate action (only where necessary); and 9: a post-visit meeting.

See Appendix 39 for a relative process, and checklist that may be used in practice.

The WOS adult at risk procedures indicate a process that should be followed, i.e.:

- Screening of a referral, which should be made to the local authority, within 1 working day, and contact with emergency services if required;

- Initial action, within 5 working days, to assess the referral and to decide whether the allegations constitute harmful or non-harmful concerns (harmful concerns would potentially lead to an investigation and non-harmful concerns, would potentially result in a referral to an appropriate agency for care and support);
- A formal investigation, to be conducted, within 8 working days of the referral;
- Appropriate action, e.g. an application for a protection order, to be made within 10 working days of the referral;
- An adult protection case conference, to be convened within 10 working days to receive the report of the investigation and to consider longer-term action; and
- An adult protection plan, to be prepared within 10 working days of the case conference.

This offers a step-by-step approach within which adults at risk may be protected, a way to proceed from a referral to an adult protection plan. Although the WOS procedures do not expressly mention it, as discussed earlier, there appears a need to apply a framework that would support and sustain long-term formal actions, in particular powers such as welfare guardianship. As discussed earlier, an adult protection/risk management framework would cover screening and initial actions, assessment of risk, adult protection planning, and implementation, monitoring and review of the plan. Additionally, adults with mental disorder may transcend a range of Acts and a range of risk, and need to be viewed in a more latitudinal way; and at each stage, procedures need to consider specifically related aspects of mentally disordered adults.

Adult at risk (with mental disorder across the Acts) process applied

From the above exploration, a relative adult at risk framework and process may be devised, i.e.:

Initial and early intervention

(1)   Initial screening and determining the initial action where:

- the referral would be explored, discussed with the referrer, agreement reached would be reached over the mandate and basis for action, there would be engagement and investigation, a suitable inquiry team allocated, etc;
- the need for initial action would be determined and, if necessary, action would be taken.

Assessment

(1)   Assessment of risk, where risk is profiled and then assessed, i.e.:
- the overall risk description (profile), i.e. identifying and profiling all risks with which the adult affected by mental disorder is exposed (being informed by risk domains and associated aspects); and

–   assessing these risks relative to (a) the relationship between the adult's risk and the effect of mental disorder on this, e.g. welfare and ability to protect him/herself, and assessing this, (b) how and why (also where and when) this risk occurs in relevant risk domains (e.g. safety, welfare, health, property, finances), (c) the adult's perception of risk, (d) making conclusions, when it is clear how and why the risk occurs.

(1)   **Initial assessment of need**, confirming how initial need may be addressed, to include informal, supportive and voluntary measures and provisions.

(2)   **Assessing powers and provisions relative to risk**, i.e.:

–   Which Act(s) is/are indicated as the most suited to the risk as assessed, e.g. the 2007 Act, where the adult is at risk of physical harm and powers are required against the harmer;

–   Which duty, power, provision is/are indicated as the most suited to the risk as assessed, e.g. duty to inquiry (s33: 2003 Act), where there is an indication of ill-treatment and neglect of an adult with mental illness; warrant for entry (s35(1): 2003 Act), where there is a need to examine medically an adult with mental illness and there is obstruction to this; welfare guardianship (s57: 2000 Act), where there is no other means to safeguard an adult with incapacity's health and welfare. Here criminal action and contact with the police may also be indicated; and

–   Exploration of the supportive or management strategies to respond to risk as assessed, e.g. pursuing Part 3 (Accounts and Funds) in the 2000 Act to manage an adult with incapacity's finances, where there is a risk to finances or assessment of needs, e.g. community care assessment/single shared assessment, and/or pulling together agency and informal networks and supports, such as family, advocacy, home care, day care, etc. Here informal and personal 'risk managers' would be added, including positive aspects of the adult's circumstances would mitigate the effects of the risk, either through the range of familial and informal networks of care, support and protection, or from the adult's personal strengths and abilities to cope with, manage or resolve risk.

Adult protection planning

(1)   **Adult protection/risk management plan**, relative to risk as assessed, and providing detail on the how risk will be managed by powers and provision of care and support. If necessary, where adult protection powers are indicated, this would include the following:

(2)   **Adult protection legislative design and plan**, detailing the legislative framework to be applied and confirming the process to obtain the powers and provision, i.e. who is involved in the process and what they need to do.

Implementation

(3) **Powers and provisions pursued and exercised** (if necessary), relative to the assessment of risk and confirmed by the legislative design and the implementation plan; where the formal orders or provisions are sought from the Sheriff or tribunal or other authorising bodies.

(4) **Adult protection/risk management implementation planning**, which would provide information on who, when, what and how the plan will meet and manage risk.

Monitoring and review

(5) **Risk and powers monitoring and reviewing**, ensuring (a) the ongoing support and protection of the adult and (b) the powers and provisions remain relative to the adult's risk.

(6) **Crisis contingency planning**, to respond to risk (and crisis), anticipated or not.

Case conferences

Adult protection case conferences for an adult with mental disorder may need to be convened, reflective of risk, needs and circumstances. The WOS procedures mention that an adult protection case conference can replace an adult with incapacity case conference. This needs to be a dedicated conference reflective of adults with mental disorder; so there needs to be a risk assessment available to it, which relates to specific risk, provided by key practitioners knowledgeable and able to provide such a risk assessment. A MHO should be a necessary attendee at such a case conference, to inform the case conference of the range of Acts and relative powers to support and protect the adult, and to make necessary recommendations. An AMP would also be a useful practitioner to have there, but this is not always possible. An MHO, however, could act as a necessary link to an AMP to obtain specialist guidance and support.

An adult with mental disorder is entitled to be at the case conference and any associated meeting. Only by exception would the adult not be at the case conference (or any other significant meeting), i.e. where the adult is incapable because of mental disorder, mental disorder prevents their attendance or where they withhold consent or cooperation, and it is necessary to meet, and where an urgent meeting is necessary. An adult is also entitled to access an independent advocacy worker (from the 2003 Act), which may assist their attendance and involvement. Arrangements should be made to ensure that the adult is linked to an advocacy worker prior to a case conference, to accompany the adult to the meeting, thereby providing support and guidance.

See Appendix 26 for (a) an adult protection framework and (b) applied process.

Care management for adults at risk with mental disorder

In many cases, care management exists side by side with protection (risk) management or is mutually inclusive within the adult protection/risk management context, thereby ensuring that an adult's need for protection is met, but also their care needs are met. A mental disorder of an adult can create risk and therefore risk management may be necessary; and it also can create need which might require a care management response. Equally, in the same way risk may prompt a need to respond to and manage the risk, risk often also creates need, which may also create a care management requirement.

In the same way this work focuses on areas or particular risk (domains), which are derived from the 'community care world', care management of adults at risk with mental disorder may also benefit from the domain approach, which focuses on particular areas of need for such adults (see appendix 36). This is important because, similar to risk, adults with mental disorder have particular needs and risks, which require a focused approach.

The writer, as an independent social worker, preparing independent community care assessments, is often asked to explain or justify his conclusions; for example, 'how has your assessment arrived at a care package at home as opposed to a residential care option?' The writer, therefore, has had to ensure an assessment process which helps determine how a person's care needs may be met, which is defensible and explainable, and which breaks down needs into specific care areas which can be assessed individually. The care management system offered here seeks to do this and to provide a focus on the needs of mentally disordered adults

In many cases care management provides the framework for support and protection, facilitating care and support services, thereby managing risk and preventing the need for formal powers, as is currently occurring in the implementation of the 2007 Act. However, for many adults, health and social care risks may require the application of powers and provisions and the delivery of services and supports.

Care management was updated in 2004 to ensure that it is targeted at people with the most complex needs and an activity undertaken by practitioners across health and social care (Scottish Executive, 2004). Care management is, therefore, an essential framework for the long-term support and protection of many adults affected by mental disorder at risk, where assessment and care planning would determine what needs have to be met, how they are going to be met, and who and what would meet these needs. It should provide an adequate and responsive framework of care and support, with clear roles, sound communication systems and regular monitoring, all inbuilt; the process tailoring services to individual needs. For adults at risk, it demands comprehensive assessment of need, intensive care planning and vigilant implementing, monitoring and reviewing.

Overall, adults with mental disorder may exist in a context of risk (the risk landscape/environment [Appendix 1]) and in a context of need (the care landscape/environment [Appendix 37]), which prompts a need for both protection and care, and which requires risk assessment and risk management to respond to risk, and care assessment and care management to respond to need. This can often be necessary for adults at risk with a range of need or where applying care management can meet and manage risk; or where, in a least restrictive way, risk management and care management can prevent the need for formal powers.

By applying the domain approach, one may clearly see key areas of need emerging for particular groups, for instance older adults with dementia, where there are need areas (for care domains see Appendix 35) that most relate to care circumstances, i.e. mental health and incapacity, safety, personal care needs, motivation and independent actions, diet and sustenance, recreation and activity, social functioning, psychological/emotional needs, physical health, familial needs and issues, financial/property, practical needs, material needs, education and employment, religion and faith, and legal and human rights; some of which are informed by Nucon and Qureshi (1996).

Whereas older adults may not have particular needs for education and employment, adults with learning disability may have particular domains that include these and others mentioned by Nucon and Qureshi, such as everyday functioning, participation in meaningful activity, home, relationships, leisure, freedom and opportunities. Although many care domains are common, e.g. risk and safety and social functioning, adults with functional mental illness may have more distinctive care domains, which might relate to fluctuating mental illness and focus more on a need for treatment and care.

For each care domain, the issue or problem that creates the need may be confirmed, the general effect of the need for the particular adult care group highlighted, the individual effect of need of the assessed adult and the level or extent of the need confirmed, leading to the individual need assessed. Thereafter, an assessment of overall need would occur, pulling together the range of needs and providing a professional opinion on how these needs would be met. This approach, of course, can also be applied to other adults with mental disorder, such as adults with alcohol brain damage or adults with personality disorder, etc.

This process could be applied in a staged way, i.e.:

- Stage 1: To determine the primary condition(s) which give rise to need, e.g. mental disorder (incapacity) and/or physical disability, etc.
- Stage 2: To delineate the individual need/problem area arising as it relates to this particular person (the domain). In doing this the assessor can focus in on the individual needs of the person, e.g. healthcare needs, need for safety, diet and sustenance, personal care needs, etc.
- Stage 3: To clarify the effect of the need/problem on the person's life and circumstances, e.g. mental disorder is affecting the person's ability to meet his/her own personal care needs, for example they are poorly motivated to wash and bathe. Other aspects of mental disorder could for example produce problems arising from disordered thought processes, e.g. delusions or hallucinations; poor memory; low or high mood; poor orientation; confusion; lack of insight; lack of cooperation; poor concentration; behavioural problems, such as aggression, etc.
- Stage 4: To provide assessor's questions. In doing this, the assessor can draw out and confirm the important aspects of the particular need, e.g. what kind of care does the adult require to meet the identified need; what are the issues in providing this care, etc.?
- Stage 5: To provide assessor's answers. In doing this, the assessor can answer the questions raised individually. This not only prompts the assessor to think about the way of resolving or meeting need and the issues arising in meeting the need. It takes

the assessor into the intellectual activity of assessing need and deliberating resolutions. This can be very important when answering questions posed later, when having to justify or defend assessment outcomes.

- Stage 6: To confirm the level and extent of seriousness or significance of the need, e.g. significant/serious need; moderate need; low need. In doing this the assessor can confirm the areas of need which may require the most assistance or care, and which may be the critical areas which need to be addressed to ensure the person remains safely at home. Or, equally, which may confirm the person's needs cannot be met at home and require to be met in another setting, e.g. residential care. Later, when the overall assessment exercise has been concluded (or, if preferred, as an on-going exercise), the assessor may reconfigure the assessment grid to place the areas of greatest need uppermost in the grid, followed by moderate, and then low levels of need.
- Stage 7: To assess each individual need, thereby to confirm how exactly the persons need would be met by assistance, support, care (or treatment), e.g. the person has a need for assistance with bathing, washing and dressing (personal care) in a regular and consistent way each day, at times agreed with the adult.
- Stage 8: To indicate the type of service or care required to meet this need and how this need should be met, e.g. a personal care assistant will be available to the person at crucial times throughout the day to assist the person wash and bathe. The service (personal carer) should encourage, prompt, and, if necessary, assist the adult to bathe and wash.
- Stage 9: To detail the care/service task required to meet the need, e.g. the personal care assistant will visit the adult each day at … (times to be agreed with the person) to assist the person to wash, bathe, do their hair, etc.
- Stage 10: To provide an assessor's comment, giving a view of objectives of the service, the issues relating to the provision of this service for the person, the difficulties that may exist in the provision of this service, etc., e.g. this service can be provided at home, and crucially it may assist the person to stay at home, there may be problems gaining access to the person at home, this person has behavioural problems and requires a sensitive and careful approach to physical assistance. The assessor may also point to the need for further assessments, specialist or otherwise, e.g. an occupational therapist's assessment.

Table 11.8 offers a schematic representation of the assessment as it would be represented on an assessment format, i.e.:

Table 11.8 Assessment of need (domain approach)

Stage 1	Stage 2	Stage 3	Stage 4	Stage 5
Primary conditions	Need / domain area arising	Individual effect of condition	Assessor's questions	Assessor's answers
Mental disorder (dementia) and physical health problems	Incapacity	Incapacity is creating poor decision making and actions, re accepting care.	1. Is it confirmed the person is incapable in this respect? 2. What problems are arising for the person?	1. A capacity assessment to confirm (or not) is needed. 2. The person is unable to accept she needs support.
	Personal care	Mental disorder is affecting the person's ability to meet his/her own personal care needs.	1. Is her mental disorder (dementia) affecting their self-care?	1. The person has lost insight into their personal care needs and forgets if he/she has washed.
	etc	etc	etc	etc
	etc	etc	etc	etc

Stage 6	Stage 7	Stage 8	Stage 9	Stage 10
Extent of seriousness of the need	Assessment of need	The type of service or care required to meet this need (and how this need should be met)	The care/service task required to meet the need	Assessors Comment
Significant	The person has a need for consistent supervision and occasional psychiatric input.	Community psychiatric nurse to be available in a regular and consistent way. Support workers / carers to be available each day.	The service(s) to provide supervision and support at crucial times (agreed with person).	Care needs (and risk) will increase without regular care and support.
Moderate	The person needs assistance with personal care.	Personal care assistants to be available at crucial times throughout the day to assist the person washes and bathe.	The service to provide encouragement, prompting or assistance to bathe and wash at times agreed with the person	This service can be provided at home, however the person has behavioural problems and requires a sensitive and careful approach to physical assistance.
	etc	etc	etc	etc
	etc	etc	etc	etc

An adult protection implementation plan

Here an adult protection plan is necessary to deliver the powers/provision and to ensure the long-term protection of the adult, initially: to allocate a named adult protection officer (council officer) to pursue short-term provisions and to prepare an adult protection plan; to allocate a MHO to assess (and pursue if necessary) long-term provision, i.e. welfare guardianship; to allocate a care manager to pursue an appropriate accommodation, and a support and care package; and to deal with financial aspects (DWP/benefits) (see Table 11.7)

The needs assessment is best done on a Microsoft Excel Spreadsheet, which allows for expansion (stages 1 to 10 [side by side rather than split], and additional columns if necessary) and analysis. When this exercise is done the assessor is in the best position to:

1. *provide an overall assessment outcome*; where the assessor provides a professional opinion on how and where the person's assessed needs should be met. This is the most crucial aspect of the assessment process which provides an assessment of need and not a list of needs or a list of resources, e.g. the adult needs a nursing home (this is not a need, this is a resource); and

2. *construct a care plan* from which the range of needs may be met. In constructing the care plan the important care planning aspects of the needs assessment may be transferred to the first part of the care plan, i.e. 2 (care domain); 5 (seriousness/significance), 6 (assessed need and service/support response), and 7 (type of service/care required), again on an individual basis into a care plan (see table 13), giving detail of how, who, where and when this service/care should be provided, e.g. a personal care service, provided by (service), at times agreed with the person in line with the person's needs, provided at home or if the service cannot be met at home to indicate the most suitable/preferred setting(s) to provide this service, e.g. supported accommodation or residential setting, etc. This should be indicated from most to least restrictive settings. See Table 11.9.

Table 11.9. Care Plan

Need Domain (area where need exists)	Level /extent of the need	Type of service or care required	The care/service task required to meet the need	Preferred setting indicated (most to least restrictive settings)			
				NHC	RC	SH	IS
Incapacity	Significant	Community psychiatric nurse to be available in a regular and consistent way. Support workers / carers to be available each day.	The service(s) to provide supervision and support at crucial times (agreed with person).		*	*	*
Personal care	Moderate	Personal care assistants to be available at crucial times throughout the day to assist the person washes and bathe.	The service to provide encouragement, prompting or assistance to bathe and wash at times agreed with the person				*
etc	etc	etc	etc	etc	etc	etc	etc
etc	etc	etc	etc	etc	etc	etc	etc

NHC: nursing home care; RC: residential care; SH: sheltered accommodation; IS: own home or other independent setting

Applying the domain approach to an assessment of need of Wilma (case example 2) one may see crucial areas of assessment emerging (see Appendix 38). In Wilma's case, there is a close association between risk and need and adult at risk proceedings may have been applied. However, meeting Wilma's needs may reduce and manage risk, may defer the need for formal adult protection action and would be the less restrictive (minimal intervention) approach. An overall assessment of need of Wilma may arrive at the application of care and support services delivered in the context of care management, ensuring adequate review and monitoring, and adult protection action taken if necessary.

See Appendix 38 for an example of a breakdown of the domain approach as applied to an assessment of need (Wilma) and Appendix 39 for assessment of need format and care plan.

An essential aspect of care management is, of course, assessment, and assessment across legislation for adults at risk needs to encompass a range of requirements, e.g. where an assessment of needs for community care services is required to access services, the basis is to be found in section 12A of the 1968 Act, amended by section 55 of the 1990 Act, where under the 2003 Act the local authority should carry out an assessment of needs (s227), where an MHO so notifies the local authority that a patient needs an assessment.

Risk, of course, may militate against needs being met. For example, an assessment of needs of an adult living alone, may indicate that an adult's needs can be met there by a provision of care and support (as indicated in the Wilma case example); however, if an adult's risk cannot be resolved by care and support, e.g. self-harm or suicidal acts, this may trump the ability to support the adult at home, and an alternative option, e.g. transfer to residential care or hospital for treatment, may need to be considered to protect the adult.

The link between assessment of risk and assessment of need is 'safety'. Where risk to safety is indicated as an effect of mental disorder, this may prompt an assessment of risk into these circumstances, e.g. an assessment of an older woman with dementia may indicate she is lacking insight (into her risks), forgetting to switch off her cooker, wandering, with a fear of becoming lost, open to self-neglect, leaving her door open, using cigarettes dangerously (in bed), not eating, not taking her medication, and not allowing carers in. All of these aspects should be picked up in a needs assessment. However, they need further examination, by profiling then assessing them individually, to arrive at both a care plan and a risk management plan which responds to and meets these risks.

An adequate care or adult protection management system needs to reflect and respond to the complexity of need and the seriousness of risk. However, in some cases, depending on the seriousness of risk factors and whether local programme criteria relate, the care programme approach (CPA) might be considered, which could exist alongside adult protection or care management. The CPA was implemented to manage risk in complex circumstances and has been indicated by the MWC in a number of deficiency in care inquiries. It can help to support and protect people with mental disorder within the 2003 and 2000 Acts, and even within the 2007 Act, providing a structured and intensive form of care management. It ensures regular reviewing and good collaboration, and provides a focused, targeted approach between agencies, and a means of standardising practice. It could be applied in three ways: (a) in many cases it may be applied as an alternative to pursuing formal interventions across the legislations; (b) it may act as a framework to delivery of formal powers for adults with mental disorders, and (c) it may exist alongside an adult protection/risk management plan.

Whatever its application, a CPA provides a comprehensive interagency care plan and a CPA coordinator, who would ensure good communication and regular reviews. It provides a risk assessment, including housing issues and a relapse management plan, which may assist vulnerable people achieve long-term continuity of care and stability, urgent attention for those at risk or who pose a risk to others, and planned, prompt and appropriate admission to hospital. Criteria to enter the programme (in certain areas) are based on the severity of the person's mental disorder, serious impairment of abilities, and an onset or long-term presence of mental disorder. A recent refocusing of the CPA enshrines its values and principles in the personalisation policy, ensuring the delivery of care is personal to the adult (CCAWI, 2009).

Chapter 12

BRIDGING THE GAPS

What agencies need to know and do

Meet their duties

Local authority agencies, of course, need to be aware of, and apply, their duties under the Acts (as described earlier in Part 2), in particular regarding the duty to inquire under each Act, i.e. section 33 of the 2003 Act, section 10 of the 2000 Act, and section 4 of the 2007 Act. Respectively, health boards need to be aware of their duty to cooperate with inquiries conducted by the local authority under the Acts, i.e. section 34 of the 2003 Act and section 5 of the 2007 Act; and, although it is not formally stated, to cooperate with a local authority investigation under section 10 of the 2000 Act. And, of course, all inquiries and investigations need to be applied in a collaborative, joint agency, and procedural context.

The statutory agencies need to be aware of their duty to provide assessments under section 228 of the 2003 Act, and their duties (as described earlier) to provide care and support services (s25 and s26, 2003 Act) in the context of Joint Implementation Plans. Local authorities, where necessary, need to make applications for intervention and guardianship orders, including for financial orders, even though they cannot act as financial guardians, and to make applications for protection orders under the 2007 Act. A recent amendment to the 2000 Act (by the 2007 Act) allows local authorities to intromit with the accounts and funds of an adult with incapacity under Part 3 of the 2000 Act.

A key responsibility for the statutory agencies is to ensure the right to independent advocacy, arising from section 259 of the 2003 Act, where it is stated that 'every person with a mental disorder shall have the right to independent advocacy'. This has pertinence for 'crossing the Acts' as it means an adult at risk with mental disorder should have access to independent advocacy whatever Act, i.e. 2003, 2000 or the 2007 Act, they may fall within. Indeed, a recent amendment to the 2000 Act allows the wishes and feeling of the adult to be expressed by an independent advocacy worker in any application to the Sheriff under the 2000 Act (s3 (5)); amended by section 55, 2007 Act.

Appoint trained and experienced key practitioners

Local authorities and health boards need to appoint adequately trained and experienced key practitioners, i.e. the local authority appoints council officers (2007 Act) and designated MHOs under section 32 (2003 Act) to operate in the 2003 and 2007 Acts, and care managers or social workers to act as named local authority welfare guardians under the 2000 Act; health boards approve medical practitioners (AMPs) under section 22 of the 2003 Act, to work under the 2003 and 2000 Acts, and, if necessary, the 2007 Act.

Provide training, support and guidance for key practitioners

Working in the practice context of adults at risk with mental disorder, especially where powers across a range of legislations, are applied is a stressful and demanding task. Local authorities and health boards need to have officers with the knowledge and expertise available to guide, advise and inform staff involved in these complex situations. In many cases, legal advice is necessary. So, therefore, these officers generally will 'need to know' what practitioners 'need to know' to inform practice, and officers will 'need to be able to do' what practitioners 'need to be able to do', to guide practice.

MHOs, through the MHO standards documents (Scottish Government, 2005), should receive adequate support and advice. Standard 7: organisation and management, states 'individual MHOs can expect that their local authority provides proper managerial, administrative and technical support which enables MHOs to fulfil their statutory duties under the legislation in accordance with the principles of the legislation and the associated Codes of Practice'. A similar standard could exist across other key practitioner groups, e.g. council officers and AMPs.

MHO support and development forums exist throughout local authorities across Scotland. They provide an excellent model, which both provides guidance and supports staff to develop as MHOs in dealing with complex situations. This model could be adopted in the area of adults at risk with mental disorder, where key adult at risk practitioner forums could assist practitioners such as council officers, GPs, MHOs and AMPs to develop skills and abilities, meet statutory duties, and ensure knowledge bases are up to date.

In working 'across the Acts', MHOs and AMPs need their role assessed to consider their involvement, which is confirmed in the 2000 and 2003 Acts, within the 2007 Act, primarily to act (and be appointed) as council officers. It is inevitable for MHOs and AMPs to be drawn into the operation of the 2007 Act, where it concerns adults with mental disorder. So guidance has to be provided as to the extent of this role, and their needs for additional training and practice guidance. Equally, the overall MHO service provision, from a strategic perspective, needs to be assessed, as it concerns adults at risk with mental disorder 'across the Acts', to ensure that local procedures in-build the MHO role and involvement, giving clarity and guidance. Equally, other key practitioners such as GPs and AMPs need to have access to legal advice and guidance, and support systems.

Agencies need to ensure that practitioners are suitably trained to work across the Acts in respect of adults with mental disorder. However, it is all very well to train practitioners in each of the Acts individually; but they need to know how to cross the Acts and how to apply the powers and provisions simultaneously.

Appendix 27 offers a relative training programme for key practitioners with which to support and protect adults with mental disorder across the Acts.

Ensure adult protection committees seriously consider adults at risk with mental disorder 'across the Acts'

Following the implementation of the 2007 Act, key agencies charged with the protection of adults at risk are represented in a local multiagency adult protection committee (APC). This group is chaired by an independent convener, and the local authority, health board, police and other agencies are represented there. The APC is charged with a range of duties as they concern adult protection practice in the area. It is charged with ensuring that adult protection procedures are implemented and monitored across agencies, ensuring that training is adequate to the needs of staff, and to:

> keep under review the procedures and practices of the public bodies and office-holders ... including, in particular .... co-operation between the Council and other public bodies or office-holders to which this section applies ... to give information or advice ... on the exercise of functions ... to make, or assist in or encourage the making of, arrangements for improving the skills and knowledge of officers or employees of the public bodies and office-holders ... who have responsibilities relating to the safeguarding of adults at risk present in the Council's area.

APCs, however, are concerned with the range of adult at risk groups, such as adults affected by disability, mental disorder, illness or physical or mental infirmity. However, as may be seen by earlier information in chapter one, the majority of adults passing through adult at risk services are adults with mental disorder. Therefore, following the key tenet of this work, that such adults need a particular and sometimes specialist approach to their needs and the risk which arise from mental disorder, APCs need to consider their duties as they concern the support and protection of adults with mental disorder across the range of legislation offered (the 2000, 2003 and 2007 Acts). They also conscious that key practitioners do not only work in the context of the 2007 Act; and, therefore, practice and procedures, information and advice, training, and improving skills and knowledge should relate and refer to the needs of key practitioners working 'across the Acts'.

Adult at risk statistics gathered, however, only relate to the 2007 Act, where many adults at risk are protected in the context of the 2003 and 2000 Acts. So, therefore, statistical information needs to provide a broader picture 'across the Acts' to give an accurate reflection of adult protection in any area.

Additionally, the specific and shared duties and provisions contained in this work (across the Acts), e.g. duties to inquire/investigate; provision of services and support; risk management; cooperation and sharing of information; the use of warrants, emergency, short term and long term orders; etc., should be drawn into the overall sphere and control of the APCs, to accurately reflect practice. To assist, this work offers a procedural guidance which relates specifically to the support and protection of adults at risk with mental disorder across the legislations.

Prepare and implement appropriate adult at risk procedures

Local vulnerable adult procedures were updated after the Scottish Border's case (SWSI, 2004) and on the implementation of the 2007 Act. Most procedures have similar processes, e.g. reporting and responding to allegations of harm in defined timescales, potentially leading to investigations, case conferences, action if necessary, and delivered in a joint agency context. There are, however, aspects of procedures that need to relate more specifically to the needs and risks of adults with mental disorder at risk, e.g. specific risk assessment and adult protection plans, specialist assessments and interventions, access to MHOs and AMPs, and access to relative resources, e.g. places of safety, etc.

Appendix 26 offers a relative adult at risk process.

What key practitioners need to know and do

Generally, across the Acts, key practitioners need to be able to protect the safety, health, welfare, finances and property of those adults with mental disorder unable or incapable of doing so themselves. They need to be able to provide care and treatment, apply the principles of the Acts, apply the COPs for the Acts, meet respective duties under the Acts and cross the Acts for people with mental disorder. No one practitioner has all the knowledge, experience or all the answers. This is why collaborative working is so important.

In supporting and protecting adults at risk affected by mental disorder, the practitioner needs to be aware of prevention, recovery and management of mental illness, and the differing perspectives and frameworks contributing to healthcare and community care assessments, and how and where to obtain specialist assessments. A practitioner needs to understand policy, perspectives and frameworks that both promote and impinge on levels of risk, e.g. barriers, poor communication, poor sharing of information, confidentially issues, data protection, etc., learning from relevant MWC deficiency in care inquiries; predominately to counter and protect against these deficiencies when dealing with risk.

Primarily, however, key practitioners need to understand the context, content and application of the 2000, 2003 and 2007 Acts, both individually and in their collective application. Their level of understanding, moreover, needs to be relative to their role and duties under the Acts; for example, a GP needs to be comfortable with the emergency provision of the Acts, in particular the 2003 Act; whereas an AMP needs to understand how longer-term provisions such a CTOs and guardianship orders may be utilised in managing risk over time; and a social worker designated as a MHO needs to be aware of primary duties under the 2003 Act; a social worker, acting as a council officer, needs to be aware of meeting duties under the 2007 Act. All practitioners working across the Acts, however, need to be aware of the range of support and protection provisions for mentally disordered people.

Importantly, key practitioners need to know how the Acts relate to the risk posed by mental disorder on an adult's life, and to engage practically and sympathetically with the adult, their partners, families and carers.

Mental disorder

Practitioners in the area of mental disorder should have a working knowledge of mental disorder in general and the legal definition (taken from the 2003 Act), in particular in respect of mental illness, personality disorder and learning disability. They, in particular medical practitioners, need to know how a diagnosis is made, and the key diagnostic categories therein. They should know how symptoms of mental illness and incapacity are demonstrated and the causal factors of these conditions, and be aware of how complex and acute conditions manifest on an adult's health, safety and welfare. They should have a comfortable and working knowledge of functional and organic mental illness, their signs, symptoms, issues arising, diagnosis and prognosis; their effect in impairing decision-making and capacity; recovery models; and their on-going management. They should have a working knowledge (specific in the field) of mental illnesses of young people, adults and older people; and of specific mental disorders: e.g. bipolar disorder, schizophrenia, dementia, depression, affective disorders, eating disorders, Diogenes Syndrome, personality disorder and co-morbid mental disorder (with alcohol and drug abuse).

Incapacity

For those affected by incapacity, they should be aware of the particular conditions which may combine mental disorder and incapacity, e.g. dementia, alcohol related brain damage, learning disability, etc., and they should understand the range of care, support and treatment options, and management and rehabilitation of adults affected thereby. Importantly, they should be able to source or provide an appropriate assessment of incapacity, following the Scottish Government guidance (xviii) thereby, and of sustaining mental health for people with incapacity, and responding to the effect of incapacity on adults, their families, partners and carers.

Policy and local strategic frameworks

Additionally, practitioners should be aware of policy and local frameworks, such as local adult at risk procedures, and provision of care and support services and the promotion of mental health and wellbeing. They should be aware of social stereotyping of those with mental disorder and its impact on people's lives, the culture and diversity issues for those adults, and the myths, attitudes and stigmas they face. They should be conversant with facts and statistics in relation to Scotland's mental health, such as suicide and suicide prevention, and trends, patterns and case law as they relate to the primary Acts.

Applying the principles

Practitioners need to understand the respective principles in and across the Acts and to apply these principles to the actions they take and the decisions they make in a practical and responsive way; in particular, during the process of seeking and securing formal provision, and while monitoring the longer-term effect of granted powers on adults and their carers and families.

Applying the codes of practice

Practitioners should apply the provisions of the Acts, informed by the COP of the respective Act they are working within.

Risk assessment and risk management

Practitioners in the field need to know about differing perspectives and frameworks that contribute to the holistic assessment of need, healthcare and community care assessment, proposed and working care plans, and obtaining specialist assessment, including risk planning and risk management and how their role, in either preparing or contributing to adult protection plans, is delivered.

They need to be able to make (or contribute to) a comprehensive assessment of risk across the range of risk posed by mental disorder, its effect on the adult's mood, thought processes, and behaviour, and its risk related to the capacity of the adult to act, make, communicate, understand and remember decisions, and in respect of the harm posed on adults with mental disorder, e.g. sexual, physical, emotional and financial. Practitioners need to be able to manage risk over time that may be posed by harmers, by self-harm, and by adults on their family, carers, partners, and towards other professionals.

They need to be aware of both the immediate and deteriorating risk to adults, families, carers, children and the public, and the range of factors, perspectives and frameworks that impinge on assessment and increase or reduce levels of risk, such as professional barriers, poor communication, poor sharing of information, confidentially issues, data protection, etc., and relevant deficiency in care inquiries, such as the Ms A case (7).

They should know about widely used risk assessment and risk management tools, in particular those provided by the JIT, and local and national policy in relation to integrated assessment and management of care and risk, and the CPA and its local application across the range of mental disorder. Primarily, key practitioners need to be able to assess risk in relation to conditions for compulsion under the 2003 Act, e.g.: health, safety, welfare, section 33 (ill-treatment, neglect, deficiency in care, to property); part 21 offences (sexual offences, etc.); grounds for guardianship under the 2000 Act; and the grounds for protection orders under the 2007 Act.

Duties and responsibilities

Practitioners should know about the roles and responsibilities of the health and local authorities, and the roles of the Sheriff, Sheriff Court and the Mental Health Tribunal, the Mental Welfare Commission, the Office of the Public Guardian, as well as relevant Scottish Government departments.

Collective working

Practitioners need to work collectively, applying knowledge of respective roles and responsibilities, thereby managing inter-professional tensions, sharing information, and resolving inter-professional dilemmas and conflicts. This is a clear problem which gets in the way of protecting adults at risk with mental disorder.

The Acts have locked certain practitioners together, e.g. MHOs and medical practitioners, like never before in the use of formal provisions and the response to risk; and within the 2003 Act, pursuing STDCs and CTOs are collaborative actions involving these key practitioners.

Jointness is particularly essential where protecting adults at risk, where many inquiries involve a social worker (council officer or MHO) alongside a medical practitioner, jointly risk assessing and responding to the impact of mental disorder on the adult's health, safety and welfare; thereby pursuing warrants, and, sometimes with police colleagues, gaining access to adults and arranging removal to a place of safety. This can be stressful and demanding work, and these practitioners need the support of health and social work colleagues in its delivery.

Collaborative working is well established between social workers, such as MHOs, and other key practitioners, such as AMPs and RMOs. However, in the area of adult support and protection one has to be mindful of problems such as highlighted in the Scottish Borders case (SWSI, 2004), e.g. poor communication, poor sharing of information and poor care planning. New adult at risk procedures, new risk assessment formats and adult protection plans, however, seek to address these problems, thereby promoting improved collaborative working.

Adult protection management and collaborative working go hand in hand; and, therefore, application of legislative duties and powers requires tight joint working, where a MHO and RMO may both lead and participate in its delivery; for example, in preparing adult protection plans (as joint assessors) and in risk management systems (as risk managers across health and social care risk).

Additionally, the social worker (MHO) and medical practitioner (RMO), in crossing the Acts with and for adults at risk, need to be aware of the functions and contribution of key bodies involved in the support and protection of adults affected by mental disorder, e.g. the Mental Health Tribunal, the Mental Welfare Commission, the Office of the Public Guardian, the Sheriff Court and voluntary and private agencies; and they should be comfortable intra-working within local authority and health board departments, and across their range of services, e.g. (local authority) legal services, community care, environmental health, childcare services, housing, etc., and (health board) primary care, specialist support, occupational therapy, etc. However, obtaining advice and support (sometimes legal) in complex and high risk cases, is essential.

Collaboration with adults, however, is the primary collaborative relationship in any legislative response. Across the Acts, this relationship is confirmed, particularly where the principle of service user participation is a common, indeed a statutory, imperative. Furthermore, key practitioners need to know about respective roles and contributions of other practitioners working with adults at risk affected by mental disorder and the functions and contribution of statutory and voluntary organisations usually involved in the adult protection field, thereby, to be able to work jointly with all of the relevant partners, while making applications, obtaining orders and warrants, protecting adults at risk, engaging within local services (e.g. health and community care agencies, specialist services, interpreters, etc.), and engaging with health and local authority departments (e.g. community care and childcare sections and teams) and partnership agencies (e.g. community mental health teams, community learning disability teams and community older people's teams).

For a more specific range of formal tasks see Appendix 28.

And specifically…

Mental health officers

In the area of 'adults at risk', the MHO role has been clearly established over the years, certainly in the context of the 2000 and 2003 Acts. In the 2007 Act, this role is less clear, because the primary social work role there is contained within the 'council officer' role. Many MHOs, however, as qualified and trained social workers, are designated as council officers. The role has been emphasised recently, as in the Ms A case (7), where the MWC (2008a, p 7) recommended that social work departments should "re-examine and clarify the role and function of the mental health officer in adult protection case conferences to ensure that their specialist training, experience and skill is used to best effect in contributing to the assessment and risk management of vulnerable adults with mental disorder in these circumstances".

    With the introduction of the 2003 Act, social workers appointed as MHOs became 'designated MHOs' and were to be more formally involved in long-term engagement with adults with mental disorder and their families. Across the Acts, MHOs often act as named welfare guardians and supervise private/relative guardians, and operate within working care plans (CTOs). MHOs, as social workers, work with mentally disordered adults providing support; many act as care managers for adults with serious and complex needs. MHOs are increasingly drawn into actions within adult at risk procedures and the 2007 Act. For MHOs, there is a longitudinal and latitudinal presence across the Acts.

Generally, MHOs should know the key rights and duties offered by the Acts e.g. duty to inquire, police powers, offences under the Act, and care and support services. Specifically, they should respond to inquiries, and only they can obtain warrants and removal orders under the 2003 Act. In particular, their work involves:

- conducting inquires (s33);
- seeking and obtaining warrants (s35) for entry, medical assessments, and access to medical records;
- seeking and obtaining authorised persons' warrants (s292);
- making an application for and seeking a removal order(s293 to Sheriff), and making an application for and seeking an urgent removal order (s294 to Justice of the Peace);
- meeting duties under emergency and short-term detentions: to provide consultation and consent (or not) to emergency detention (s36) and short-term detention (s44); and

- meeting the duty and its associated tasks in applying for the provisions of a CTO (s57).

MHOs are designated to work with the 2000 and 2003 Acts (reports, etc.), and have specific duties and independent actions and opinions to make therein, e.g. to consent to short-term and emergency detentions, to give views on medical reports, and to provide reports and opinions on the appropriateness of welfare intervention and guardianship orders and (where not a local authority applicant) the suitability of a proposed welfare proxy. Although not confirmed in the 2007 Act, a MHO may be appointed a council officer, to operate in the context of the 2007 Act. Indeed, where the adult has a mental disorder, an MHO's involvement may be essential in 'crossing the Acts', ensuring the correct legal framework is employed that is reflective of the adult's needs and risks.

Social workers (and council officers)

A trained and qualified social worker, acting as a council officer (including a MHO), should be able to investigate under the 2007 Act, thereby obtaining and providing relative risk assessments, obtaining warrants for entry, and urgent cases entry and removal orders, and prompting and assessing for application for protection orders under the Act, i.e. assessment orders, removals orders, banning orders and temporary banning orders, and thereby providing evidence in court; thereafter, to exercise protection orders and prompt the revoking, reviewing and reapplying for orders. Social workers, however, have an important role in the assessment of care needs, thereafter acting as care managers; and, as appointed council officers, preparing an assessment of risk and an adult protection plan.

MHOs and social workers, working across the Acts, need to incorporate the role into the context of local care management systems and structures, to ensure this important link with services and resources is made.

Consultant psychiatrists (RMOs/AMPs)

Consultant psychiatrists and other consultants can act as AMPs under the 2000 and 2003 Acts (approved under section 22 of the 2003 as having such 'qualifications, experience and training'), thereby granting short-term detentions (and emergency detentions), preparing medical reports and working care plans (giving medical treatment) in CTOs, as well as other tasks (see Appendix 28), and providing reports for guardianship and intervention orders, and may act as 'health professionals' under the 2007 Act, thereby conducting medical examinations, etc.

General practitioners

GPs may grant emergency detentions under the 2003 Act (where a short-term detention is not available) and assess capacity under the 2000 Act. They may provide medical assessments in formal inquiries under the 2003 Acts and where the police remove mentally disordered adults to a place of safety (such as a police station). They may provide the second medical reports for applications for CTOs, or guardianship or intervention orders under the 2000 Act. They may also provide medical certificates for other measures in the 2000 Act, i.e. Parts 3, 4 and 5; and may act as 'health professionals' under the 2007 Act, thereby conducting medical examinations, etc. They have duties to cooperate and report adults at risk (subject to General Medical Council confidentiality guidance) to the local authority under section 5 of the 2007 Act.

Managers/practitioners

In the complex area of protecting adults with mental disorder, practitioners need to be able to get on with the practice and delivery of adult protection without getting entangled by 'red tape' and the administrative process. Managers need to lead and 'manage'. Key practitioners and allocated managers need to operate in consort with each other, one assisting the other, both with similar objectives, i.e. to protect the adult at risk and preventing duplication of effort.

See Appendix 29 for a risk management process for (a) managers and (b) key practitioners

A Crossing the Acts process

From this work it appears clear that adults with mental disorder have particular risks, i.e. caused by (a) mental disorder or incapacity, (b) the effects of mental disorder or (c) because they have mental disorder, which leaves them particularly open to risk and harm, and which may need to be met across a range of legislations and by local authority and healthcare agencies and practitioners. Consequentially, there needs to be an 'across the Acts' process (as indicated by this work) applied by agencies and practitioners to the support and protection of adults at risk with mental disorder in the community.

To (or do):

- create and apply particular and relative adult at risk (mental disorder) procedures and frameworks (as described in Chapter 11), to include applying relative risk assessment tools and adult protection plans;
- ensure partner agencies and key practitioners know what they need to know and do what they need to do (as described in Chapter 12, by avoiding the pitfalls of previous poor practice, meeting duties across the Acts, and applying risk assessment and risk management across the range of risk experienced by adults with mental disorder;
- seek safe and secure authority and powers (as described in Chapter 10), across the Acts, as they relate to adults with mental disorder, assessing particular risk and powers relative to this risk, and allocating and supporting 'key practitioners' to make collective decisions, thereby seeking adequate authority to protect, etc.;
- apply adult protection (adults with mental disorder) in an applied and practical way, thereby confirming mental disorder and risk; obtaining correct and adequate legal mandates; confirming a need to visit, assess and act; and acting from a basis of correct and adequate legal powers, responding to immediate, ongoing and significant risk/harm and need; and
- oversee the adult protection milieu to include an 'across the Acts' and adult at risk with mental disorder perspective.

CASE EXAMPLES

1. WALTER

Walter is a man aged 57, who has an alcohol related brain damage and is affected by bouts of agitation and depression. His alcohol abuse manifests in self-harming and behavioural difficulties, disinhibition and poor self-care. He also has asthma and heart disease. His GP believes he is incapable of understanding he needs treatment. He had spent a good part of his life in a long stay hospital, leaving some ten years ago. Walter's house is continually untidy and is very basic; comprising a television, a settee and a coffee table littered with cigarettes, no carpet, and cans of lager litter the floor. He is thin and unkempt. He cannot walk very far because of his asthma. His main outing each day is to collect his cans (a twelve-pack), which he purchases each morning to last him throughout the day. He eats only when his home help prepares food for him. His cooker was isolated some time ago and he is not allowed to cook. He is incontinent of urine when he sleeps. He does not eat, is constantly wet, and only lets his community nurse in when he is fearful he may harm himself by taking paracetamol. Walter's brother, Peter, acts as his power of attorney (continuing and welfare). Walter is open to exploitation and it has been reported that his brother has accompanied him to a cash machine and he could not account for money he lost. It is believed that his brother is using Walter's cash to buy alcohol for him and his 'friends', who use Walter's house as a drinking den. Walter is generally non-compliant and resistant with support. His RMO fears he may kill himself without treatment for his depression. He generally refuses to consent to support or to the caring agencies sharing any information on him.

The 2000 Act is indicated, i.e.:

- Assessment of capacity;
- Inquiry under s10:
  - personal welfare at risk and
  - into the exercise of the attorney's proxy powers;
- Office of the Public Guardian investigation (s6);
- Offences of ill-treatment and neglect (s83);
- Welfare guardianship (interim and full powers);
- Part 3 (funds and accounts);
- Part 5 (s47) medical treatment (physical problems).

The 2003 Act is indicated, i.e.:

- A potential need for s35 warrant for entry and medical examination;
- a removal order (s293/4);
- medical treatment, potentially under compulsion;
- offences of ill-treatment and neglect;
- care and support services under s25.

The 2007 Act is also indicated, i.e.:

- Inquiry under s4;
- Protection orders, i.e. Banning order

The 1968 Act and 1990 Act are also indicated, i.e.:

- Assessment of need, access to care and support services;
- Local adult at risk procedures are also indicated: e.g. investigation, risk assessment and adult protection plan.

2. WILMA

Wilma is aged 72, has dementia, heart disease and abuses alcohol, which manifests in poor self-care. She is generally non-compliant and resistant of supports. Her house is continually untidy and is very basic. She is thin and unkempt. She doesn't do much each day and remains at home most of the time, because she can't walk very far because of her asthma. She eats only when her home help prepares food for her. She is incontinent of urine when she sleeps. Recently she doesn't eat, is constantly wet and only lately let the home help in. She has a male friend, much younger than her, who generally visits her on Friday nights. Wilma has told home helps this man wants sex from her and she says she is frightened. She also thinks the man may be taking money from her. She feels his company helps reduce her loneliness.

The 2007 Act is indicated: i.e.

- Inquiry under s4;
- Protection orders, i.e. banning order.

The 2000 Act is indicated, i.e.

- Assessment of capacity;
- Inquiry under s10;
- Welfare guardianship (powers of non-consorting, access, etc.);
- Part 5 (s47) medical treatment (physical health problems).

The 2003 Act is indicated, i.e.

- Inquiry under s33;
- Removal order (s293/4);
- Assessment for offences under s311;
- care and support services under s25;
- independent advocacy services.

The 1968 Act and 1990 Act are indicated, i.e.
• Assessment of need access to care and support services.

Local adult at risk procedures are indicated, e.g.
• Investigation, risk assessment and an adult protection plan.

3. MARY

Mary is aged 23 and is affected by learning disability, which affects her ability to make important decisions regarding her safety and welfare. She lives with her aunt and uncle. They are emotionally harming her, threatening to throw her out, which scares her because she doesn't want to be homeless. They are financially abusing her, by using her benefits for their needs and not hers. She would like to leave the house and set up on her own, but is scared of being on her own, and is denied this by her domineering uncle. Her cousin is sexually exploiting her. The aunt and uncle know about this, but do not do anything to stop this, other than forcing her to take oral contraception tablets. She says she is scared to go home to a day centre officer and indicates she 'doesn't like' what is going on.

The 2007 Act is indicated, i.e.

- Inquiry under s4;
- Protection orders, i.e. Assessment, Removal and Banning orders.

The 2000 Act is indicated, i.e.

- Assessment of capacity;
- Welfare guardianship;
- Part 3 (funds and accounts).

The 2003 Act is indicated, i.e.

- a potential need for s33 inquiry; S35 warrant for entry and medical examination;
- a removal order (s293/4);
- assessment for offences under s311;
- care and support services (s25) and promoting well-being and social development (s26).

Local adult at risk procedures are indicated:
• e.g. investigation, risk assessment and an adult protection plan.

4. LESLEY

Lesley is aged 34 and is affected by learning disability. She resides with Tom who is aged 54 and abuses alcohol. Tom was homeless and obtained a housing association flat, then Lesley moved in with him. Lesley previously received psychiatric support, then Tom refused services, which were about to be withdrawn anyway because he sexually assaulted a care worker. Now neither of them wishes to receive any support or services. He is known to be aggressively dominant of her. There was a serious fire in the house, caused by an overfull chip pan, which had been left on by Tom, when he was drinking alcohol. This was the third time this had happened, although on previous occasions there had been no serious outcome. The fire service extinguished the fire, which caused damage to the kitchen of the flat, and windows were broken. Lesley suffered burns while trying to put out the fire and agreed to go to the accident and emergency department, where her burns were treated; and, although she was well enough to go home, hospital staff were concerned about her safety and welfare. Her burns were treated in hospital and she went home. She refused to agree to a social worker visiting her at home. The following day a fire prevention officer called to see them. He was concerned that the couple neither understood nor was coping with the seriousness of the situation. He reported that the flat was no longer weather tight (it being winter), the wiring in the kitchen was unsafe, and the house was in a deplorable condition: there being little furniture, it being extremely cold, there being piles of papers lying around, and no evidence of food or provisions. On speaking to Lesley the fire officer found her withdrawn and talking to herself. Tom resented certain questions and told the fire officer to 'get out and leave them alone', that he is the master of this house and her.

The 2007 Act is indicated, i.e.:

- Inquiry under s4;
- Protection orders, assessment and removal order.

The 2000 Act is indicated, i.e.:

- Assessment of capacity;
- Welfare guardianship.

The 2003 Act is indicated, i.e.:

- s33 inquiry; S35 warrant for entry and medical examination;
- Removal order (s293/294)
- Short-term detention
- Care and support services under s25.

Local adult at risk procedures are indicated, i.e.
• investigation, risk assessment, an adult protection plan

The 1990 Act and 1968 Act are indicated, i.e.
• Assessment of need, access to care and support services

5. JOHN

John is a man aged 24 with learning disability/Asperger's syndrome who poses a risk to women and thereby is open to attack in his local community, has welfare needs, has needs for treatment and care on a compulsory basis, was discharged into the community from a secure hospital setting subject to a community based compulsory treatment order, with requirements to allow access, attend for treatment and attend an adult learning centre. The emphasis of the order is the protection of him and others. However, he also has welfare needs/risks not met by the CTO, such as his care, residence, responding to physical health issues such as diabetes, and requiring him not to consort with women, all of which need to be met in the context of welfare guardianship, but with the emphasis on protection of health and welfare. His father acts as his welfare guardian. A MHO supervises him on behalf of the local authority and also acts as designated MHO in respect of the CTO, alongside the RMO and a community psychiatric nurse. Part 3 of the 2000 Act provides authority for his father to manage his finances. These powers were set in the context of the local care programme approach. This formal framework may be viewed as highly restrictive, but this has to be balanced with the benefits of him living in the community, at home, rather than living in a secure hospital setting.

The use of (and need for) the 2000 Act is confirmed, i.e.

- Welfare guardianship, with powers to:
    - Decide on care and accommodation;
    - Decide on contact with others;
    - Consent to medical treatment;
    - Decide on social, cultural and educational activities;
    - Supervise, accompany and support the adult on a 24-hour basis;
- Part 3 to manage funds and accounts.
    - Here local adult at risk procedures are confirmed, i.e: risk management (HCR 20 etc.) and adult protection planning.

The use of (and need for) the 2003 Act is confirmed, i.e.

- Community compulsory treatment order, with powers to:
    - Give medical treatment;
    - Require attendance for medical treatment;
    - Require attendance for community care services;
    - Require adult to reside in specified place;
    - Allow visits by RMO, MHO, etc.;
    - Obtain approval of MHO to change address.

- Local care management and care programme approach is indicated.

6. MR H

Mr H is man in his mid-seventies with a long history of alcohol abuse, who became affected by ARBD. He has been drinking since approximately the age of 14 and his health records as early as 1985 refer to his 'long history of alcoholism'. They report suicidal wishes, overdoses, duodenal ulcer, non-insulin-dependent diabetes, arthritis and various injuries, including fractures resulting from fights and falls, most often associated with alcohol abuse. Social work contact dates from the mid-1980s and appears to have been related to his offending, often associated with alcohol abuse. It was subsequently established that he was affected by ARBD. There were quite frequent contacts with his GP, social work department and housing department prior to the point when he was placed on guardianship in March 2004. The MWC (2006) found that health and social care services did not pay enough attention to his mental function and capacity, and there was poor risk assessment and inadequate knowledge of the relevant legislation.

The 2000 Act is indicated, i.e.

- Assessment of capacity;
- Inquiry under s10;
- Welfare guardianship;
- Part 5 (s47) medical treatment (physical problems);

The 2003 Act is indicated, i.e.

- Care and support services under s25;
- Potentially (at a point in his care a short term detention for assessment related to medical treatment).

The 1990 Act and the 1968 Act are indicated, i.e.

- Assessment of need access to care and support services.

Local adult at risk procedures are indicated, i.e.

- Investigation, risk assessment and adult protection planning.

7.   MS A

Ms A is a 67-year-old woman with a learning disability who had reported being raped. Similar assaults were alleged to have taken place previously. It appeared from initial investigations, that the services responsible for her had been unable to protect her from a series of serious sexual assaults. The responses of health, social care and criminal justice services combined to deny her access to justice. No-one was prosecuted for the alleged offences against her. Those who pose a known risk to her safety remain at large within her community, while she continues to endure a protective regime that effectively deprives her of much of her liberty.   There was never a proper, considered discussion about potential offences under the 2003 Act. This represented a fundamental flaw in the health and social work team's management of this case (MWC, 2008a).

The 2007 Act is indicated, i.e.	**The 2003 Act is indicated, i.e.**	**The 2000 Act is indicated, i.e.**
• Inquiry under s4; • Protection orders, i.e. Assessment, Removal and Banning orders (also temporary banning order).	• Assessment for offences under s311; • Care and support services (s25) and promoting wellbeing and social development (s26).	• Assessment of capacity; • Welfare guardianship; • Interim guardianship powers.

- Local adult at risk procedures are indicated: e.g.: investigation, risk assessment and an adult protection plan.

References

CCAWI (Centre for Clinical and Academic Workforce Innovation) (www.lincoln.ac.uk/ccawi/publications/unit%201%20personalisation.pdf)

Douglas, K S, Guy L S and Weir, J (undated) HCR-20 Violence Risk Assessment Scheme: overview and annotated bibliography Burnaby, BC, Canada, Simon Fraser University (www.violence-risk.com/hcr20annotated.pdf)

DWP (Department for Work and Pension (no date) 'Third party access – help with collecting benefit or pension payments', London, DWP (www.dwp.gov.uk/docs/third-party-access.pdf; accessed 6 October 2010)

JIT (Joint Improvement Team) Edinburgh, JIT (www.jitscotland.org.uk/knowledge-bank/publications/adult)

Keenan, T (1999) 'The predominate use of emergency detention under the Mental Health (Scot) Act 1984', Master's thesis, University of Glasgow

Killeen, J, Myers, F with Brisbane, A, Coulson, K, Fearnley, K, Gordon, J, Keith, D, Maclean, J, Thom, M and Woodhouse, A (2004) The Adults with Incapacity (Scotland) Act 2000: learning from experience Edinburgh, Scottish Executive

Millan, B (2001) New Directions: report on the review of the Mental Health (Scotland) Act, 1984, SE/2001/56, Edinburgh, Scottish Executive

MWC (Mental Welfare Commission) (2001) Report of the Inquiry into the Care and Treatment of Mr B Edinburgh, MWC

MWC (2004) Annual Report 2003–2004 Edinburgh, MWC

MWC (2006) Investigation into the Care and Treatment of Mr H Edinburgh, MWC

MWC (2007) Investigation into the Care and Treatment of Mrs T Edinburgh, MWC

MWC (2008a) Justice Denied: a summary of our investigation into the care and treatment of Ms A Edinburgh, MWC (www.mwcscot.org.uk/web/FILES/Publications/Justice_Denied_Summary_FINAL.pdf; accessed 23 September 2010)

MWC (2008b) Our Review of Mental Welfare in Scotland 2007–08 Edinburgh, MWC (www.mwcscot.org.uk/web/FILES/Annual_reports/MWC_Overview_web.pdf; accessed 23 September 2010)

MWC (2009a) Annual Report 2008–2009 Edinburgh, MWC

MWC (2009b) Mental Health Act Care Plans Edinburgh, MWC (www.mwcscot.org.uk/web/FILES/Publications/Care_Plan_Guide.pdf; accessed 6 October 2010)

Nocon, A and Qureshi, H (1996) Outcomes of Community Care for Users and Carers, Milton Keynes, Open University Press

Patrick, H. (2004) Authorising Significant Interventions for Adults who Lack Capacity Edinburgh, MWC

Professional Social Work (2010) 'Dealing with risk', July, p 24

Scottish Executive (2001) Consultation on Vulnerable Adults Edinburgh, Scottish Executive

Scottish Executive (2004) Guidance of Care Management in Community Care, Circular, Edinburgh, Scottish Executive (www.sehd.scot.nhs.uk/publications/CC2004_08.pdf; accessed 6 October 2010)

Scottish Executive (2005a) Mental Health (Care and Treatment) (Scotland) Act 2003: code of practice: volume 2 Edinburgh, Scottish Executive

Scottish Executive (2005b) Mental Health (Care and Treatment) (Scotland) Act 2003: code of practice: volume 1 Edinburgh, Scottish Executive

Scottish Government (2005) Standards for Mental Health Officer services provided by local authorities in partnership with health Edinburgh, Scottish Government
(web only) www.scotland.gov.uk/Publications/2005/05/1393048

Scottish Government (2006) Letter (www.sehd.scot.nhs.uk/mels/HDL2006_56.pdf; accessed 23 September 2010)

Scottish Government (2007) With Inclusion in Mind: the local authorities' role in promoting wellbeing and social development Edinburgh, Scottish Government (www.scotland.gov.uk/Publications/2007/10/18092957/0; accessed 23 September 2010)

Scottish Government (2008a) Adults with Incapacity (Scotland) Act 2000: communication and assessing capacity: a guide for social work and health care staff Edinburgh, Scottish Government (www.scotland.gov.uk/Publications/2008/02/01151101/0; accessed 6 October 2010)

Scottish Government (2008b) Adults with Incapacity (Scotland) Act 2000: code of practice: for local authorities exercising functions under the 2000 Act Edinburgh, Scottish Government

Scottish Government (2008c) Protection of Vulnerable Groups (Scotland) Act 2007: Scottish Vetting and Barring Scheme Edinburgh, Scottish Government

Scottish Government (2009) Adult Support and Protection (Scotland) Act 2007: code of practice, 2009/01/30112831, Edinburgh, Scottish Government

SLC (Scottish Law Commission) (1997) Report on Vulnerable Adults, Edinburgh, SLC

SWSI (Social Work Services Inspectorate) (2004) Report of the Inspection of Scottish Borders Council Social Work Services for People Affected by Learning Disabilities Edinburgh, Scottish Executive

APPENDICES

The Acts:

- **The Social Work (Scotland) Act 1968 (the 1968 Act);**

- **The NHS and Community Care Act 1990 (the 1990 Act);**

- **The Adults with Incapacity (Scotland) Act 2000 (the 2000 Act);**

- **The Community Care and Health (Scotland) Act 2002 (the 2002 Act)**

- **The Mental Health (Care and Treatment) (Scotland) Act 2003 (the 2003 Act)**

The Adult Support and Protection (Scotland) Act 2007 (the 2007 Act).

Appendix 1: The Adult (with mental disorder) Risk Landscape

© Tom Keenan 2010

Appendix 2: Areas of Risk and Harm

- **Physical harm:** from assaulting, e.g. punching, slapping, burning, pushing, grabbing, biting; or ill treatment, abuse of medication, use of weapons, use of physical force, restraint, force feeding or starving, domestic abuse;

- **Risk to finances:** from theft, exploitation, forcing to give money, misappropriation (of funds), extortion, embezzlement; abuse of powers (e.g. DWP appointee, intromission with funds, power of attorney or financial guardianship); to savings, accounts, benefits, rent, security; or from imprudence or debt;

- **Risk to property:** house, tenancy, mortgage, and inheritance;

- **Risk to personal things**: to equipment, goods, pets, clothes;

- **Sexual harm:** from sexual exploitation to multiple rape, from the use of sexual language, forcing to watch pornography, lack of consent or incapacity to consent; touching and trying to touch; sometimes from disinhibition and lack of insight into safety;**Emotional harm:** from psychological force/abuse, causing fear, alarm and distress; the use of blackmail, threatening to harm adult and to harm others the adults care for, excluding the adult or preventing contact with others, to dashing confidence, undermining, running down and belittling, treating with a lack of dignity, the application of tyranny;

- **Risk from neglect of needs:** wilful neglect, needs not being met, lack of care and support, lack of personal care (washing, getting out of bed, dressing, eating, toileting, housework, travel); lack of treatment and mismanagement of medication; causing squalor, lack of hygiene, insanitary condition, and services being cut off;

- **Self-harm:** e.g. from para-suicide, suicide attempts, cutting wrists, overdosing, reluctance or inability to self-care;

- **Verbal or oral harm:** e.g. from shouting, swearing, brow-beating, name calling;

- **Risk to health:** from abuse of alcohol or drugs, lack of treatment, from cold or hyperthermia; from poor diet and nutrition; causing illness and mental illness or relapse;

- **Risk to safety**: from frailty (falls), fire: from dropped cigarettes, cooker and fires; from wandering and traffic;

- **Risk to welfare:**, losing relationships; causing divorce, unemployment, homelessness; from abuse of powers (e.g. welfare power of attorney);

- **Risk to other persons**: to carers, family, children, e.g. lack of childcare or education, to public and neighbours; causing emotional harm, stress, fatigue, from behaviour (anti-social), sometimes sexual and physical harm;

- **Risk to rights:** civil and legal; to being protected; to education, independence, privacy, social contact, social inclusion, leisure, choice, control, friends, employment, ownership, freedom; from abuse, discrimination, inequality and stigma;

- **Institutional harm:** from dire care services, strict systems and regimes, poor standards and patterns of care; ill-treatment and neglect, omissions to act to protect;

- **General aspects or effects of harm:** from a crises or short term episode, from committing offences and falling into the criminal justice system, from a long term risk scenario, to harm being perpetrated in a particular way, or from bodies, persons or proxies, or persons promoting or facilitating the harm.

Appendix 3: Areas of Harm (Risk Domains)

Domains (type of harm)	Risk and harm aspects (from risk landscape)
Physical harm	e.g. physical assault, punching, grabbing, force feeding, starving, biting, use of weapons, domestic violence, etc
Financial Harm	e.g. theft, exploitation, extortion, misappropriation of funds or benefits, abuse of powers (e.g. continuing power of attorney), from imprudence (mental disorder), etc.
Material Harm	e.g. property: house, tenancy, inheritance; things: pets, cars, equipment, clothes, etc.
Sexual harm	e.g. sexual exploitation, assault, rape, sexual language, touching and trying to touch, arising from disinhibition, lack of insight, no consent or incapacity
Emotional harm	e.g. psychological, causing fear, alarm, distress, threats to adult and others, blackmail, belittling, excluding, undue pressure, tyranny, etc.
Welfare Harm	e.g. losing or damaging relationships, neglect of personal needs, unemployment, homelessness, abuse of welfare powers (e.g. welfare guardian), etc.
Rights Harm	e.g. civil and legal: protection, education, independence, liberty, privacy, social contact, freedoms, friends, choice, control, ownership, discrimination, inequality, stigma, etc.
Health Harm	e.g. deprivation of or lack of treatment, from illness and disease, from poor diet and nutrition, abuse of medication, from alcohol or drugs, etc.
Self Harm	e.g. from para-suicide, suicide attempt, cutting wrists, overdosing, reluctance or inability to self-care, etc.
Safety Harm	e.g. from fire: e.g. cookers, dropping cigarettes, fires; wandering, traffic, falls, etc.
Harm to Others	e.g. children (welfare, education, childcare); carers (physical, emotional, etc.), family, neighbours, public (from behaviour), sexual and physical harm, etc.
Institutional Harm	e.g. poor care services/providers, overly strict systems and regimes, neglect and ill-treatment, poor stands and quality of care, omission to protect, etc.

Appendix 4: Risk profile / types / examples / Acts

Risk	Type	Examples	Predominant Acts (secondary Acts)
from others	abuse / harm	targeted abuse	2007
	assault	physical, sexual, financial, psychological harm	2007
	offences	sexual offences and rape, etc	2007 (2003)
	neglect	not providing care	2007 (2003)
	deficiency in care / omissions to act	not acting to protect or safeguard a person with mental disorder	2007 (2003)
from self	self neglect or lack of care	lack of hygiene, not eating appropriately;	2003 (2007)
	behaviours (incapacity)	disinhibition, scratching, head hitting	2000
	harming	taking pills, cutting, parasuicide / suicide attempts	2003
to personal welfare	unable to self care	not looking after self, house, finances	2003 (2000)
	living alone without care	not looking after self, house, finances	2003 (2000)
	deficiency in care and treatment	poor or inadequate care provision	2003
	incapable in respect of	lack of capacity to act or make decisions about person welfare	2000 (2003)
to health	lack of treatment	medication /assessment / detention	2003 (2000)
to property and finances	not paying bills	lack of ability or capacity to manage finances	2000 (if incapable) (2003)
	abuse	theft, extortion, fraud, misappropriation of funds, etc	2007 (2000 if incapable)
to others	from behaviours	harming carers	2000 (if incapable) (2003)
	assault	posing harm to others	2003 (2000 if incapable)

Appendix 5: Harm, risk and relative powers across the Acts (all examples only)

Harm	Acts	Risk of	Warrants; access & entry; assessment	Removal	Emergency and short term powers	Long term orders
From others	2007 Act	Abuse; Assault;	Access and entry; Assessment order;	Removal order (SH or JOP);		Banning order;
	2003 Act	Neglect; Offence Assault	Access and entry; Assessment / medical examination;	s293/4 or 297;	Emergency or short term detention;	CTO; — Access; Residence;
	2000 Act	Personal welfare;				Welfare: W Guardianship; Finance: Part 3; F Guardianship;
From self	2007 Act	Harm;	Access and entry; Assessment order	Removal order (SH or JOP);		CTO;
	2003 Act	Self;	Access and entry; Assessment / medical examination;	s293/4 or 297;	Emergency or short term detention;	CTO;
	2000 Act	Neglect / personal welfare;				Finance: Part 3/ F Guardianship; Health: Part 5; Welfare: W Guardianship;
From lack of (or deficiency in) care or treatment; or neglect; or living alone and unable to care; unable to protect oneself	2007 Act	Unable to protect;	Access and entry; Assessment order;	Removal order (SH or JOP);		
	2003 Act	Unable to care;	Access and entry; Assessment / medical examination;	s293/4 or 297;	Emergency or short term detention;	CTO; — Access; Treatment / care; Residence;
	2000 Act	Personal welfare;				Health: Part 5; Welfare: W Guardianship;
To property and Finances	2007 Act	Financial Abuse;	Access and entry; Assessment order;			Banning order;
	2003 Act	Risk to;	Access and entry; Assessment;			
	2000 Act	Risk to;			Intervention Orders	F Guardianship; Funds & Accounts;
To Others	2007 Act	To carers;	Access and entry; Assessment order;	Removal order (SH or JOP);		
	2003 Act	From mental disorder;	Access and entry; Assessment / medical examination (incapacity?);	s293/4 or 297;	Emergency or short term detention;	CTO; — Treatment; Residence; Access;
	2000 Act	From Incapacity;				Welfare guardianship;

Appendix 6: Provision of support, care and treatment

	2003 Act	2000 Act	2007 Act	1968 / 1990 / 2002 Acts
Support	advocacy; MWC, LA, HB, MHTS duties; named person; MHOs; AMPs/RMOs; GPs	information and advice; OPG, LA, MWC, HB duties; MHOs; GPs; AMPs	access to services (advocacy): LA & HB duties; cooperation; Council Officer.	assessment and access to services; care management
Protection	duty to inquire; risk to health safety, welfare; (finance/property) offences by others	duty to inquire; welfare, property & finance powers and provisions; proxy powers; offences	duty to inquire; duty to report; cooperation; risk of harm from others and self; assessment, removal, banning orders; access to records; offences	duty of care (protection); care programme approach
Care	assessment; care and support services / promotion of well-being and social development; compulsory powers (CTO)	welfare guardian powers	access to services	in the community: at home / residential and nursing home care; carer assessment/ support; direct payment; care management; SSA; CPA
Treatment	for mental disorder; definition of medical treatment; informal and compulsory treatment (STD/CTO); advance statements	treatment for physical and mental health on a non-compulsory basis	medical examination	access to treatment following community care assessment; CPA

Appendix 7: The Links across the Acts

The 2003 Act	The 2000 Act	The 2007 Act
Accessing the 2003 Act, where persons affected by mental disorder have access to the provisions therein, relies on confirming the existence of 'mental disorder' defined under s328 as either: ☐ mental illness, ☐ personality disorder, or ☐ learning disability, ☐ or a combination of each however caused or manifested, but not just by reason of sexual orientation, sexual deviancy, transsexualism, transvestitism, dependence on, or use of, alcohol or drugs, behaviours that causes, or likely to cause, harassment, alarm or distress to any other person, or acting as no prudent person would act. The Act does not determine severity as a means to access its services nor does it require a test of risk; being affected by 'mental disorder' is enough.	Accessing the 2000 Act, where a person or an organisation acting on behalf of an 'adult with incapacity', is able to access the provisions of the Act relies on confirming an adult with incapacity, so defined in the Act (under s.1) as a person who has attained the age of 16, who is incapable of ☐ acting; or ☐ making decisions; or ☐ communicating decisions; or ☐ understanding decisions; or ☐ retaining the memory of decisions, in relation to any particular matter, by reason of mental disorder or of inability to communicate because of physical disability.	Accessing the 2007 Act, where an 'adult at risk' is confirmed as an adult, so defined (s.3), who is: a. unable to safeguard her/his own well-being, property, rights or other interests, b. at risk of harm, and c. because s/he is affected by disability, mental disorder, illness or physical or mental infirmity, is more vulnerable to being harmed than adults who are not so affected. An adult is at risk of harm for these purposes if another person's conduct is causing (or likely to cause) the harm or the adult is engaging (or likely to engage) in self harm. The term 'abuse' is not favoured within the Act. 'Harm' is, however, which includes all harmful conduct, including neglect and other failures to act and, in particular a) conduct which causes physical harm, b) conduct which causes psychological harm, c) unlawful conduct which appropriates or adversely affects property, rights of interests, and d) conduct which causes self-harm.

Appendix 8: Principles across the Acts

2003 Act	2000 Act	2007 Act
The principles of the 2003 Act need to be applied when protecting an adult with mental disorder within the formal provisions by having regard to:	There should be no intervention in the affairs of an adult unless the intervention the intervention will:	A person may intervene, or authorise intervention, only if satisfied the intervention:
a. the present / past wishes / feelings of patient, by any means of communication / in a way most likely to be understood;	a. benefit the adult and that such benefit cannot be reasonably achieved without the intervention; such intervention under the Act shall be the least restrictive	a. will provide benefit to the adult which could not reasonably be provided without intervening in the adult's affairs, and
b. the views of relevant others;	b. such intervention under the Act shall be the least restrictive option in relation to the freedom of the adult, consistent with the purpose of the intervention;	b. is, of the range of options likely to fulfil the object of the intervention, the least restrictive to the adult's freedom.
c. ensuring the patient's participation in the discharge of the function;		Where a public body or officeholder performs a function under the Act, have regard to:
d. providing information and support of patient to participate; considering a range of options; providing maximum benefit;	c. where intervention is to be made, account shall be taken of the present and past wishes and feelings of the adult;	a. the adult's ascertainable wishes and feelings
e. ensuring equality;	d. where intervention is to be made, account shall be taken of the views of others;	b. views of nearest relative primary carer, guardian / attorney; others with an interest;
f. respecting diversity;	e. where the proxy must encourage the adult to exercise whatever skills he/she has; and the development of new skills.	c. the adult participating as fully as possible in the performance of the function,
g. discharging in a manner that involves minimum restriction (where subject to compulsion);		d. providing the adult with such information and support as is necessary to participate
h. considering the needs and circumstances of the patient's carer;		e. adult not to be treated less favourably than any other in a comparable situation;
i. having regard to provision of appropriate services and continuing care;		f. the adult's abilities, background and characteristics.
j. best securing the welfare of the child.		

Appendix 9: Duty to Inquire across the Acts

The 2003 Act	The 2000 Act	The 2007 Act
The 2003 Act places a duty on a local authority to inquire into the circumstances of a person, where it appears that the person is aged 16 or over has a mental disorder and is living in the community, and any of the following circumstances apply: a. where that person may be or may have been, subject, or exposed, to ill treatment, neglect or some other deficiency in care or treatment; b. that because of mental disorder, the persons property may be, or may have suffered loss or damage, or may be, or may have been at risk of suffering loss or damage; c. that the person may be living alone or without care; and unable to look after himself or his property or financial affairs; d. that because of mental disorder the safety of some other person may be at risk. (s33: 2003 Act)	The 2000 Act imposes on the local authority the function to investigate any circumstances made known to it where the personal welfare of an adult (incapable under section 1) seems to be at risk. This is to ascertain whether there is any need to take action either under the 2000 Act or otherwise to safeguard the personal welfare of the adult. This deals with situations where the adult is found to have impaired capacity (because of mental disorder) and there is risk to personal welfare. (s10: 2000 Act) The duty to inquire and to act under the 2000 Act may be applied where the adult's personal welfare is in jeopardy or where the adult, impaired by incapacity, needs support and protection, e.g. an adult a. whose living circumstances has deteriorated or is at risk of harm from others, (e.g. financial or sexual exploitation); b. is at risk from poor safety and security, e.g. wandering, mismanaging cookers, fires, etc.; c. is being neglected or ill treated; or d. has a proxy misusing powers against them under the Act.	The 2007 Act places a duty on the Council to make inquiries about a person's well-being, property or financial affairs if a. it knows or believes that the person is an adult (aged 16 or over) at risk of harm and b. it might need to intervene in order to protect the adult's well-being, property or financial affairs. (s4: 2007 Act) An adult is an adult at risk under this Act, where all of the following 3 sets of circumstances apply: a. the adult is unable to safeguard her/his own well-being, property, rights or other interests; b. the adult is at risk of harm, where harm includes all harmful conduct (which includes neglect and other failures to act) and, in particular conduct which causes c. physical harm; d. conduct which causes psychological harm (for example by causing fear, alarm or distress); e. unlawful conduct which appropriates or adversely affects property, rights of interests (for example theft, fraud, embezzlement or extortion); f. conduct which causes self-harm.); and g. the adult, because s/he is affected by disability, mental disorder, illness or physical or mental infirmity, is more vulnerable to being harmed than adults who are not so affected. (s3(1): 2007 Act) The adult is at risk of harm for these purposes if: a. another person's conduct is causing (or is likely to cause) the adult to be harmed or b. the adult is engaging (or is likely to engage) in conduct which causes (or is likely to cause) self-harm. (s3(2): 2007 Act)

Appendix 10: Duty to Inquire criteria across the Acts

	1	2	3	4	5	Confirm
2003 Act	where it appears a) person is aged 16 or over	b) has mental disorder living in the community	may be or may have been subject, or exposed to ill treatment neglect some other deficiency in care or treatment living alone or without care	property at risk or has suffered loss or damage unable to look after property or financial affairs	safety of some other person may be at risk	*1,2 and either 3, 4 or 5*
2007 Act	known or believed an adult intervention may be necessary to protect	adult is unable to safeguard her/his own well-being property rights other interests	at risk of harm (as defined under section 53 of 2007 Act)	being affected by disability mental disorder illness physical or mental infirmity are more vulnerable to being harmed than adults who are not so affected	where another person's conduct is causing the adult's harm or likely to adult is engaging in conduct which causes likely to cause self-harm	*All 2,3,4 (the 3 point test)*
2000 Act	circumstances made known to local authority	impaired capacity (mental disorder)	need to take action to safeguard the personal welfare of the adult	personal welfare of an adult seems to be at risk		*2, 3*

Appendix 11: Investigations across the Acts

	Investigations	
2003 Act	**2000 Act** General	**2007 Act**
Purpose of investigation **Where the local authority have established there is a duty to inquire** Where the local authority considers that assistance from 'specified persons' is necessary or would assist in their inquiries under section 33, this allows the authority to request that assistance from those specified in the section. This includes the Mental Welfare Commission, the Public Guardian, the Scottish Commission for the Regulation of Care, and the local NHS Board and Service. The 'person' shall comply which this request. (s34) Under section 317, sanctions apply to any failure to comply with the Act. A person commits an **offence** where he/she: refuses to allow a person authorised access to any premises; refuses to allow access to a mentally disordered person by a person authorised to have such access; refuses to allow the interview or examination of a mentally disordered person by a person authorised to interview or examine such person; persists in being present when requested to withdraw by a person authorised to interview or examine, in private, a mentally disordered person; refuses to produce any document or record or record to require the production of such document or record; or otherwise obstructs a person in the exercise of any functions conferred on them by virtue of this Act The patient themselves will not have committed an offence should they do any of the above. (S37 and 07 chp15 COP vol1) The steps resulting from the duty to inquire could alternatively involve a wide range of voluntary or compulsory interventions. For example, care and support under the Social Work (Scotland) Act 1968 may be provided on an informal basis. Intervention under the Adults with Incapacity (Scotland) Act 2000 might also need to be considered. If intervention under the 2003 Act is required, consideration of an emergency or short-term detention certificate or even an application for a CTO may be appropriate.	**Purpose of investigation** The **purpose of the investigation** is to ascertain whether there is any need to take action either under the 2000 Act or otherwise to safeguard the personal welfare of the adult. This deals with situations where the adult is found to have impaired capacity. It is possible that an investigation could find that the adult's capacity is not impaired in relation to the cause for concern, but is vulnerable for some other reason, for example physical infirmity or mental illness. The code does not deal with the action required where the adult is at risk for some other reason than incapacity as defined by the 2000 Act. In such circumstances, intervention under the 2007 Act or 2003 Act will need to be considered. Where an adult may lack capacity due to mental disorder an intervention under the 2003 Act may be appropriate. The duty social worker will need to make an assessment of which route will be most appropriate. To receive and investigate any complaints about the exercise of functions relating to the personal welfare of an adult made in relation to welfare attorneys, guardians or persons authorised under intervention orders. The investigation of complaints is a matter for local procedure. There is statutory obligation to **co-operate** with the local authority in respect of inquiry. However, there is responsibility on Councils, the Commissions and the Public Guardian, to consult and co-operate in certain cases, e.g. respective inquiries. (LA code of practice [check]) Under section 83 of the 2000 Act it is an **offence** for any person exercising powers under the 2000 Act relating to the personal welfare of an individual to ill -treat or wilfully neglect him/her. The offence is punishable on summary conviction to a fine not exceeding £5000 or a term of imprisonment not exceeding 6 months, and on indictment to a fine or a term of imprisonment not exceeding 2 years. The duty of the local authority to investigate circumstances where the personal welfare of an adult appears to be at risk is a statutory function under the 2000 Act. In cases which indicate that urgent action is needed to protect the person from harm, then action may be taken under the 2003 or the 2007Act as appropriate. (Chap 9 COP) If the adult has capacity, but is at risk, the 2000 Act is not able to offer any assistance. The officer should consider what other social work or medical interventions can be offered and should follow local procedures with regard to adults in need of support and protection, i.e. on the use of the 2003 or 2007 Acts. In cases where the 2003 Act appears to be relevant, the investigating officer should consult a MHO if he/she is not one, and liaise with appropriate medical practitioners	**Purpose of investigation ...** Where public bodies and office holders, so far as consistent with the proper exercise of their functions, must **cooperate** with a Council making an inquiry under section 4 and with each other, where such cooperation is likely to enable or assist the Council making the inquiry, under section 4. Public bodies include all Councils, the Commissions stated above, the Public Guardian, chief constables of the police forces and relevant Health Board. (s5) A Council officer may **enter** any place for the purpose of enabling or assisting a Council conducting inquiries under section 4 to decide whether it needs to do anything (by performing functions under this Part or otherwise) in order to protect an adult at risk from harm. (s7 (1)). A Council officer, and any person accompanying the officer, may interview, in private, any adult found in a place being visited under section 7. (s8(1)) Where (a) a Council officer finds a person whom the officer knows or believes to be an adult at risk in a place being visited under section 7, and (b) the officer, or any person accompanying the officer, is a health professional, that health professional may conduct a private **medical examination** of the person.(s9 (1)) A Council officer may require any person holding health, financial or other **records** relating to an individual whom the officer knows or believes to be an adult at risk to give the records, or copies of them, to the officer. Such a requirement may be made during a visit or at any other time. Requirements made at such other times must be made in writing. (s10) Section 49 provides that it is an **offence** to **prevent or obstruct** any person from doing anything they are authorised or entitled to do under the Act. It is also an offence to refuse, without reasonable excuse, to comply with a request to provide information made under Section 10 (examination of records etc). However if the adult at risk prevents or obstructs a person, or refuses to comply with a request to provide access to any records, then the adult will not have committed an offence. Where the person has a mental disorder, action under the Mental Health (Care and Treatment) (Scotland) Act 2003 may be appropriate. Where a person has impaired capacity, an order or the appointment of a proxy under the Adults with Incapacity (Scotland) Act 2000 may be appropriate. It may be that it would be appropriate to provide care and support under the Social Work (Scotland) Act 1968. In some cases, particularly in those where the adult has capacity, assistance may be provided to the adult by, for example, ensuring that they have access to suitable advice and support, should they wish to access it. (10 ch4 COP)

Appendix 12: Entry and Assessment

2003 Act	2007 Act

Warrants of entry, to detain, access to medical records
The 2003 Act makes further provision in relation to inquiries by providing a warrant, that may only be sought by a relevant MHO, if it is thought that entry to premises, access to medical records, or a medical examination, are/is necessary and access has been or is likely to be denied. However, this warrant does not authorise the removal of the person at risk to a place of safety. (s35)
 	
There are three separate warrants which can be issued:
 	
    A warrant to enter premises, where it is necessary to enter premises for the purposes of pursuing the local authority's duty to inquire(s35(1)); or/and
 	
The Sheriff or Justice of the Peace must grant a warrant where he/she is satisfied that the MHO's application meets the following conditions: it is necessary to enter the premises for the purposes of pursuing the local authority's duty to inquire; and the MHO cannot obtain entry to the premises or reasonably believes that he/she will not be able to access the premises. (COP 22 chap 15)
 	
    A warrant to detain a person; pending, and for the purpose of carrying out a medical examination, for a period of up to 3 hours(s35 (4)); or/and
 	
Where an application is made on these grounds, the Sheriff or the Justice of the Peace must grant the warrant where he/she is satisfied that: it is necessary for a medical practitioner to carry out a medical examination of the person who is the subject of the local authority's duty to inquire; and the MHO cannot obtain the consent of that person to the medical examination. (COP 26 chap 15)
 	
    A warrant to gain access to a person's medical records for a medical practitioner. (s35(7))
 	
Where an application is made on these grounds, the Sheriff or Justice of the Peace must grant the warrant where he/she is satisfied that: it is necessary for a medical practitioner to have access to the person's medical records; and the MHO cannot obtain the consent of that person to accessing their medical records. (COP 29 chap 15)
	Warrant for entry
	A warrant for entry may be granted by a Sheriff for entry where is satisfied that a Council officer has been, or reasonably expects to be refused entry or otherwise will be unable to enter; or any attempt by a Council officer to visit the place without such a warrant would defeat the object of the visit. A warrant for entry granted by a Sheriff expires 72 hours after it has been granted. Once a warrant has been executed, it cannot be used again. (s37)
	
	The warrant authorises a Council officer to visit any place specified in the warrant, accompanied by a constable. The accompanying constable may use reasonable force where necessary to fulfil the object of the visit. This may include the constable opening lock-fast places, therefore it would be expected that the Council would take all reasonable steps to ensure the security of the person's premises and belongings if force has been required to enter the premises. Wherever possible, entry to premises should first be attempted without force.
	
	Urgent cases
	An urgent case application for a warrant for entry may be made to a Justice of the Peace if it is impracticable to make the application to the Sheriff and that an adult at risk is likely to be harmed if there is any delay in granting the warrant. A warrant for entry granted by a Justice of the Peace expires 12 hours after it has been granted. Once a warrant has been executed, it cannot be used again. (s40 (1b))
	
	Assessment order
	The Council may make an application to a Sheriff for an assessment order to help the Council to decide whether the person is an adult at risk and to take an adult at risk of serious harm to a more suitable place to allow a Council officer or Council nominee to conduct a private interview. The order also provides that a health professional may carry out a medical examination in private. The order gives a warrant for entry.
	
	The Sheriff must be satisfied that the Council has reasonable cause to suspect the subject of the order is an adult at risk who is being, or is likely to be, seriously harmed; the order is required to establish whether the person is an adult at risk who is being, or is likely to be, seriously harmed. The order is valid for up to seven days; however, it is expected that the assessment would be carried out in the shortest possible time. (s11)

Appendix 13: Warrants and removal criteria across the 2003 and 2007 Acts

For the purposes of inquiry (s35) (where it appears: person is aged 16 or over ... has mental disorder ... living in the community ... may be or may have been ... subject, or exposed ... to ill treatment ... neglect ... some other deficiency in care or treatment ...; property at risk or has suffered loss or damage ... living alone or without care ... unable to look after property or financial affairs ... safety of some other person may be at risk) it is necessary to enter premises ...

the MHO will be unable (or reasonably apprehends) to obtain entry to those premises (s35[1]) ...

necessary that a medical practitioner carry out a medical examination ... consent not available to the MHO (s35 [4]); ...

necessary a medical practitioner has access to a person's medical records ... consent not available to the MHO (s35[7]).

Where it is necessary to remove to a place of safety (s293) a person, aged 16 or over, who has mental disorder...subject, or exposed ... to ill treatment ... neglect ... some other deficiency in care or treatment ...;because of mental disorder the person's property is at risk or has suffered loss or damage ... person is living alone or without care ...unable to look after property or financial affairs

Where application to the Sheriff is impracticable (s294)...any delay would be prejudicial to the person...application may be made to a Justice of the Peace.

Where the police may take person to a place of safety (s297) ...if that person is in a public place...appears to be mentally disordered... in immediate need of care or treatment... in the interests of the person ... necessary for the protection of any other person...to allow a medical practitioner ...to examine the person ... to make arrangements for care and treatment.

Where it is known or believed an adult is at risk of harm and intervention may be necessary to protect (s4)...;adult is unable to safeguard her/his own well-being...property... rights...other interests ... where another person's conduct is causing the adult's harm .... or likely to ... adult is engaging ... likely to ... in conduct which causes ... likely to cause... self -harm .. harm includes ... all harmful conduct ... conduct which causes physical harm ... conduct which causes psychological harm ... fear, alarm or distress ... unlawful conduct which appropriates or adversely affects property, rights of interests ... theft, fraud, embezzlement or extortion ... conduct which causes self-harm ... affected by disability ... mental disorder ... illness ... physical or mental infirmity ... more vulnerable to being harmed than adults who are not so affected.

warrant of entry...application to Sheriff (s37)...only Council can appl ... Council officer has been, or reasonably expects to be refused entry or otherwise will be unable to enter...any attempt by a Council officer to visit the place without such a warrant would defeat the object of the visit.

warrant for entry ... application to a Justice of the Peace. (s40[1b])... where impracticable to make the application to the Sheriff ... adult at risk is likely to be harmed if delay.

removal order ...application to a Justice of the Peace. (s40[1a1] ... where not practicable to make application to the Sheriff ... adult at risk is likely to be harmed if delay ...order cannot be made if adult withholds consent. Unless adult is under undue pressure to refuse consent or ... lacks capacity to consent ... where undue pressure does not apply.

Appendix 14: Removal Provisions and Powers

	Removal Orders	
2003 Act	**2000 Act**	**2007 Act**
	General	
The 2003 Act offers the most substantive range of emergency and short provision to protect adults at risk affected by mental disorder. The Act does not rely on consent of the adult nor does the adult need to lack capacity. The Act, however, lack powers against harmers.	Although the 2000 Act does not expressly provide for urgent action, the investigating officer may consider that an intervention order or interim guardianship should immediately be sought. (9.14 LA COP)	The 2007 Act offers the primary framework for protecting adults at risk. It lacks robust emergency powers, however, especially where the adult withholds consent to action or is incapable because of mental disorder.
	Removal	
Removal to a place of safety	**Removal of incapable adult**	**Removal of an adult at risk to a 'suitable place'.**
Removal from a private place

A removal order may be sought by a MHO to a Sheriff for the removal of the adult at risk to a place of safety for up to seven days. The need for the order may stem from a section 33 inquiry, where access to the person has been achieved in the context of local authority duties or from the use of section 35 warrants. If there is sufficient information which suggests the person needs and risks are such to move directly to a removal order instead of using warrants under section 35, the MHO may proceed directly to obtain this order. The removal order authorises the MHO specified in the order, any other person so specified, and any constable of the relevant police force, to remove the person at risk to a place of safety specified in the order. The removal order only authorises entry to the patient's premises and the patient's removal to a place of safety. It does not permit access to a patient's medical records nor does it permit detention for the purpose of carrying out a medical examination. (s293)

Removal from a public place

The police may take a person to a place of safety if a person is in a public place and appears to be mentally disordered and in immediate need of care or treatment and where they consider that it would be in the interests of the person or necessary for the protection of any other person to remove the person to a place of safety. The person may be detained there for a period of up to 24 hours. The purpose of this detention is to allow a medical practitioner to examine the person and to make arrangements for their care and treatment. Arrangements should be in place to ensure that police officers can rapidly ascertain the location of designated places of safety. (s297)

Warrant to enter premises for purposes of taking patient

A warrant is available to allow a person to enter premises where that person has already been given authority under another section of the Act or associated regulations to take (or retake) a patient to any place or into custody. (s292) | Although the 2000 Act does not expressly provide for urgent action to remove an incapable adult, some authorities, however, have been able to pursue and obtain welfare guardianship orders on a fast track basis, in some cases obtaining either interim or full powers to protect an adult at risk. This requires speedy access to assessments and reports, and efficient collaborative working. Where the person has a mental disorder, the 2003 Act would allow local authorities to seek an order for the immediate removal of the adult to a place of safety for a prescribed period. **Intervention orders** and **Interim welfare guardianship** powers may also be used in this context (see below).

....

Place of safety (2003 Act)

A **place of safety** is defined as: a) a hospital; b) premises which are used for the purpose of providing a care home service (as defined in section 2(3) of the Regulation of Care (Scotland) Act 2001 (asp 8)); or c) any other suitable place (other than a police station) the occupier of which is willing temporarily to receive a mentally disordered person.

Suitable place (2007 Act)

Assessment Order: This may in some circumstances require written confirmation from the person who owns or manages this place that they are willing to receive the adult for assessment purposes. For example, the place could be a friend's or relative's house or a care home. The suitability of the place to conduct a private examination could also be confirmed in writing. This would be desirable but it may not always be practicable in potentially urgent or emergency situations (19; COP chap9). **Removal Order:** Good practice would be that the Council provides a suitability report of both the place and the person willing to care for the adult at risk and also obtain a written agreement from the owner of the proposed specified place where it is for example, a private home or independent care provider to confirm the owner's willingness to receive the adult at risk for up to 7 days. The place to which the adult should be taken will be specified in the order and the adult must only be taken to the place specified on the order; however there may be circumstances where, before the order is executed, the adult consents to being taken to another place. (22; Chap 10) | **Urgent removal to a suitable place**

An adult at risk may be removed urgently to a suitable place on an application by a Council to a Justice of the Peace where it is not practicable to make application to the Sheriff; and the adult at risk is likely to be harmed if there is any delay in granting the order. The Justice of the Peace must be satisfied that the person is an adult at risk who is likely to be seriously harmed if not moved to another place and that the adult is to be removed to a place that is suitable and available. The adult at risk must be removed within 12 hours of the grant of the removal order and the order expires after 24 hours. (s40 (1a))

A removal order cannot be made by the Sheriff if the adult withholds consent, unless a) the adult is under undue pressure to refuse consent or b) where the adult lacks capacity to consent (evidence provided), where the need to establish undue pressure does not apply. (s35 (1))

Removal to a suitable place

A Council may apply to the Sheriff for a removal order which authorises a Council officer, or any Council nominee, to move a specified person to a specified place within 72 hours of the order being made, and the Council to take such reasonable steps as it thinks fit for the purpose of protecting the moved person from harm. A removal order expires 7 days (or such shorter period as may be specified in the order) after the day on which the specified person is moved in pursuance of the order. The Sheriff may grant a removal order only if satisfied that the person in respect of whom the order is sought is an adult at risk who is likely to be seriously harmed if not moved to another place, and as to the availability and suitability of the place to which the adult at risk is to be moved. (s14) |

Appendix 15: welfare guardianship, compulsory treatment orders and banning orders

Provision	Grounds	Provides	Powers
Welfare Guardianship	Mental disorder and incapacity: ☐ of acting; ☐ or of making, ☐ or communicating, ☐ or understanding, ☐ or retaining the memory, of decisions. Necessity Where the principles applied	Care and welfare (under direction) Treatment (without compulsion)	As requested by the applicant and granted by the Sheriff; for example, to: ☐ Decide where adult should live; ☐ Apply for community care assessment; ☐ Manage a direct payment; ☐ Access to personal information; ☐ Consent medical treatment; ☐ Pursue legal action (welfare); ☐ Make decisions on the adults dress, diet and personal appearance; ☐ Make decision on social and cultural activities; ☐ Arrange adult to undertake work, education or training; ☐ Decide with whom the adult should or not consent; etc
Compulsory Treatment Order	☐ Mental disorder; ☐ and because of this, inability to make decision about treatment is significantly impaired; ☐ significant risk to health, safety or welfare of patient, or safety of others; ☐ non compliance / necessity; ☐ availability and benefit of treatment. Where the principles are applied	Care and Treatment (medical and care). Informal and under compulsion	As requested by the MHO applicant and granted by the Mental Health Tribunal (can either be a hospital or community based order). ☐ The detention in hospital ☐ Giving of medical treatment ☐ Attendance for medical treatment; ☐ Attendance for community care services, relevant services, etc; ☐ Residence in a specified place; ☐ Access where the patient resides; ☐ Informing/getting permission from the MHO on residence.
Banning Order	☐ Where an adult at risk is being, or is likely to be, seriously harmed by another person; ☐ That the adult at risk's well-being or property would be better safeguarded by banning that other person from a place occupied by the adult than it would be by moving the adult from that place; and ☐ That either (i) the adult at risk is entitled, or permitted by a third party, or (ii) neither the adult at risk nor the subject is entitled, or permitted by a third party, to occupy the place from which the subject is to be banned. ☐ Where the principles are applied.	Protection against a harmer (a subject)	☐ Which bans the subject from being in a specified place; *the order may also:* * ban the subject from being in a specified area in the vicinity of the specified place * authorise the summary ejection of the subject from the specified place and the specified area * prohibit the subject from moving any specified thing from the specified place * direct any specified person to take specified measures to preserve any moveable property owned or controlled by the subject which remains in the specified place while the order has effect * to be made subject to any specified conditions * require or authorise any person to do, or to refrain from doing, anything else which the Sheriff thinks necessary for the proper enforcement of the order. ☐ A condition specified in a banning order may, in particular, authorise the subject to be in the place or area from which the subject is banned in specified circumstances (for example, while being supervised by another person or during specified times).

Appendix 16: Powers and Provisions across the Acts

Type	The Power of Provision	Act	Section	Who applies	Who grants
Inquiry (investigation)	To cause inquiries to be made	2003	S33	Local Authority	Local Authority
	To make inquiries about wellbeing, property or financial affairs	2007	S4	Council	Local Authority
	To investigate any circumstances: personal welfare at risk	2000	S1	Local Authority	Local Authority
Cooperation (inquiry)	To provide assistance to local authority	2003	S34	Local Authority	Health Board and Trust, MWC, OPG, SCRG
	To cooperate with Council & each other	2007	S5	Local Authority	Public bodies and Office Holders
	Warrant for entry	2003	S35 (1)	MHO	Sheriff or Justice of the Peace
	Warrant for entry	2007	S37	Council	Sheriff
	Warrant for entry	2007	S40 (1b))	Council	Justice of the Peace (impracticable /delay to apply to Sheriff)
	Warrant to medically examine	2003	S35 (4)	MHO	Sheriff or Justice of the Peace
	Warrant to access medical records	2003	S35 (7)	MHO	Sheriff or Justice of the Peace
	Removal to a place of safety	2003	S293	MHO	Sheriff
	Removal to a place of safety	2003	S294	MHO	Justice of the Peace (impracticable / delay to apply to Sheriff)
Immediate Powers	Warrant to enter and remove patient	2003	S292	Authorised Person	Sheriff or Justice of the Peace
	Removal from public place	2003	S297	A constable	A constable
	Assessment Order	2007	S11	Council	Sheriff
	Removal Order (Urgent Cases)	2007	S40 (1a)	Council	Justice of the Peace (impracticable /delay to apply to Sheriff)
	Emergency detention to/in hospital	2003	S36	To a GP	Medical Practitioner (with MHO consent, unless impracticable)
	Removal Order	2007	S14	Council	Sheriff
	Short term detention	2003	S44	Applicant to a AMP	Approved medical practitioner (with MHO consent)
	Intervention Order	2000	S53	Local Authority / others	Sheriff
Short Term Powers	Interim Compulsory Treatment Order	2003	S65	Applicant	Mental Health Tribunal for Scotland
	Interim Guardianship	2000	S57	Local Authority / others	Sheriff
	Temporary Banning Order	2007	S21	Council / others	Sheriff
	Guardianship (welfare / financial)	2000	S57	Local Authority / others	Sheriff
Long Term Powers	Compulsory Treatment Order	2003	S63	MHO (AMP)	Mental Health Tribunal for Scotland
	Banning Order	2007	S19	Council / others	Sheriff
Supportive provisions	Assessment of needs	1990	S55	Applicant	Local Authority
	Assessment of needs	2003	S227	MHO	Local Authority
	Request for an assessment of need	2003	S228	Application in writing	Local Authority and Health Board
	Authority for Accounts and Funds	2000	Part 3	Applicant	Office of the Public Guardian
	Medical Treatment	2000	Part 5	Applicant	Medical Practitioner

Appendix 17: The Links across the Acts

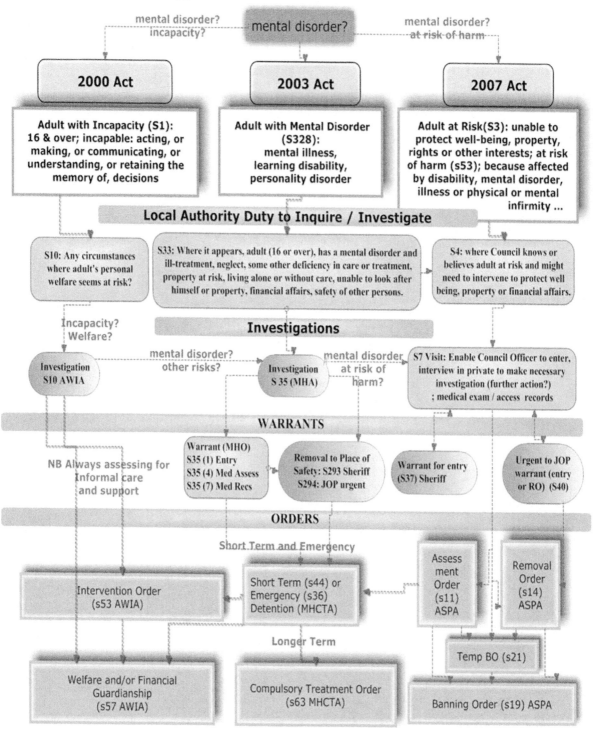

Appendix 18: The Inter-relationships of the Acts

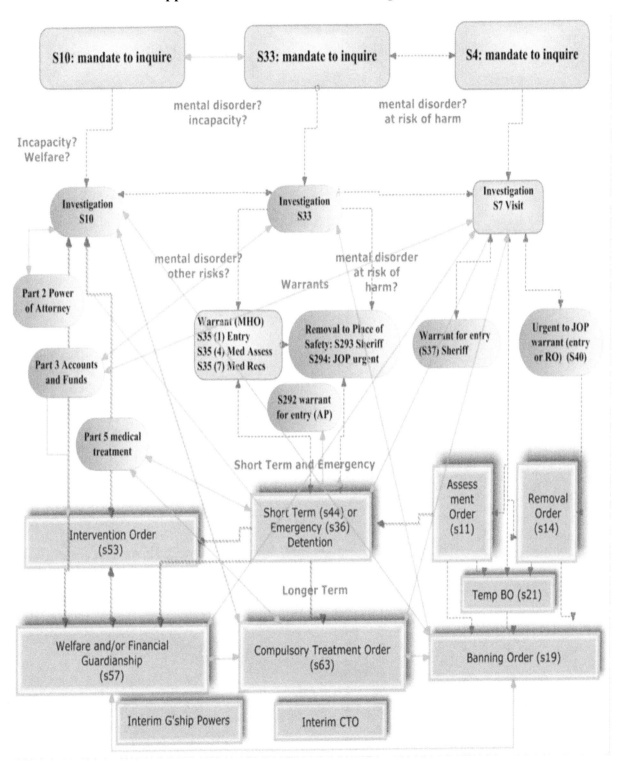

Appendix 19: To Prepare a Legislative Design

Risk (for example)	Power (for example)	ACT	Provision (for example)	Task / purpose (for example)
Risk of self harm, e.g. parasuicide	To require adult to attend for treatment	2003	CTO (community)	To improve mental health / treat mental illness
RTisk to others, e.g. from paranoia	To admit adult to hospital for treatment	2003	Short term detention / Emergency detention	To treat under compulsion
Risk to health, e.g. an incaoable adult with a physical or mental illness who needs treatment.	To authorise treatment	2000	Part 5	To treat physical health problems / mental illness
Risk from financial exploitation, e.g. misusing and incapable adults funds.	To authorise the management of funds	2000	Part 3	To protect finances
Risk to health and welfare, e.g. from neglect.	To access (and enter premises) in emergency	2003	Warrant of entry under S35 (1)	To assess
Risk to health, e.g. need for medical treatment for mental disorder.	To medical examine	2003	Warrant to medically examine under S35 (4)	To establish mental disorder and need for treatment
Rrisk from a harmer, e.g. where the harmers prevents access.	To access to assess	2007	Warrant for entry to premises under s37 (Sheriff) or s40 (JOP)	To establish if adult at risk
Risk to welfare, e.g. incapable adult is refusing required services.	To access adult (long term)	2000	Welfare Guardianship	To monitor health and welfare
Risk to mental health, e.g. refusing access to RMO / CPN.	To access adult (long term)	2003	CTO (community)	To monitor mental disorder
Risk to health and safety, e.g. ill-treatment or neglect.	To remove to a place of safety	2003	S293 (Sheriff) S294 (JOP)	To protect adult at risk
Risk from others, e.g. a harmer is not allowing access to the adult or environment isn't suitable for medical examination.	To require the adult to transfer to a suitable place for assessment	2007	Assessment order (S11)	Remove to assess or medically examine in a suitable place
Risk from others, e.g. where the adult needs to be removed to protect him/her from significant harm.	To require the adult to transfer to a suitable place for protection	2007	Removal order (S14) (Sheriff) Urgent Removal Order (s40) (Just of the Peace)	Remove to protect
Risk arising from mental illness, e.g. to protect the adult from ncn compliance of medication, self harm or harm to others.	To require the adult to reside in another place for treatment	2003	CTO (community)	To improve mental health and health
Risk to welfare, e.g. an incapable adult who lacks ability to live at home is at risk from others.	To require the adult to reside in another place for care	2000	Welfare Guardianship	To protect health and welfare (and safety)
Risk to health and welfare, e.g. cannot desist from the use of alcohol to the detriment to health and safety.	To require adult to refrain from alcohol/drug use	2000	Welfare Guardianship	To improve health and welfare (and safety)
Risk to welfare, e.g. adult needs ongoing and daily community care supports.	To require adult to attend community care services	2003	CTO (community)	To develop skills and abilities /access leisure & recreation
Risk to an incapable adult's welfare, e.g. an incapable adult needs daily support to improve skills and abilites	To require adult to attend day care	2000	Welfare Guardianship	To improve skills and abilites
Risk form others, e.g. an incapable adult who needs not to allow a-cess to a harmer to his/her house	To require adult not to consort with another	2000	Welfare Guardianship	To protect health and welfare of adult at risk
Risk to finances or/and property, e.g. large financial estates or house or property are at risk from others.	To manage adult's financial estate / property	2000	Financial Guardianship	To protect finances/ property of adult
Risk from a harmers, e.g. a harmers is physically abusing an adult at risk.	To require subject of banning order not to be in adult's house & subject to conditions	2007	Banning order (S19) on named subject(s)	To protect adult at risk

Appendix 20: The criteria across the Acts

2003 Act — Short term, emergency, long term powers

Criteria	STDC	EDC	CTO
The patient has a **mental disorder**	✓	✓	✓
Because of the mental disorder, the patient's ability to make decisions about the provision of medical treatment is significantly impaired	✓	✓	✓
Medical treatment which would be likely to prevent the disorder worsening or alleviate any of the symptoms, or effects, of the disorder, is available		✓	✓
It is necessary to detain the patient in hospital for the purpose of determining what medical treatment should be given to the patient or giving medical treatment to the patient;	✓		
If the patient were not detained in hospital there would be a significant risk to the health, safety or welfare of the patient or to the safety of any other person	✓		
If the patient were provided with such medical treatment there would be a significant risk to the health, safety or welfare of the patient or to the safety of any other person			✓
The granting of a short-term detention certificate is necessary.	✓		
It is necessary as a matter of urgency to detain the patient in hospital in order to determine what medical treatment requires to be provided;		✓	
making arrangements with a view to granting a short-term detention certificate would involve undesirable delay.	✓		
Where the medical practitioner has consulted a MHO and s/he has consented to the detention	✓		✓
Unless it has been impracticable to do so		✓	
The making of the compulsory treatment order is necessary			✓

2000 Act — Intervention or Guardianship Orders

a. An adult (who has attained the age of 16)

b. Who is incapable (by reason of **mental disorder** [or inability to communicate because of physical disability]) of

- acting (to protect themselves from risk to their welfare, finances or property); or
- making decisions (where the lack of decision making capacity places the adult's welfare, finances or property at risk); or
- Communicating decisions (where the lack of ability to communicate decisions places the adult's welfare, finances or property at risk) or
- understanding decisions (where the lack of ability to understand decisions places the adult's welfare, finances or property at risk); or
- Retaining the memory of decisions (where the lack of retention of memory of decisions places the adult's welfare, finances or property at risk).

Where the Sheriff confirms:

a. an 'adult with incapacity' is at risk to their welfare, finances or property;

b. the order is necessary (and there are no other means under the Act) and the proposed intervener/guardian (excepting the local authority) is suitable to protect the adult's welfare, finances, or property; and

c. the principles apply; e.g. management of risk is a benefit to the adult and is of the least restrictive option in relation to the freedom of the adult.

2007 Act — Protection Orders

Adults at risk are adults who

a. are unable to safeguard their own well-being, property, rights or other interests, and

b. are at risk of harm (which includes all harmful conduct and, in particular, includes i) conduct which causes physical harm, ii) conduct which causes psychological harm, iii) unlawful conduct which appropriates or adversely affects property, rights or interests, and iv) conduct which causes self-harm); and

c. because they are affected by disability, **mental disorder**, illness or physical or mental infirmity, are more vulnerable to being harmed than adults who are not so affected.

An adult is at risk of harm if

a. another person's conduct is causing (or is likely to cause) the adult to be harmed, or

b. the adult is engaging (or is likely to engage) in conduct which causes (or is likely to cause) self-harm

Assessment order, which the Sheriff may grant only if satisfied

a. that the Council has reasonable cause to suspect that the person in respect of whom the order is sought is an adult at risk who is being, or is likely to be, seriously harmed,

b. that the assessment order is required in order to establish whether the person is an adult at risk who is being, or is likely to be, seriously harmed, and

c. as to the availability and suitability of the place at which the person is to be interviewed and examined.

Removal order, which the Sheriff may grant only if satisfied

a. that the person in respect of whom the order is sought is an adult at risk who is likely to be seriously harmed if not moved to another place, and

b. as to the availability and suitability of the place to which the adult at risk is to be moved

Banning order, which the Sheriff may grant only if satisfied

a. that an adult at risk is being, or is likely to be, seriously harmed by another person,

b. that the adult at risk's well-being or property would be better safeguarded by banning that other person from a place occupied by the adult than it would be by moving the adult from that place, and

c. that either the adult at risk is entitled, or permitted by a third party, or neither the adult at risk nor the subject is entitled, or permitted by a third party, to occupy the place from which the subject is to be banned.

Appendix 21: An 'across the Acts' criteria assessment

Across the Acts: The Acts' criteria assessment	Tick v	2003 Act							2007 Act					2000 Act		
1. Tick which aspect(s) applies; 2. Go across to see which provision(s) applies, then 3. Go up and down the provision(s) to see what other aspects of the provision(s) need to apply to obtain the provision(s); then 4. Agree and pursue the provision(s).		S33 Inq	S 35	S2 93 RO	S2 97 RO	S 36 ED C	S4 STD	CT O	S4 Inq	S 11 AO	S 14 RO	S 19 BO	S 37 S40 1b	S 10 Inv	S 57 WG	S 57 IG
Mental Disorder (Police: reasonably suspects; Sheriff: where satisfied)		*		*	*	*	*	*	*	*	*	*			*	*
Over 16		*		*	*	*	*	*	*	*	*	*		*	*	*
Incapable (decisions / actions)														*	*	*
Personal welfare of an adult at risk														*	*	*
Ill-treatment, neglect, deficiency in care and treatment		*		*												
Living alone or without care		*		*												
Unable to look after self, prop, finances		*		*												
Significant harm if adult not removed to a place of safety				*												
Unable to enter premises to assess /medically examine adult/ obtain medical records			*													
Unable to enter premises for assessment of adult at risk (also urgent case warrant)													*			
Immediate need of care and treatment																
Interests of person/ others to remove adult to a place of safety					*											
Significant risk to health, safety or welfare	o				*	o	or	o								
Significant risk to other persons	r					r		r								
To pursue STDC would cause undesirable delay						*										
Patient's ability to make treatment decisions significantly impaired							*	*								
Necessary to detain to determine or give treatment							*	*								
Medical treatment is available and would benefit patient						*	*	*								
Order is necessary						*	*	*								
Unable to safeguard own wellbeing, property, rights, interests									*	*	*	*				
At risk of harm (physical, psychological, unlawful conduct, self -harm)									*	*	*	*				
Local authority might need to intervene									*							
A need to remove to a place of safety (or specified place)				*												
A need to take adult from a place to assess or medical examine										*						
To decide adult at risk and if LA needs to protect adult from harm										*						
Exposed to serious harm (harm for RO urgent cases)									*	*	*	*				
Available/suitable place									*	*	*					
Adult's wellbeing or property better safeguarded by banning harmer											*					
Adult entitled to occupy place											*					
Adult might also be incapable											*	*				
No other means to safeguard /promote welfare, property or finances		*					*	*	*	*	*	*			*	*
Having regard to (and taking account of) principles of Act		*		*			*	*	*	*	*	*		*	*	*

Appendix 22: The Joint Implementation Team:
Risk Assessment and Adult Protection Plans

RISK ASSESSMENT	PROTECTION PLAN
1. COMMUNICATION, CAPACITY, AND INVOLVEMENT **e.g.** Has the person being assessed any particular communication and support needs?(e.g. for interpreter, advocate, appropriate adult, Makaton, sign, speech and language therapist; or as a result of dementia, head injury etc	**1. PERSONAL DETAILS – ADULT AT RISK** **2. AGENCY/STAFF INVOLVEMENT** **3. ACTIONS**
2. CHRONOLOGY OF SIGNIFICANT EVENTS Chronology of relevant events/significant event history (Attach if available; **or** list significant relevant events under: date, brief detail, agencies/people involved, and outcome/consequences)	Actions and Roles, which define services to be in place and procedures to be followed, with responsibilities, timescales and outcomes identified involving service users, carers, members of the core group and all other agencies involved in the Protection Plan. These should include immediate or longer term actions; both benefit enhancing and harm reducing measures, and roles of services, the adult, advocates, unpaid carers attorneys and guardians, as appropriate.
3. CURRENT RISKS OR CONCERNS e.g. Physical injury; violence/aggressive behaviour	
4. CURRENT RISK DESCRIPTION e.g. What behaviour, allegation, complaint, circumstances or event has prompted this risk assessment? (detail the nature of the behaviour or incidents which put the person at risk, e.g. the nature and extent of sexual/physical/financial abuse; the specific areas of self-neglect (eating, medication, wandering)	**4. VIEWS AND ROLES OF ADULT AT RISK AND OTHERS** **5. CONTINGENCY PLAN** To identify significant changes which might occur and what additional or alternative action should be taken in that event, such as case conference or legal action.
5. RISK ASSESSMENT e.g. What is your assessment of the risk? How severe might the consequences/injuries/harm/damage be if no action is taken to reduce the risk, or increase protection? How probable is it that these circumstances will recur? What is your view and any agreed view about the degree of risk and urgency of action?	**6. DISTRIBUTION OF PROTECTION PLAN** Distribution to be identified which takes account of confidentiality and third party information issues.
6. RECOMMENDATION/ACTIONS **e.g.** Detail any immediate actions that have already been taken in order to protect, or reduce the risk (include whether this situation/risk/concern been referred to another service, or agency, and if so, with what result)	

Appendix 23: A Risk Assessment Format

a) **Overall risk description** (using risk domains and risk landscape)

    i.   e.g. type and aspects: frequency; consent and capacity; potential harmer(s); (repeat for each risk domain); the what, who, when, where, and in particular the 'whys';

b) **Assessment of risk, relative to**

    i.   the relationship between the adult's risk and the effect of mental disorder on this, e.g. welfare and ability to protect him/herself, and assessing this;

    ii.   the adult's perception of risk and abilities to manage risk;

    iii.   *how* and *why* (also *where* and *when*) this risk occurs in relevant risk domains (e.g. safety, welfare, health, property, finances); and

    iv.   providing conclusions, when it is clear *how* and *why* the risk occurs; then

c) **Assessment of powers and provisions,** relative to risk as assessed to determine whether formal provisions or powers are indicated or not, and if so

    i.   which Act(s) is/are indicated;

    ii.   which duty, power or provision is/are indicated; and

    iii.   exploration of the supportive or management strategies to respond to risk as assessed, to include factors which would mitigate risk. Following this, the preparation of adult protection / risk management planning and implementation;

For example:

Response: e.g. an adult lacks capacity to (a) understand the risk associated with the harmful conduct and (b) to make decisions to protect him/herself from this harm; and as his/her capacity is permanent, relating to his/her learning disability, formal action is indicated; and where

Formal action is indicated: e.g.: an adult has a mental disorder, therefore the 2003 Act is indicated, e.g. short term: duty of inquiry (s33); (potential): warrant of entry (s35 [1]; medical assessment (s35 [4]); removal to place of safety (s293); e.g. longer term: advocacy, assessment, and provision of care and support services; an adult is incapable, therefore the 2000 Act is indicated: e.g. short term: assessment of capacity; e.g. longer term: welfare guardianship (2000 Act), to make decision as to where he/she should reside.

Appendix 24: Adult Protection / Risk Management Plan

ADULT PROTECTION PLAN / RISK MANAGEMENT FORMAT

Adult Protection / Risk Management Plan

1. **Personal Details – Adult at Risk**
2. **gency/Staff Involvement**
3. **Adult Protection Plan**

a) **Findings of the risk assessment** (relative to risk domains)
e.g. sexual, physical, emotional, financial (relative to mental disorder);

b) **Protective actions;**
⇒ Informal and supportive (and adult's role in managing risk)
⇒ Formal (indicating Acts, and powers and provisions needed)

c) **Objectives of the protection plan;**
d) **Roles and Responsibilities** (in delivering the plan);
e) **Timescales;**

e.g. (to be prepared on separate sheet):

Risk (domains and aspects), e.g.:	Protection actions (informal and formal)	Objectives	Roles and Responsibilities	Timescales
Sexual:				
Physical:				
Emotional:				
Financial:				
Others:				

(to be preared Adult Protection / Risk Management Implementation)

4. **Adult protection legislative design and plan:** detailing the legislative framework to be applied and confirming the process of obtaining the powers and provisions (i.e. who is involved and what do they need to do).

5. **Adult protection plan implementation:** with emphasis on informal and formal delivery; adult's role; confirming formal duties/officers acting in a formal capacity; delivery and expiry of formal powers, etc.

6. **Risk and powers monitoring and review:** ensuring a) the ongoing support and protection of the adult, and b) the powers and provisions remain relative to the adult's risk.

7. **Crisis Contingency Plan:** identifying potential risk scenarios and respective risk management plans.

Appendix 25: An example of an Adult Protection Plan

Risk (Domain and aspects)	Protection actions (informal and formal)	Objectives	Roles and Responsibilities	Timescales
Sexual: Sexual exploitation	Banning order (2007 Act)	Removal of risk of sexual harm	Council officer to pursue and monitor a Banning Order	For 6 months (then review)
Financial: Misappropriation of funds; loss of money	DWP appointee arrangement or Part 3 (accounts and funds) 2000 Act	Reinstatement of funds	Council officer / care manager to pursue and deliver relative provisions	For 3 years (then review)
Emotional harm: Causing fear, threat, distress	Care and support, and advocacy (2003 Act)	To assist adult develop sufficient strengths and confidence	Advocacy worker and Care worker to assist adult	Ongoing
Welfare (and human rights) harm: Risk to welfare, opportunity, freedom, independence	Welfare guardianship (2000 Act); Care management (1990 Act)	To assist adult achieve optimum independence	Mental health officer; Council Officer / care manager (named welfare guardian) to pursue and deliver guardianship; to pursue and deliver care provision	For 3 years (then review)

Appendix 26: Adult Protection Framework and Process Applied

10 Point Adult Protection Framework applied	10 Point Adult Protection Process applied
A. Initial Action 1. Screening and initial action	**A. Initial and early intervention** (within 24 hours or 5 working days of referral, depending on risk): 1. Screening and initial action:

B. Assessment
 	
2. Assessment of risk
 	
  Risk description and profiling
 	
  Assessment of risk (including adult's perceptions)
 	
3. Assessment of need
 	
4. Assessment of powers and provisions against risk (plus positive, supportive & informal aspects)
	a) Confirm adult at risk (mental disorder) (take initial early action if required);
	  b) Confirm relative duty to inquire;
	  c) Confirm need for investigation (initial meeting if possible);
	  d) Allocate suitable coordinating manager;
	  e) Allocate suitable investigating team;
	  f) Deliver investigation (visit) and take immediate actions if required); and
	  g) Post visit meeting.
	
	B. Assessment (between 5 to 10 working days of referral):
	
	1. Assess risk:
	  a) Prepare risk description and profile; and
	  b) Ass*ess risk (including adult's perceptions);*
	3. Assess initial need; and
	4. Assess powers and provisions against risk (plus positive, supportive & informal aspects)

C. Adult protection planning 5. Adult protection plan 6. Legislative design	**C. Adult protection planning** (within 10 working days of referral): 5. Hold a case conference, and 6. Prepare an adult protection plan and legislative design.

D. Implementation
 	
7. Powers and provisions pursued
 	
8. Implementation plan (and exercise of powers)
 	
9. Monitoring and reviewing
 	
  The plan
 	
  The powers
 	
10. Crisis contingency plan (CCP)
	D. Implementation (to commence within 10 working days of referral):
	
	7. Pursue powers and provisions;
	8. Implement the protection plan (and exercise the powers);
	9. Monitor and review
	    the adult protection plan;
	    the legislative design and applied powers; and
	10. Prepare the crisis contingency plan (CCP) (to implement if and when necessary).

Appendix 27: A Training Programme for Key Practitioners:
To Support and Protect Adults with Mental Disorder

The training is for 'key practitioners', e.g. mental health officers, council officers, social workers, approved medical practitioners, general practitioners, etc. It offers a one day programme and a practical (what needs to be done and how to do it) approach; how to avoid pitfalls, what works, etc.; working together in investigations; how to seek immediate, short term, long term powers across the Acts, in an adult protection / risk management (crisis contingency plans, etc) framework, and a step by step application, etc, with handouts, guides, and wall charts). It offers specific forms of risk assessment and adult protection plans, again to respond to the specific risks of adults with mental disorder. This is a one day programme for a maximum 12 staff, because it is intensive and participative, and delivered in an interagency and multidisciplinary basis.

Session 1	The Context	'The knowledge'	• The risk landscape • Development and pitfalls • The primary and supportive Acts
Session 2	The Powers	'The authority'	• Inquiry and investigations • Immediate & short term powers • Long term & multiple provisions and powers • Powers and provisions 'across the Acts'
Session 3	The Framework	'The process'	• Assessment of risk and risk management • Formats • Adult at risk / protection management process
Session 4	The Crossing	'The gaps'	• What to do and know • Bridging the gaps • A 'crossing the Acts' process

Appendix 28: Specifically what key practitioners need to do

Social workers, mental health officers (MHOs), and Council Officers	General practitioners (GPs) and approved medical practitioners (AMPs)
2003 Act	
Inquiries (duty to inquire)	
Social workers or MHOs	*GPs or AMPs*
☐ Conduct inquires under s33;	☐ Accompany and assist inquires under s33 (s34);
Immediate Powers	
MHOS	*GPs or AMPS*
☐ to seek and obtain warrants under s35 for entry, medical examinations, medical records; ☐ to seek and obtain authorised person's warrants (s292);	☐ to carry out medical examination under s35 (4); ☐ to have access to and to read medical records under s35 (7); ☐ to accompany an authorised person (authorised person's warrant (s292);
Removal orders	
☐ to make an application and seek an order (s293 to Sheriff); ☐ to make an application and seek an order (s294 to Justice of the Peace)	☐ to medically examine an adult removed from a public place by the police to a place of safety. This may be in a Police station. (s297)
Short Term Powers	
MHOS	*AMPs and GPs*
Emergency and short term detentions: ☐ to provide consultation and consent (or not), to emergency detention (s36); ☐ short term detention (s44); ☐ extension of short term detention (S47); ☐ to interview the patient (s45); ☐ to ascertain name of named person; ☐ to inform patient of and to access advocacy;	Emergency and short term detentions: ☐ to medically examine and grant (or not), a emergency detention (s36) (GP: medical practitioner); ☐ thereby obtaining a MHO consent (unless impracticable) short term detention (s44) (AMP); ☐ thereby obtaining a MHO consent (mandatory); ☐ extension of short term detention (S47) (AMP); ☐ to pass certificate to hospital managers; ☐ to arrange transfer to hospital (if in the community);

Appendix 28: Specifically what key practitioners need to do

Long Term powers

MHOS	AMPs (and RMOs)and GPs
to apply for a compulsory treatment order (s57);	to carry out medical examinations of the patient (2 AMPs or AMP and GP. NB a GP may make a medical examination);
to apply the Act's principles;	to be satisfied the conditions under s57 are met;
to interview the patient; inform patient of rights; inform of and access advocacy;	to consider whether notice should be given to the patient of the application (s57 [5]);
to identify named person (s59);	to consider the patient capable of instructing a solicitor (s57 [5]);
to give notification (s60);	to attend the Tribunal and give evidence;
to prepare MHO report (s61); to provide a view on medical reports;	to consult with MHO over the proposed care plan (s62), advising on treatment plan, recorded matters, etc;
to prepare a proposed care plan (s62), to consult medical practitioners and other persons providing care and treatment;	as RMO, after grant by the Tribunal, to prepare a 'working' care plan setting out medical treatment (s76);
to make and submit the application to the MHTS (s63);	as RMO, to meet duties on reviews of order (s77, s78, s83);
to lead and produce evidence at a MHTS hearing;	to meet duties on extensions and variations (s84, s86, s90, s93);
to meet duties on extension of order (s85);	to arrange suspensions of the order (s127, s128);
to meet duties on extension and variation of order (s89);	to reference to Tribunal where recorded matters are not being provided (s96);
to consult on recorded matters (s96);	to meet duties on non-compliance measures (s112, s113, and s114).
to provide consent on non-compliance measures (s112 and s114) of a CTO or ICTO.	

Other duties (2003 Act)

MHOs	AMPs
To act as designated MHO for patients case (s229);	To act as patient's responsible medical officer (s230);
To notify local authority that the patient may be in need of community care services (s 227);	To carry out assessment of need (s228);
To provide assessment of need (social worker or MHO) (s228);	To meet duties regarding safeguarded medical treatment (part 16);
To provide social circumstances reports (s 231).	Meeting duties to patient re advance statements (s276 and s277).

Appendix 28: Specifically what key practitioners need to do

2000 Act

Social workers and MHOs	AMPs and GPs
☐ To investigate (complaints against welfare proxies and circumstances of risk to welfare, s10);	☐ To cooperate with investigations;
☐ Provide information and advice to welfare proxy (s10);	☐ To provide medical assessments;
☐ Act as local authority supervisor of a private welfare guardia (s10);	☐ To provide assessments of capacity;
☐ Act as named welfare guardian (s59);	☐ To provide medical certificates under
☐ To countersign part 3 (s27a of the 2007 Act);	☐ Part 3 (accounts and funds);
☐ To assess and apply S13ZA procedure (s64 of the 2007 Act);	☐ Part 4 (management of residents Funds) and
☐ To prompt the revoking, reviewing and extension, of all welfare proxy powers	☐ Part 5 (medical treatment);
☐ To protect finances through Part 3, Part 4 or Part 6 (and property), prompting appropriate applications by the local authority, in particular for a financial intervention order or financial guardianship;	☐ To provide medical treatment (part 5); and
☐ To prompt appropriate medical authority under Part 5; and	☐ To provide medical reports (one by AMP) for
☐ To provide a welfare guardianship report (S57) (NB only a MHO can provide this report).	☐ Intervention orders (s53) and
	☐ Guardianship order applications (s 57 (3) and (4).

2007 Act

Social workers (who may be MHOs) acting as Council Officers	AMPs and GPs
To:	To:
☐ conduct an inquiry (s4);	☐ cooperate with the local authority making inquiries (s5);
☐ cooperate with other public bodies (s5);	☐ where the doctor believes the person is an adult at risk and action is needed to protect the adult from harm, to report to the local authority the facts and circumstances of the adult (s5) (subject to GMC guidance);
☐ consider importance of providing advocacy and other services (s6);	
☐ investigate (visit and assess)(s7);	☐ provide a medical examination (s9);
☐ interview (with consent) (s35);	☐ obtain consent of adult to medical examination (s35);
☐ interview in private (s8) if required;	☐ give up medical records (s10);
☐ seek a medical examination if required (s9);	☐ read medical records (s10); and
☐ required any person to give up health, financial or other records (s10);	☐ provide medical evidence the adult is incapable of providing consent to protection orders.
☐ obtain warrants for entry (s37) and urgent cases entry (s40b) and removal order (s40a);	
☐ seek consent of adult for a protection order (unless there is undue pressure or the adult is incapable) (s35);	
☐ prompt and assess for an application by the Council for a protection order (assessment order, removal order, banning order, temporary banning order);	
☐ provide evidence in Court; and	
☐ exercise and monitor protection orders.	

Appendix 29: A manager / key practitioner adult protection / risk management process

Managers' Adult Protection Process	Key Practitioners' Adult Protection Process
1. Screen and consider initial action (local authority officer): Discuss with referrer and other agencies, a) confirm an adult at risk (using the definition offered in the 2007 Act); and, if mental disorder exists, b) i) confirm a relative duty to inquire within the three Acts; ii) consider the makeup of the visiting team, i.e. two suitable workers (e.g. mho/amp) shared health and social care perspective; iii) allocate; and iv) support and manage an appropriate formal investigation (practitioners to pursuing initial action, considering warrants and orders available across the 2003 and 2007 Act).	**1. Investigation: visit adult and consider initial action:** a) assess and agree initial actions (or not), including informal supports; b) confirm an adult at risk, using the definition offered in the 2007 Act, and c) if mental disorder exists, confirm a relative duty to inquire within the three Acts; and d) respond to initial risk, providing appropriate action, i.e. consider the range of warrants and orders available within the 2003 Act, and the 2007 Act.
2. Assess and manage presenting risk: Manage and support a specific risk assessment to respond to the particular needs of adults with mental disorder, which may need to be met across the Acts. Respond to presenting and immediate risk.	**2. Assess risk and provide a professional opinion:** a) assess risk and the effect of mental disorder on this, which may need to be met across the 2003, 2000 or 2007 Acts; b) assess the relationship between the adult's risk and the effect of mental disorder on this, e.g. welfare and ability to protect him/herself, and assessing this; and
3. Assess powers and provisions against risk: Manage and support an exploration/assessment of the range of powers and provisions against the adult's risks.	c) assess the *how* and *why* (also *where* and *when*) this risk occurs in relevant risk domains (e.g. safety, welfare, health, property, finances); and
4. Pursue necessary powers and provisions: As many adults with mental disorder have immediate and long term risks, in the need to ensure appropriate response with risk associated with mental disorder across the legislations, consider and confirm a dual path approach to actions (immediate / short term and long term actions). Prompt and support the pursuit of these powers.	d) make conclusions, when it is clear *how* and *why* the risk occurs; then **3. Assess powers and provisions against risk: i.e.** weigh and balance powers and provisions against the adult's risks. Then agree and confirm a legislative design, confirming primary and secondary Acts and powers.
5. Provide and manage adult protection / risk management: • **convene** a **case conference:** reflective of risk, needs and circumstances (mental disorder), involve key practitioners (visiting team); determine an • **allocate and support an adult protection plan** relative to risks of the adult affected by mental disorder, ensure this is coordinated by an appropriate key practitioner, e.g. a MHO; • **implement the adult protection plan,** confirm and oversee implementation; • **monitor and review,** coordinate and manage reviews, ensure appropriate monitoring arrangements; and • **confirm and manage a crisis contingency plan** to respond to immediate and unforeseen risk; • **provide support, advice and guidance** to key practitioners delivering the adult protection plan; • **coordinate and confirming distribution, recording and sharing of information,** ensuring suitable and agreed arrangements.	**4. Pursue powers and provisions:** a) confirm powers to protect the adult on an immediate or short term basis, and then b) explore and confirm long term actions (long term powers); c) thereby ensuring an appropriate response with risk associated with mental disorder across the legislations, i.e. a dual path approach (immediate / short term and long term actions). **5. Adult protection planning and risk management:** a) attend the AP case conference, providing the risk assessment, giving evidence and making recommendations for longer term actions, etc., discuss adult protection plan; b) prepare an adult protection plan, relative to risks of the adult affected by mental disorder, coordinate contributions of core group / key practitioners; c) coordinate the delivery of the adult protection plan (with core group); d) monitor and review, cooperate with or coordinate reviews and monitoring arrangements; e) prepare a crisis contingency plan; coordinate and implement when and where necessary; f) write up, record and file, pass to manager to sign and confirm.

Appendix 30a: Across the Acts: adults affected by mental disorder at risk guide

2003 Act	2000 Act	2007 Act
Client groups (affected by)		
1. Mental illness (functional, e.g. bipolar disorder and schizophrenia illness); 2 Mental Illness (organic, e.g. dementia); 3. Learning disability, personality disorder, etc.	Mental disorder: i.e. 1. Learning Disability; 2. Mental Illness (organic e.g. a. Dementia and b. ARBD /ABI).	1. Mental disorder (a. capable or b. incapable); or 2. disability, illness, or mental or physical impairments.
Adults in need of treatment (protection *and* care)	Adults in need of care (protection and treatment)	Adults in need of protection (care and treatment)
Duty to Inquire		
Immediate Powers		
Warrant of entry		
Where adult is refusing access	None	Harmer or third party is refusing access
Local authority assessment		
To assess risk, and need for treatment and care and support services	To assess risk to personal welfare	To assess risk and establish adult at risk and need for protection orders.
Medical Examination		
• To establish mental disorder and need for treatment; • To establish need for compulsory powers.	• To assess the adult's mental capacity; • To assess the adults physical and mental health; • To provide treatment by informal means or under s47, the 2003 Act.	• To establish the adult's need of immediate medical treatment for a physical illness or mental disorder; • To provide evidence of harm to inform a criminal prosecution; • To assess the adult's physical health needs; or • To assess the adult's mental capacity.
Emergency Detention		
Emergency detention to or in hospital (s36)	None	None
Removal to assess		
None (although s293 could be used for this purpose)	None	Assessment order (s11), to a more suitable place for a private interview or medical examination in private.
Removal to protect		
a. Removal (s 293/s294) to a hospital (or residential care or someone's home); if incapable to residential care (or hospital); b. From a public place (s297) to hospital (if no place of safety available, by exception to a police station). NB. Place of safety is defined under s300.	o immediate powers to remove.	Removal (urgent cases, s40, 1a) to a 'specified place'. The Sheriff is satisfied as to the availability / suitability of the place, which is specified in the order. Council provides a suitability report of the place and the person willing to care for the adult and a written agreement from the owner of the proposed specified place.

Appendix 30b: Across the Acts: adults affected by mental disorder at risk guide

Short Term Powers

2003 Act	2000 Act	2007 Act
☐ Short term detention (s44) ☐ Interim compulsory treatment order (s65)	☐ Intervention Order (s53) ☐ Interim guardianship (s57)	☐ Temporary banning order (s21)

Long Term Powers

2003 Act	2000 Act	2007 Act

☐ Compulsory Treatment Order (hospital based) (s63) (detention and medical treatment); or
☐ Compulsory Treatment Order (community based) (s63) e.g. treatment, to attend for treatment; to attend for community care services, etc; to reside at a specified place; to allow MHO, RMO, person authorised by RMO; requirements on approval or informing MHO on/about change of address.
	☐ Welfare Guardianship (s57) (either by private individual (relative etc) or local authority); or
	☐ Financial Guardianship (s57); or
	☐ Welfare and Financial Guardianship (s57) (combined).
		☐ Banning order (s19):
		   ☐ To ban a subject from being in a specified place;
		   ☐ The order may also ban the subject from being in a specified area; summary ejection; made subject to specified conditions, etc.

Supportive Provisions

2003 Act	2000 Act	2007 Act
☐ Care and support services (s25); ☐ Services designed to promote wellbeing and social development (s26); ☐ Assistance with travel (s27); ☐ Assessment of needs (1990 Act) governed here by s227 (MHO referral); ☐ Request for assessment of need to local authority and health board (s228); ☐ Independent advocacy service (s259); ☐ Advance statement (medical treatment) (s275); ☐ Named person (s250) NB. Underpinned by assessment and care management and care programme approach	☐ Part 2: Power of attorney; ☐ Part 3: Accounts and Funds; ☐ Part 4: Management of residents funds; ☐ Part 5: Medical treatment (s47). Underpinned by assessment and care management (1990 Act).	☐ Local authority duty to have regard to the importance of providing appropriate service, including in particular independent advocacy services (s6). Underpinned by assessment and care management (1990 Act).

Appendix 31: Risk Assessment (adults with mental disorder at risk)

Assessment of Risk

a)   The overall risk description, thereby identifying and profiling all the risks with which the adult affected by mental disorder is exposed (being informed by risk domains and associated aspects);

```



```

b)   **Assessment of risk (assessing the overall range and degree of risk),** relative to (a) the relationship between the adult's risk and the effect of mental disorder on this, and (b) *how* and *why* (also *where* and *when*) this risk occurs in relevant risk domains (e.g. safety, welfare, health, property, finances); (c) the adult's perception of risk; and (d) making conclusions, when it is clear *how* and *why* the risk occurs;

```



```

c)   **Assessment of powers or provisions against risk as assessed, to determine** whether (a) formal provisions or powers are indicated or not, and, if so, (b) which Act(s) is/are indicated; (c) which provisions / powers are indicated.

```



```

d)   **Exploration of the remedies or management strategies to respond to risk as assessed** (supportive/informal provisions and strategies, including managing aspects, e.g. self-protective abilities)

```



```

Appendix 32: Adult Protection / Risk Management Plan
(adults at risk with mental disorder)

a)   **Adult protection plan**, relative to risk as assessed in the risk assessment, and providing the *how* risk will be managed or met:

1.   Findings of the risk assessment (reflective of risk domains and aspect, e.g. sexual, financial, physical, etc)

```



```

2.   Protective actions (informal and formal)

```



```

3.   Objectives of the protection plan

```



```

4.   Roles and Responsibilities

```



```

5.   Timescales

```



```

b)   **Adult protection legislative design and plan**

```



```

Appendix 33: Crisis Contingency plan

Risk scenario 1

a)   Crisis scenario

```
```

b)   Crisis management plan

```
```

Risk scenario 2

a)   Crisis scenario

```
```

b)   Crisis management plan

```
```

And other risk scenarios and crisis management plans to be added

Appendix 34: Across the Acts: adults at risk with mental disorder framework

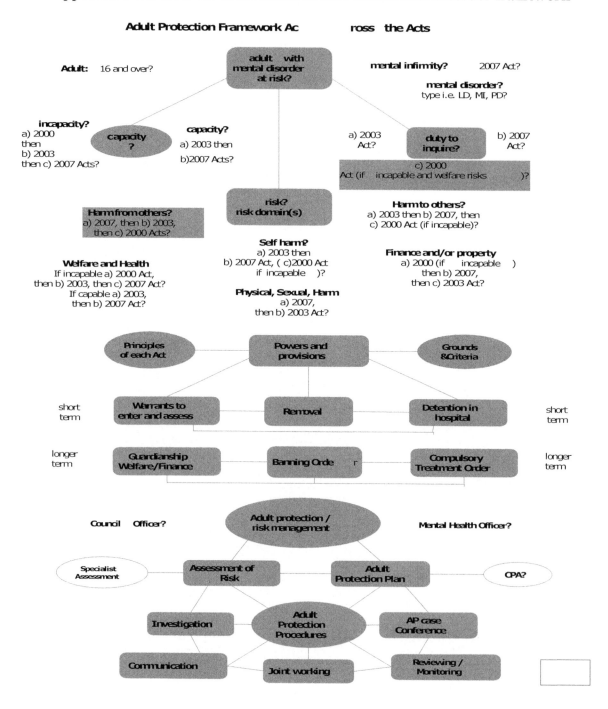

Appendix 35: Areas of Care (Care Domains) (adult / mental disorder)

Domains (area of need)	Care aspects (from care landscape)
Physical health	e.g. illness (acute, chronic, terminal) and injury, pain (acute, chronic), consider: skin, sight, hearing, stomach, bowels, continence, teeth, and breathing problems; leading to lack of ability to self-care, etc.
Mental health and cognition	e.g. poor mental health and wellbeing, low or high mood, confusion, problems with thought processes, disorientation, hallucinations delusions, agitation, behavioural problems, anxiety, grief, etc.; leading to lack of ability to take decisions, meet needs, pay bills, take medication, lead one's life, aggression, unhappiness, sometimes placing oneself and others at risk, etc.
Safety	e.g. fragility: standing, walking; transferring, feeding; poor self-care; cookers, fires, dropped cigarettes; from others, wandering, self-harm; leading to e.g. risk of falls (floor /bed / stairs); losing weight ; risk of fire; to others; exploitation, neglect / abuse; getting lost; risk of suicide /accidental death. NB: risk to safety in some cases should lead to assessment of risk.
Physical ability and mobility	e.g. physical impairment, problems walking, climbing stairs, getting out and about, transferring (bed, chair, bath/shower), frailty; leading to falls, fear of falls, etc
Diet and sustenance	e.g. inability to prepare food and drink; lack of ability to shop, store safely, have balanced diet; leading to poor nutrition, starvation, illness, etc
Personal care	e.g. problems with hygiene, dressing, washing, bathing, hair, nails, etc.; leading to inappropriate clothes and shoes (circumstances and weather), being unkempt, lack of cleanliness, being untidy, etc.
Motivation and independent living skills	e.g. lack of motivation, opportunity to do things, inability to retain skills and abilities; leading to institutionalisation, becoming dependent, etc.
Social functioning	e.g. lack of socialisation, engagement; poor social support and networks; lack of social activity, poor contact and communication; leading to not getting out / meeting people, leading to e.g. isolation, becoming housebound, etc.
Recreational activities	e.g. lack of access to fun and games, exercise, art and culture, reading, etc., leading to boredom, poor mental health and wellbeing, lack of human rights, etc.
Material	e.g. poverty, lack of furniture; poor or no equipment; lack of access to things/personal possession; clothes / shoes, etc.; leading to detrimental effects on welfare, health, safety, etc.
Practical needs	e.g. poor housework; not shopping; not paying bills nor collecting prescriptions; leading to house becoming, unkempt or unclean; lack of food, and supplies. etc.
Legal and human rights	e.g. lack of ability to challenge powers/orders, lack of liberty, poor access to private space, private and family life, etc.; leading to inability to challenge orders / powers / court actions., discrimination, lack of human rights, etc.
Financial/ Property	e.g. poor access to cash; problems in day to day budgeting; inability to protect finances, house /home; leading to poverty; stress; homelessness; loss of home/house, debt, etc.

Appendix 36. The Care Landscape (adults with mental disorder)

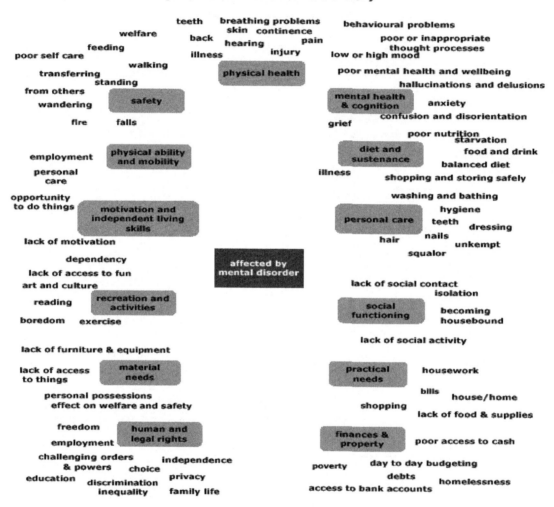

**Care Landscape
(adults with mental disorder)**

© Tom Keenan 2010

Appendix 37. Assessment of need (domain approach)case example: Wilma: older person (aged 71) with dementia living alone.

Primary Conditions	Need / domain area	Individual effect of need	Assessment of need (each need assessed)	Level / extent of the need)	Assessed response to need (service).	Type of service required.	Assessors Comment
	a) Incapacity	Poor decisions / actions / poor safety and hygiene.	A need for consistent supervision and occasional psychiatric input.	Significant	Supervision and support.	Community Psychiatric nursing.	Risk and care needs will increase without care and support.
	b) Safety	At risk of exploitation (sexual / financial) self neglect, feeding, and poor hygiene.	A need because of incapacity and poor memory posing major risk living alone in an independent tenancy.	Significant	Inhouse support/ care staff available throughout the day.	A risk assessment is required to confirm.	Poor memory /incapacity may lead to risk at home or unsupervised setting. Adult at risk procedures have been instigated.
	c) Personal care	At risk without supervision and prompting.	Personal care needs need to be met.	Significant	Personal care service.	A personal care assistant available at crucial times throughout the day to assist the person wash and bathe.	This may need to be provided in a care setting.
	d) Motivation and independent living skills	Doesn't do the things she used to do, e.g. cooking shopping, etc.	Lack of stimulation may lead to a lack of morale; reduced mental health and wellbeing.	Significant	Opportunity to do practical things.	Home care.	Is restricted in present environment.
	e) Diet and sustenance	She is losing weight.	Needs food and drinks provided.	Significant	Provision of meals throughout the day	Meals service (home care/ meals and wheels)	Poor memory may present problems re food at home.
Mental disorder (dementia) and physical health problems	f) Recreational activities	Her access to activities and recreation is limited.	She needs access to more recreation and activity.	Significant	To access activities and recreation.	Support staff / carers/ befrienders	Is poor presently.
	g) Social functioning	She is lonely and lacks access to social contact and networks.	She needs access to more suitable social contact.	Moderate	To access activities and recreation.	Support staff / carers/ befrienders	Is restricted presently.
	h) Psychological / emotional	Gets anxious about her predicament.	She lacks insight and is scared.	Moderate	To support and assist access to activities.	Support staff / carers/ befrienders	Her 'fears' need to be addressed.
	i) Physical health	She has asthma and can't walk far.	Needs primary care input	Moderate	Treatment and medication	Primary health care (carers assisting taking medication)	Will need supervision when taking medication.
	j) Familial issues	She has lost contact with her family (sons) because of her alcohol use.	Need to discuss family contact with her.	Moderate	Assistance in regaining contact with family.	Support staff.	This needs to be addressed carefully and will her approval.
	l) Financial/ Property	Has no ability to manage money / being exploited?	She needs support to have her finances managed and protected.	Moderate	Assistance with her finances.	Debts advice; welfare rights officer.	Adult at risk procedures have been instigated to assess risk from this man.
	k) Practical needs	Her house is untidy and she can't shop.	She needs support to shop, housework, bills, etc.	Moderate	Assistance/ provision of housework and shopping.	Home care/support service (home carer).	Has been unwilling to accept home care support in the past.
	m) Material needs	Her furniture and equipment are basic but adequate.	She doesn't wish assistance (at this stage).	Low	No need (at this time)	No service (at this time)	Her house is equipped but everything may need replaced in future.
	p) Legal and human rights	Rights challenged, but she values her independence and privacy.	Sensitive adult protection approach, protecting her rights.	Low	Protection of human and legal rights.	Advocacy; legal representation; named person.	Rights may protected through independent advocacy worker.
Primary Conditions	**Need / domain area**	**Individual effect of need**	**Assessment of need (each need assessed)**	**Level / extent of the need)**	**Assessed response to need (service).**	**Type of service required.**	**Assessors Comment**

Appendix 38. Assessment of need and care planning (domain approach)case example: Wilma: older person (aged 71) with dementia living alone.

Stage 1	2	3	4	5	6	7	8	9	10
Primary conditions	Need / domain area arising	Individual effect of condition	Assessor's questions	Assessor's answers	Assessment of need	Seriousness/ significance	Assessed service response to need.	Type of service required	Assessor's Comment
e.g. Mental disorder (demented) and physical health problems	e.g. Incapacity	Incapacity is creating poor decisions and actions.			There is a need for consistent supervision and occasional psychiatric input.	Significant	The service to provide supervision and support.	Community psychiatric nurse to be available each day.	Care needs (and risk) will increase without regular care and support.
	e.g. Personal care	Mental disorder is affecting the person's ability to meet his/her own personal care needs,			The person needs assistance with personal care.	Moderate	The service to provide encouragement, prompting or assistance to bathe and wash.	A personal care assistant to be available at crucial times throughout the day to assist the person wash and bathe.	This service can be provided at home, however the person has behavioural problems and requires a sensitive and careful approach to physical assistance.
	etc	etc			etc	etc	etc	etc	etc

Care Plan (person's name)

Level / extent of the need	Assessed service response to need.	Service required	Preferred setting indicated (most to least restrictive settings)				
			NHC	RC	SH	IS	
Significant	The service to provide supervision and support.	Community psychiatric nurse to be available each day.		*		*	
Moderate	The service to provide encouragement, prompting or assistance to bathe and wash.	A personal care assistant to be available at crucial times throughout the day to assist the person wash and bathe.				*	
etc	etc	etc					
etc	etc	etc					

NHC: nursing home care; RC: residential care; SH: sheltered accommodation; IS: own home or other independent setting

Appendix 39: Providing support and protection of adults at risk across the Scottish legislative frameworks

a) Make secure 'legal' decisions?	b) ... in a procedural context?	c) ... get agencies and practitioners to do what the need to do?	.... d) and confirm engagement and actions in an applied and practical way:
1. Ensure adult centrality;	1. Screen and determine the initial action;	Ensure agencies know what they need to know and do what they need to do, i.e.:	Engage (from a position of correct and adequate legal authority):
2. Ensure 'only where necessary' approach;	2. Assess risk, both profiled and then assessed;	1. Meet duties (i.e. to inquire, cooperate and assess; and provide care, support and advocacy);	1. Confirm mental disorder?
3. Avoid the pitfalls;	3. Assess powers and provisions relative to risk;	2. Appoint trained and experienced key practitioners;	2. Confirm risk?
4. Be inventive *and* pragmatic;	4. Plan adult protection / risk management;	3. Ensure adult protection committees respond to adult at risk with mental disorder;	3. Confirm the correct legal mandate to engage?
5. Consider what works;	5. Implement adult protection / risk management;	4. Prepare and implement procedures reflective of adult at risk with mental disorder; and	4. Confirm the mandate gives sufficient authority?
6. Explore the options;	6. Pursue adult protection powers (if necessary);	5. Train, support, guide, and empower key practitioners.	5. Confirm there a need to visit / assess / act?
7. Assess powers against risk;	7. Monitor and review risk and powers; and	Ensure practitioners know what they need to know and do what they need to do, i.e.:	Act (from a basis of correct and adequate legal powers):
8. Use the principles;	8. Plan and provide crisis contingency.	1. Know about mental disorder and incapacity, and their associated risks;	6. Confirm a) immediate; b) ongoing and c) significant risk/ harm?
9. Ask the questions;		2. Understand the pitfalls of adult protection work as it relates to adult at risk with mental disorder;	7. Confirm a) immediate; b) ongoing and c) significant need?
10. Compare and contrast;		3. Know the 2003, 2000, 2007 Acts, their relationships, and how to cross the Acts;	8. Confirm how will this be met on the a) immediate, b) short term and c) long term?
11. Confirm grounds and criteria, together; and		4. Apply their codes of practice;	9. Confirm need for a) immediate, b) short term; and c) long term powers?
12. Ensure appropraite authority.		5. Apply the principles;	10. Confirm how will they be sought and exercised?
		6. Know about and implement local adult at risk procedures;	
		7. Apply risk assessment and risk management, across the range of risk posed by mental disorder;	
		8. Know about the effect of risk on carers and families and respond to this;	
		9. Meet their duties and responsibilities under the Acts; and	
		10. Work together.	

Appendix 40a: Adults with Mental Disorder at Risk:
Early Intervention Procedure and Checklist.
(Timescale: within 24 hours or 5 working days of referral, depending on risk)

	Event	Officer		Action	Tick
1	Referral received by the Council (SWD)	Reception / adult care / community care services	a. b.	Receive and acknowledge the referral; and Pass forward to screen.	
2	Screen referral	Senior social worker / operational manager	a. b. c. d. e. f.	Discuss with referrer; Discuss with others with knowledge of the case; Apply the 3 point test (confirm adult at risk with mental disorder); Discuss senior manager; Pass forward for allocation; and If no ASP action, either close or pass to the appropriate team / service for other actions e.g. CCA or health care assessment.	
3	Allocate suitable senior manager	Head of service / operational manager	a.	Allocate suitable senior manager to coordinate ASP response;	
4	Allocate suitable practitioners	Senior Manager	a. b.	Allocate suitable key practitioners, relative to the circumstances, needs and risks of adult, e.g. council officer and MHO; and Link with health care and other agencies: to allocate suitable health care practitioners, e.g. GP or AMP; and/o Police constable.	
5	Agree mandate for inquiry	Senior Manager	a. b.	Consider the referral information; and Agree suitable inquiry mandate, i.e. 2007, 2003 or 2000 Act (duty to inquire).	
6	Pre-visit meeting	Senior manager and key practitioners / and relative others (e.g. referrer)	a. b. c. d. e. f. g. h. i.	Arrange and conduct a previsit meeting; Agree the type of visit (e.g. s7, 2007 Act); Discuss the risk circumstances; Agree objective of visit; Agree roles; Agree contact arrangements, e.g. telephone, letter, or no contact (if prior contact would prejudice the safety of adult); Agree need for Police support (or not); Consider the need for warrants (or not); and Coordinate visit.	

Appendix 40b: Adults with Mental Disorder at Risk: Early Intervention Procedure and Checklist.

(Timescale: within 24 hours or 5 working days of referral, depending on risk)

	Event	Officer	Action	Tick
7	Visit	Key practitioners	a. See adult (in private if necessary / with consent) b. Obtain consent for interview and/or medical examination; c. Assess immediate ☐ ☐ risk; ☐ ☐ needs; ☐ ☐ carer support needs; d. Discuss the need for supportive/protective action with adult (and with carer); e. Pursue immediate action (where necessary).	
8	Immediate action: (to enter or remove), where: a) visit obstructed or b) where there is a need to remove for assessment or protection. Only where necessary	Key practitioners in consultation with senior manager and Police Where grounds/criteria are met	a. (2007 Act) warrant for entry: ☐ ☐to Sheriff (s37) or ☐ ☐to JOP (s40 1b); by Council; or b. (2003 Act) warrants: ☐ ☐for entry (s35 (1); and/or ☐ ☐for medical examination (s35 (4); and/or ☐ ☐for access to medical records (s35 (7); to Sheriff or JOP by MHO; or c. (20007 Act) assessment order (s11) or removal order (s14); either with consent of adult, or where there is undue pressure, or where there is incapacity; by Council to Sheriff, or urgent cases for removal order to JOP by Council (s40 1a); or d. (2003 Act) removal order: ☐ ☐To the Sheriff (s293); or ☐ ☐To a JOP (s294); by a MHO; e. Police involvement to effect entry or order; and/or f. Offences, under the relevant Act.	
9	Post-visit meeting	Senior manager and key practitioners / and relative others (e.g. Police)	a. Discuss visit findings and initial actions; b. Agree pro tem support and protection actions; c. Consider longer term action (or not); d. Senior manager to consider adult protection case conference; and e. Write up risk assessment / adult protection report.	

Appendix 41a: A step by step application (ask the questions to get the answers) (preparing for and delivering the visit)

Early intervention

1 — Initial visit

Obtain correct and adequate legal authority (mandate)

1.	is there indication the person has mental disorder?	1.	i.e. mental illness, dementia, learning disability;
2.	Is there indication of an adult at risk?	2.	i.e. at risk of harm;
3.	What is the correct mandate to engage?	3.	i.e. s4 (2007 Act); s33 (2003 Act); s10 (2000 act);
4.	Does this mandate give sufficient authority?	4.	i.e. to protect the adult;
5.	Is there a need to visit / assess / act?	5.	i.e. to see / interview / protect adult;

2 — preparation

Visit and Assess

1.	What is the initial and apparent risk?	1.	i.e. to do an initial risk (for protection) assessment;
2.	What is the initial and apparent need?	2.	i.e. to do an initial need (for support) assessment;
3.	Is there a need for immediate powers?	3.	i.e. to assess for (using the grounds and criteria): □ 2007 Act: warrant for entry (s37 / s40(1b)); assessment order (s11); removal order (s14 / s40 (1a)); □ 2003 Act: warrants for entry, assess, medical exam, etc. (s35); removal order (s293/4); emergency (s36) or short term (s44) detention;
4.	Will they work?	4.	i.e. to decide what power would work and what won't (which may help decide which power to seek);
5.	Is there a need for particular input?	5.	i.e.: □ Police (criminal offence /obstruction / need to enter); □ Mental health officer involvement (needed for 2003 Act powers); □ General practitioner or approved medical practitioner; □ Necessary others: e.g. independent advocacy worker, relative, friend, CPN, nurse, etc.

Appendix 41b: A step by step application (ask the questions to get the answers) (on the short term and the longer term)

3		**Take necessary/ immediate steps to protect the adult**		
	1.	What is the significant risk?	1.	i.e. full risk assessment;
	2.	What is the significant need?	2.	i.e. full community care / single shared / needs assessment;
	3.	Is there a need for short term powers?	3.	i.e. to assess for (using the grounds and criteria):
		Further visits/interviews		□ 2007 Act: assessment order (s11); removal order (s14 / s40 (1a)); temporary banning order (s21)
				□ 2003 Act: removal order (s293/4); short term detention (s44);
				□ 2000 Act: intervention order (s53); interim guardianship (s57);
	4.	Will they work?	4.	i.e. to decide what power would work and what won't (which may help decide which power to seek);
4		**Take necessary short term action(s) to support and protect the adult**		
	1.	What is the ongoing and significant risk?	1.	i.e. full risk assessment;
	2.	How will this be met?	2.	i.e. adult protection plan;
	3.	What is the ongoing and significant need?	3.	i.e. full community care / single shared / needs assessment;
	4.	How will this be met?	4.	i.e. care plan or care programme;
	5.	Is there a need for long term powers?	5.	i.e. to assess for (using the grounds and criteria):
		Further visits/interviews		□□ 2007Act: banning order (s19);
				□□ 2003 Act: compulsory treatment order (s63);
				□□ 2000 Act: guardianship order(s) (s57);
	6.	Will they work?	6.	i.e. to decide what power would work and what won't (which may help decide which power to seek);
	6.	How will they be sought and exercised?	7.	i.e. legislative design (involving legal section where necessary) and an adult protection plan.
5		**1 Take necessary long term action(s) to support and protect the adult**		

Long term / *Short term*

Appendix 42

An adult with mental disorder at risk in a legal context

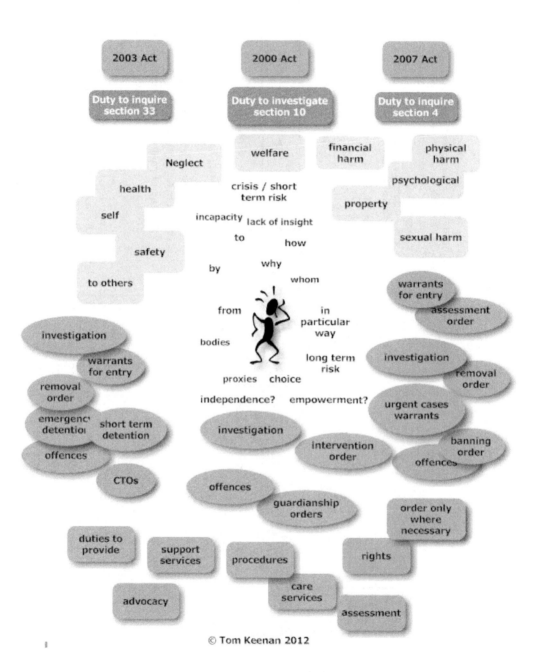

© Tom Keenan 2012

Legend

Legislations	Practitioners
2007 Act: The Adult Support and Protection (Scotland) Act 2007;	**AMP:** approved medical practitioner;
2004 Act: The Vulnerable Witness (Scotland) Act 2004;	**RMO:** responsible medical officer;
2003 Act: The Mental Health (Care and Treatment) (Scotland) Act;	**GP:** general practitioner;
2002 Act: Community Care and Health (Scotland) Act 2002;	**CPN;** community psychiatric nurse;
2000 Act: The Adult with Incapacity (Scotland) Act 2000;	**MHO:** mental health officer;
1990 Act: The NHS and Community Care Act 1990;	**COs:** council officer.
1984 Act: The Mental Health (Scotland) Act 1984;	
1968 Act: The Social work (Scotland) Act 1968;	
1948 Act: The National Assistance Act 1948.	

Key legal provisions		
2003 Act	**2000 Act**	**2007 Act**
S1: General principles	Part 1: General:	S1 and S2: Principles
S25: Care and support services	S1: Principles and definitions	S3: Adults at risk (definition)
S26: Promoting well-being and social development	S3: Powers of Sheriff	S4: Council duty to make inquiries
S33: Duty to inquire	S10: Functions of local authorities	S5: Cooperation
S35: Warrants (inquiries under s33)	S12: Investigations	S6: Advocacy and other services
S36: Emergency detention in hospital	Part 2: Power of Attorney:	S7: Visits
S44: Short term detention	S15: Continuing power of attorney	S8: Interviews
CTO: S57:	S16: creation and exercise of welfare power of attorney	S9: medical examinations
MHO duty to apply for a compulsory treatment order	Part 3: Access to Funds (substituted by Part 2 2007 Act:	S10: Examinations of records
CTO: S63:	Part 4: Management of Residents' Funds	AO: S11: Assessment orders
Application for compulsory treatment orders	Part 5: Medical Treatment:	RO: S14: Removal orders
ICTO: S65:	S47: Authority for medical treatment;	BO: S19: Banning orders
interim compulsory treatment	Part 6: Intervention and Guardianship Orders:	TBO: S21: Temporary banning orders
S292: Warrant to enter for purposes of taking patient	IO: S53: Intervention orders	
S293: Removal order:	WG: S57: Welfare guardianship	
S294: Removal order: application to justice of the peace	FG: S57: Financial guardianship	
S297: Removal from public place	S70: non-compliance with welfare guardians powers	

iMaster's Thesis. University of Glasgow. The Predominate use of emergency detention under the Mental Health (Scot) Act 1984. Tom Keenan, 1999.

iiConsultation on vulnerable adults. Scottish Executive. ISBN 0-7559-0318-8. 2001

iiiScottish Government Publications. Report of the Inspection of Scottish Borders Council Social Work Services for People Affected by Learning Disabilities. April 2004.

ivScottish Government Publications. The Adults with Incapacity (Scotland) Act 2000: Learning From Experience. October 2004.

v Scottish Law Commission Report on Vulnerable Adults: ISBN 0-10-257997-0. 1997

viReview of the Mental Health (Scotland) Act 1984.January 2001 se/2001/56.

viiScottish Government Publications. Adult Support and Protection (Scotland) Act 2007. 2009/01/30112831

viiiScottish Government Publications. Mental Health (Care and Treatment) (Scotland) Act 2003: Code of Practice Volume 2. 2005. ISBN 0-7559-4568-9.

ix http://reports.mwcscot.org.uk/Investigationsreports/LossofFocus/LossofFocusIntro.aspx

xScottish Government Publications. Communication and Assessing Capacity: A guide for social work and health care staff. ISBN 978 0 7559 1605 4.

Printed in Great Britain
by Amazon

14938318R00133